INTRODUCTION TO ISLAMIC CIVILISATION

Introduction to

ISLAMIC CIVILISATION

EDITED BY R. M. SAVORY

CAMBRIDGE UNIVERSITY PRESS
CAMBRIDGE
LONDON · NEW YORK · MELBOURNE

Published by the Syndics of the Cambridge University Press
The Pitt Building, Trumpington Street, Cambridge CB2 1RP
Bentley House, 200 Euston Road, London NW1 2DB
32 East 57th Street, New York, NY10022, USA
296 Beaconsfield Parade, Middle Park, Melbourne 3206, Australia

First published 1976

Set in Great Britain at Tradespools Ltd
and printed and bound in
the United States of America

Library of Congress Cataloguing in Publication Data

Main entry under title:

Introduction to Islamic civilisation.

Bibliography: p.

Includes index.

1. Civilization, Islamic. 2. Near East – Civilization – 1798–

I. Savory, R. M.

DS36.85.157 909'.09'7671 74–25662

ISBN 0 521 20777 0 hard covers
ISBN 0 521 09948 X paperback

CONTENTS

ACKNOWLEDGEMENTS

I acknowledge with gratitude the assistance rendered by all the contributors to this volume at various stages of its preparation. My special thanks are due to my colleagues on the editorial committee, who have given so generously of their time; to Professor E. Birnbaum, for putting the bibliography into its final form; to Professor G. M. Wickens, for his help with the glossary; to Professor E. Birnbaum and Mr S. I. Gellens, for preparing the index; and to Mrs L. Michisor, for her expert typing of the manuscript.

I would also like to express my thanks to all the members of the Cambridge University Press who have been concerned with the production of this book.

Toronto 1975 *R. M. Savory*

INTRODUCTION

In 1970, ten members of the Department of Islamic Studies at the University of Toronto, at the request of the organisers of Radiostudy, the 'open university' adult education programme of Ryerson Polytechnical Institute in Toronto, prepared a series of talks on the Middle East. These talks were broadcast over CJRT Radio, in the form of twenty-four half-hour programmes, between 29 September 1970 and 13 April 1971, and re-broadcast in revised form in 1974–5.

Even before the series went on the air, we had an enquiry from the Cambridge University Press as to whether we thought it might form the basis for a book, since it was felt that there was a need for a good introductory handbook on Islamic civilisation. The suggestion was that the original radio scripts be recast in the form of essays, scholarly in content but written in a form manageable by the general reader. In order to make the proposed book readily available to undergraduates and the general public, it was suggested that it be published as a paperback.

The change of medium, and the limit of 100,000 words imposed by the Cambridge University Press, made necessary a drastic reshaping of the original material, and an editorial committee consisting of Professors E. Birnbaum, M. E. Marmura, R. M. Savory, G. M. Wickens and, from 1973, L. M. Kenny, supervised this task. The editors decided to make the chapters on the high-cultural and social aspects of Islamic civilisation the core of the book. The original three background chapters on political history have been conflated into one chapter which aims at underlining the main themes of Islamic history, and the five scripts on individual 'key' countries have been omitted; chapter 4 is a conflation of what were originally two scripts. Four new chapters have been added: three of these deal with the impact of nationalism and modernisation in the Arab lands, Iran and Turkey respectively, with particular emphasis on the ways in which these factors have led to a departure from the norms of Islamic civilisation, and their psychological effects on intellectuals and others in those areas. An attempt has been made in these chapters to assess the extent to which the pressures of nationalism and modern political and economic structures have undermined, and bid fair to destroy, that unity and cohesiveness of Islamic civilisation with which the greater part of the book is concerned. The fourth chapter deals with the continued existence of tribal society in one modern Islamic country – Iraq.

In the course of restructuring the original Radiostudy material, the editorial committee decided to seek authors outside the Department of Islamic Studies in a few cases: chapters have been contributed by two other Canadian scholars as well as one British scholar who has been a Visiting Professor in the Department.

In its present form, *Introduction to Islamic Civilisation* begins with the geographic, ethnic and linguistic background of the Middle East. For practical and other reasons, the book has been limited to the central Islamic lands of the Middle East; such areas of the Islamic world as Moorish Spain and the Maghrib (Muslim North Africa) have therefore not been given special treatment but have been referred to in their logical context. After a brief historical résumé of the Islamic period, the book moves on to examine the religious, philosophical and legal foundations of Islamic society and its contributions to world civilisation in the field of literature, art, science and medicine. It also deals with the interaction between the East and the Christian West from the Crusades in medieval times down to the massive encroachment of the West upon the Muslim world at all levels – military, political, economic and cultural – in the modern era. Throughout the book, the canvas has been painted with broad strokes, so that the reader will not get lost in a mass of detail. It is hoped that he will become familiar with the basic facts and problems of Islamic studies, and will at the same time be stimulated to the study of particular trends and ideas as elaborated in more specialised literature.

A few words regarding the system of transliteration used are in order: Islamic names and terms which are in common use in English (e.g. Mecca) are given in their English forms. Other Arabic and Persian words are rendered generally according to the 'romanisation' schemes approved jointly by both the American and Canadian Library Associations and the U.S. Library of Congress.[1] As these schemes are used in the catalogues of nearly all major libraries in North America and many libraries elsewhere, their use will enable the reader easily to locate in his own institution books by or about Islamic authors or subjects mentioned in the present text. Ottoman Turkish is rendered according to the 'Ottoman Turkish Transliteration Scheme' devised by Eleazar Birnbaum.[2] The official (Latin) 'Turkish alphabet' of 1928 is used for modern Turkish. Islamic words common to these three languages will consequently appear in some cases, in slightly different forms: e.g. Aḥmad and 'Uthmān (Arabic), Aḥmed and 'Os̱mān (Turkish).

1 See U.S. Library of Congress, Processing Department, *Cataloging Service*. Bulletin 91 [Arabic Romanisation], 92 [Persian Romanisation]. Washington, September 1970.

2 See E. Birnbaum, 'The Transliteration of Ottoman Turkish for Library and General Purposes', *Journal of the American Oriental Society*, vol. 87, no. 2 (1967) pp. 123ff.: (Transliteration Scheme, pp. 134–56). The major libraries both within and outside Turkey have not yet adopted a consistent romanisation.

PUBLISHER'S NOTE

The publisher and editors are grateful to the following for permission to reproduce photographs in their possession, on the pages listed:

Aerofilms Ltd, 131; Rev. J. C. Allan, 38, 40 (above & below), 136, 166, 185 (above); Miss Anne Bolt, 3, 9, 11, 13, 155, 159; Peter Baker, 31; Bibliotheque Nationale, Paris, 100, 101; The British Library, 63, 64, 66, 110; Cambridge University Library, 117; J. Allan Cash, cover, 21, 45, 96, 168, 173 (above & below), 185 (below); The Chester Beatty Library, Dublin, 178; Alastair Duncan (The Middle East Archive), 95, 109 (above & below), 143, 149, 157 (above & below); The Fitzwilliam Museum, Cambridge, 90, 92, 99; Giraudon, Paris, 78, 97 (above); A. F. Kersting, 16, 22, 181; The Mansell Collection, 32, 115, 118, 139, 151, 183; The National Maritime Museum, London, 133; Österreichische Nationalbibliothek, 5, 106; Photo Mas, Barcelona, 91, 97 (below), 126; The Pierpoint Morgan Library, 103, 104; Topkapı Saray Museum, Istanbul, 28, 178; R. Wood, 14; Victoria and Albert Museum, 88, 93 (above & below), 107; Photo Yan, 129

I

Introduction to the Middle East

G. M. WICKENS

Location and significant geography

The term 'Middle East' is not local to the area itself but seems to have been coined by the American naval historian A. T. Mahan, about 1900, as part of his strategic analysis into Near, Middle and Far East. In much the same sense, it was taken up by British and other strategists during and after the First World War. The term itself has remained, even being adopted (somewhat illogically) by the Russians, the Chinese, and the peoples of the Middle East themselves; but its significance, while nearly always including *certain* countries, nowadays varies a good deal in extent as compared with former usage. (One may mention in passing that the term 'Near East' is much less often met with than formerly, except in reference to Ancient Egypt, Palestine, Anatolia and Mesopotamia, i.e. for a large part of the region in the pre-Christian and early-Christian era.) The following is a *maximum* list of Middle Eastern countries according to present usage (many would restrict it considerably): In North Africa, Libya, Egypt, the Sudan, and perhaps Ethiopia, Somalia, and the 'horn' of Africa generally; in Asia, Saudi Arabia and such smaller neighbours as Yemen, Kuwait, and the Persian Gulf states; further north, Israel, Jordan, Syria and Lebanon; further north still, and running westwards into Europe, modern Turkey. Returning to Asia, and moving east from Jordan and Syria, we come to Iraq, Iran (or Persia), Afghanistan and Pakistan. (The latter state, of course, since the secession of Bangladesh, corresponds only to the former West Pakistan.) This is an enormous and shapeless mass enough, but – even so – some would add Cyprus and parts of the Balkans in the west, the Caucasus and five southern Soviet republics in the centre, and Kashmir and other bits and pieces in the east. Broadly speaking, then, the Middle East runs from the Central Mediterranean to North-west India, and from Central Africa to Central Asia; in a narrower sense, it refers to the Eastern Mediterranean area and western or south-western Asia.

So much for location: what of the significant geography? First, one must stress the diversity of this region: it is emphatically not one great sand-desert, nor even one great desert at all – though it does lie in one of the world's arid belts, where cultivation must depend, nearly everywhere, on irrigation works of varying degrees of complexity. Throughout the whole area, there are only three great river-systems: the Nile, mostly in Egypt and the Sudan; the Tigris–Euphrates, mostly in Iraq; and the Indus complex, mostly in Pakistan. These three river-systems, of course, gave birth to three of the great original civilisations of mankind, many centuries before the coming of Islam; and the civilisatory drive of the area has been one of the few constants throughout all the vicissitudes of nature and history. In comparison with the cultivators of these great valleys and of many scattered lesser areas, the nomads that Western convention associates with the region as a whole form a marked and constantly decreasing minority. Even more characteristic, this is the region where the concept of the city was born, and many of the greatest of the original foundations still survive and thrive (sometimes with populations that have for centuries been numbered in the millions): Cairo, Alexandria, Jerusalem, Damascus, Baghdad, Istanbul, Ankara, Tehran, Iṣfahān, Samarqand, Bukhārā and Karachi – to say nothing of dozens of others somewhat smaller, such as Baṣra, Hamadan, Kermanshah, Shiraz, Tabriz, Smyrna, Beirut, Port Said, Aden, and so on. Moreover, even this tally takes no account of the many once famous places that have fallen foul of military

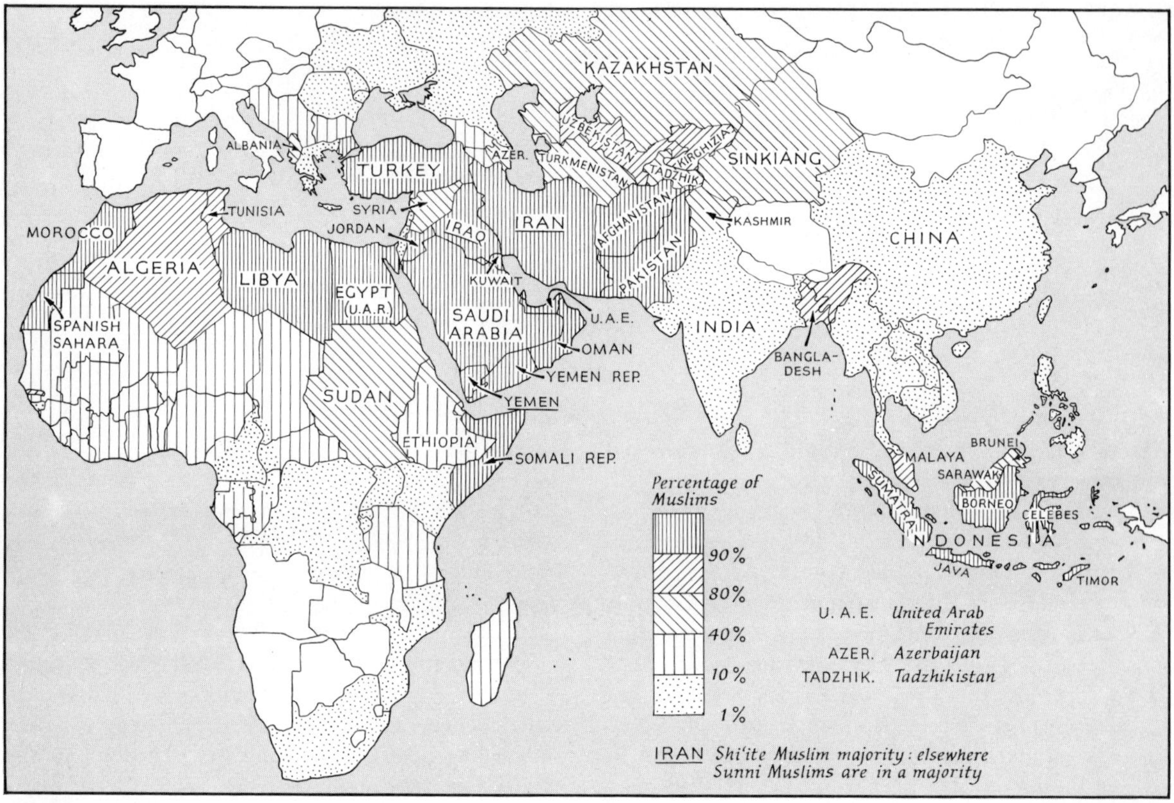

Distribution of Islam in the world today

devastation or economic change: Kūfah, Nīshāpūr, Ṭūs, Sīrāf, Rayy, Marv, Marāghah, and the rest.

To come back to our original theme: there is, then, great geographical diversity, and it is marked not only over the extreme ranges from north to south or east to west, but often over small or medium-sized areas within the individual countries themselves. Turkey, for example, has a 'mediterranean'-type coastal strip both on the Mediterranean itself and along the Black Sea, but inland it is one great mountainous plateau with often the bitterest of weather conditions. In its northern section Iran has snow-capped peaks, one of which, Demavand, is nearly two-thirds as high as Everest; in its southern reaches it shares with Iraq a well-watered and fertile, but uncomfortably hot and humid, area that provides some of the world's best dates. Iraq itself has almost as great a range of contrasts; and the short journey from the Mediterranean coast up and over the Lebanon and Anti-Lebanon mountains traverses a diversity of climate and terrain that is classic throughout the tourist world. Only in specific regions like the Sahara or Central Arabia can one count on enormous unbroken tracts of sandy or dusty waste; only in the Persian Gulf, the Red Sea or the Southern Sudan can one predict relentless heat at all times of the day and year.

Again, one must repeat, most of this vast area, outside the cities, is peopled – wherever habitation is possible at all – not so much by nomads as by industrious and skilful cultivators. Inevitably, tradition still rules the lives of such people (as it does the world over); but the new technology in both agriculture and industry, as well as changing economic and political forces generally, is subjecting the old patterns of their lives to severe strains and distortions.

Over such a vast and varied area, it goes without saying that communications have been difficult, and even downright poor, for most of its history. Yet for many centuries some very efficient post-roads and military routes were maintained by governments,

Morocco. Chaouen, a small town in the Rif Mountains, Lower Atlas

and used extensively by the ubiquitous merchants and pilgrims. One of these in particular, with a main trunk and several branches, is still in use along much of its length: the Great Silk Road from China to the Mediterranean. The rivers, though not always navigable for their entire length, have also either been used extensively in themselves or have provided suitable routes to be followed by roads, and later by railways. But many roads – especially those most used over the centuries by the caravans of wandering merchants, scholars, mystics, pilgrims and rogues – have struck out boldly across wilderness and mountains, thereby exposing the travellers to even greater hardship and danger than usual on the long hauls from one oasis to the next. The more one considers the natural obstacles to communication (and, of course, to settlement) in the Middle East, the more one must acknowledge the accomplishments of past ages in both spreading and holding together a culture whose underlying oneness is no less remarkable than its vigorous variety. But more of this later. Sea-travel has been less used for local movement, though the Middle East did develop extensive sea-trade with both India and the Far East, as well as with southern Europe. In recent years the communications picture has been transformed, partly by the internal-combustion engine and by cable and radio (to say nothing of satellites), but most importantly by the use of the airplane.

Ethnic groupings and cultures

The basic substratum of ethnic groupings in the Middle East takes in *all* the peoples of antiquity, including many now completely lost as recognisable entities: Egyptians, Nubians, Berbers, Arabs, Ethiopians, Jews, Babylonians, Phoenicians, Assyrians, Greeks, Hittites, Medes and Persians, Scythians, Armenians, Indians, Georgians, and so on. This human mishmash – to which we owe most of the basic arts of civilisation (government, writing, agriculture, metal-working, building, philosophy, and the rest) – was briefly and superficially unified, over three centuries before Christ, by Alexander's conquests. In the early centuries of the Christian era, moreover, it was permeated more thoroughly, if less extensively, by Hellenistic culture and by the conflicting forces of Roman and Persian organisation. At the time of the initial Islamic expansion, in the early seventh century of our era, the Middle East divides essentially into two halves: a Western, Christian half, often torn by internal quarrels, but essentially sound and vigorous; and an Eastern, Persian Zoroastrian half, still apparently formidable and monolithic, but in fact somewhat hollow within. Yet, culturally, a great paradox revealed itself: Islam, with certain clearly defined limits, set its own (as we might say) 'Arab' mark on the Western half; in the Eastern half, however, it was the Persian culture of Iran that set its own enduring and protean mark on Islam.

So we have come to the rise of Islam, the faith and culture that has given this vast, disparate, shapeless, often divided area its one overriding common interest that is only nowadays being seriously eroded by modernisation and materialism, whether these be capitalistic or Communist. Islam began as an exclusively Arab religious movement, in the commercial centres (not among the nomads) of central Arabia, and Arabic has remained its official holy tongue, the language of its original revelation. Islam was also in the early decades spread abroad, to the west, the north and the east, by bands – often quite modest-sized bands – of Arabs from Arabia and the area where Arabia joins the modern states of Jordan, Syria and Iraq. But the faith and its associated culture very swiftly outgrew the Arabs as such, and ultimately transcended their classical, written language and their several spoken dialects; and this faith and culture now belong, on any showing, to the peoples of the area as a whole and to many millions even further afield. At the present day, in the area itself, it is particularly associated not only with the several so-called Arab lands, but with Persia, Turkey, Afghanistan and Pakistan – all of which have their very distinctive Islamic cultures and languages.

Perhaps a little more should be said about these central problems of Islamic identity and 'Arabness', for they contain the seeds of grave misunderstanding, whether considered at the level of pure academics or in terms of practical politics. The relatively few Arab conquerors did not exterminate or drive out the original inhabitants of other lands, but – after a period of racial exclusiveness – mingled freely with them. Accordingly, save in their own areas of origin (as mentioned above), it is virtually impossible to speak of 'Arabs' with any significant degree of precision. Few of the inhabitants of North Africa, from Egypt to Morocco, enjoy an undisputed ethnic title to be Arabs, though most of them are Muslims, and they read and write Arabic (if they are literate) and speak different dialects of it. But the Persians, Afghans and

Horseman, from a tenth-century Arabic manuscript

Pakistanis are certainly not Arabs at all (though they may have some Arab blood, together with Turkish and Mongol strains), nor do they normally write or speak Arabic: indeed, many Arabs and other Muslims even grudge some of them membership of the Islamic family in any full sense. The Turks, starting from their distant ancestral homes in central and north-east Asia, did not arrive on the Middle Eastern scene in any dominant way before the ninth century of our era at the earliest: not only are they non-Arab and non-Arabic-using, but nowadays they do not even write in the Arabic script. Individually, many of them are still practising Muslims in some sense, but of all the Islamic states Turkey has gone farthest towards deliberate secularisation.

If so many Middle Eastern Muslims are not Arabs, this applies even more to several clearly defined non-Muslim communities, such as the Armenians, the Assyrians, the Arameans, and possibly the Copts. But one word, just to complicate the picture, on the other side: sizeable communities of Arabs are not, and have never been, Muslim but Christian. There is a heavy concentration of these in Lebanon and Jordan, but smaller groupings are found in other countries: they range from Eastern Catholics, independent or in union with Rome or with the Greek Orthodox Church, through Anglicans and Lutherans, to such venerable foundations as the Nestorians and the Monophysites. So strong is the cultural attraction of Islam that these Christian Arabs, though often distrusted and victimised by their Muslim brethren, have always been in the vanguard of Islamic cultural advances. At the present time, they provide many of the most passionate Arab nationalists.

In comparatively modern times, say over the last two or three centuries, the West has been destroying the traditional life-pattern of this multi-ethnic, multi-cultural civilisation by the introduction (part-deliberate, part-unconscious) of its own modern technology – both peaceful and military – of its principles of divisive nationalism and ballot-box political democracy, and of a gigantic, radically new economic structure. In many instances, of course, the West has had willing allies and successors among Middle Eastern leaders themselves, but this has not made the process any easier or ultimately more successful. All is now in flux; and violence (as we all know) is often bitter, continuous, and on a massive scale. But until these forces made themselves felt, the traditional culture of this vast area, for something like 1000 years, was flourishing, stable and flexible. It has been well described as 'diversity in unity'.

At the human and humane level, though in all this vast area, over the central 1000 years of its Islamic history, blood was shed in dynastic wars, in brigandage, in riots and in assassinations, these things were not the rule but the exception, and their scale and ferocity by the standards of our own age was very limited indeed. However exaggerated the claims of modern Muslim apologists for the natural and inherent tolerance of their society, it could in practice certainly stand comparison with our own. During all this time the greatest violence came to the Middle East from outside invasions, from the Mongols on several occasions between about 1220 and 1400, and from the ostensibly Christian Crusaders between about 1100 and 1300.

Brief history of the area over the last 13–14 centuries

Some pointers to this have already been given. At the Prophet's death in 632 of our era, the young Islamic religion, with its nascent state-machine and culture, was almost wholly Arab, confined (somewhat patchily) to the Arabian peninsula, and based on the mid-Arabian cities of Mecca and Medina. Within 30 years 'Islamdom' had spread throughout the peninsula, into and beyond Egypt, up the Mediterranean coast to Asia Minor, through Iraq up to the Caucasus, into Iran, and beyond into Central Asia and North-western India. The campaigns themselves, conducted by an Arab élite, were swift and nearly always outstandingly successful, not least because the conquered populations by and large improved their lot, at any rate during the initial years of the new régime.

The century that followed, i.e. from about 660 to 750, was the one great period of Arab pre-eminence, under the Umayyad Caliphs (or 'successors' of the Prophet), who moved the seat of authority to Damascus. During these years the conquered cultures were in disarray and Arabic culture was very much to the fore, its chief mode of expression being in an idiosyncratic poetry and rhetoric, which was beginning to graft vigorous new shoots onto a sturdy trunk of tradition. But there were also radical and total innovations in art and architecture, and in life-styles generally, nearly all traceable in some measure to Byzantium or Persia, or both. Above all, the Arab establishment was indebted to these two civilisations in particular for the sorts of men and methods needed to govern a large urbanised empire. During these 90 years up to A.D. 750 the Islamic civilisation spread through North Africa into Spain and across Asia to the borders of the T'ang Empire of China. Throughout all this time, whatever strengths Europe was secretly developing, it stood, and would stand for some nine or ten centuries to come, uneasily on guard, both physically and intellectually, against an almost constantly victorious Islamic Middle East.

The Umayyad dynasty collapsed in 750 under pressure from a number of forces: the conquered peoples were reasserting themselves in their resentment at being treated as second-class Muslim citizens, even when they had been made 'clients' (*mawālī*), or honorary Arabs; the more conservative Muslims, particularly of Arabia, were shocked by the worldly and innovative tendencies of the Damascus Caliphs; and the Shi'ites (some of Arab and other races, but a markedly high proportion of them Persian) could not accept either the current method of choosing the Prophet's successors, or the men chosen, or the functions assigned to them. The new dynasty, the 'Abbasids, reigned in Baghdad (but soon did little ruling) for just over 500 years. It soon became evident that they were far from satisfying any of the revolutionary groups whose dissidence had brought them to power, but they – or their 'controllers' – were clever politicians and efficient enforcers of other types of cohesion. Above all, they gave the Islamic world a focus that was at the very least cultural. Spain, Egypt and Iran (and later other provinces) all soon asserted varying but growing forms of independence – and this not only in politics and administration, and in the arts and crafts of living, but in several cases in spiritual and legistic allegiance; and in one remarkable instance, Iran, in that most intimate and pervasive of all human creations, language. But, whatever the prides and glories of Cordova or Cairo or Damascus or Ṭūs, all roads led, in all manner of significant connections, to and from Baghdad. Culturally and administratively, this period from 750 to 1250 was marked by Persian ascendancy and assimilation; militarily, the Turkic warriors progressively gained control; and in both aspects this holds not only for the heart of the Empire, but far out into the provinces, the classic exception being – in this, as in so many other things – the Iberian Peninsula in the far west. But socially, and even economically, the whole area was one; and for most of these 500 years there was an incredible richness of action and interaction in literature, philosophy, science, mathematics, medicine, theology, building, craftsmanship and commerce. The Golden Age, whether one uses the term idealistically or with some measure of realism, is commonly regarded as the reign of Hārūn al-Rashīd, or the slightly longer period from about 780 to 830; but in fact the whole half-millennium was one of the great periods of steady forward movement in the history of man.

Until very recently Islamic historiography and sociology remained abnormally unsophisticated, and it was usually maintained, quite simplistically, that this great Middle Eastern civilisation associated with Islam fossilised and declined as a result of the Mongol invasions and the rise of the Ottoman Turks (and similar dynasties in Iran and India). But such statements beg a number of questions. Was there in fact a fossilisation and decline after 1250, and more particularly after 1500? Were the Mongols and the Turks and others responsible, or were other, far more subtle and complicated, processes at work? Could these Central Asian peoples have had any serious effect on matters at all if the structure had not been gravely impaired already? What do such assertions, and such questions, mean anyway when subjected to rigid logical and semantic analysis?

What *can* be said with some confidence is this: after 1258 the centre of gravity of Islamic culture and prosperity was no longer embodied in a Caliph in Baghdad, but moved variously to Iran, Afghanistan, Central Asia and India; and, from about 1450 onwards, it could be measured most constantly and most centrally – but by no means exclusively – in and around Asia Minor, and particularly in Constantinople, soon to be generally known as Istanbul. Over the area as a whole, there was no commercial decline (quite the reverse), though the centres of prosperity changed. Culturally too, the story was much the same, if not more so. Indeed, until well into the last century, the Middle East was efficiently busy enough about its own affairs, whether worldly, intellectual or spiritual. But they were very much its *own* affairs. With very few exceptions, the mind of the Middle East from about 1450 to 1850 was largely closed to the realities of the world around it, even where those realities lay close and painfully to hand. Moreover, even within its own orbit, the dynamics of thrust, originality and inventiveness were running down, and this at a time when the West was confidently discovering and applying motive springs of change that were apparently inexhaustible – however mindless and destructive they might prove to be in the long run.

Social structure of the traditional Middle East

By and large, this was a society based on agriculture, craftsmanship and commerce, with a tendency to centralised administration, to religiously based legalism, and to the maintenance of large professional armies. Having to maintain these three weighty and unproductive institutions (a largely tax-*gathering* administration, an elaborate religio-legal corps, and a demanding soldiery), as well as to provide great luxury for its upper classes, it was a conservative and heavily taxed society – one in which effort seemed most profitably applied not in trying to make fundamental changes, but in scheming to outwit the bureaucrat, the lawyer and the soldier, and to live one's life and do one's work in peace. Except among the Shi'ite minority, there was no official religious caste, though there were in fact everywhere, after the ideally simple early years, large corporations of religious and legal functionaries (the two categories often overlapping). To judge from literature of all kinds, the most typical 'middle' figures of this society were the merchant, the scholar, and the wandering or settled mystic. If Islam did not by any means confer all the equality its apologists nowadays often claim, it was nevertheless an open society in the sense that most people could see and know other people's business, whether private or professional; and it was also a society where the tendency to centralised administration was offset by a simplicity of life-style, and by the bonds of family, local community and professional occupation. It seems that, in a world that was essentially so much poorer and rougher than our own, most people who had the ability to profit by it could get a good, inexpensive education, and many sick people or wanderers stood a good chance of having their needs met cheaply and efficiently – and all this without elaborate administrative machinery or fantastic public outlay. The West's greatest disservice to the Middle East was the destruction, witting or otherwise, of this way of life and the failure to replace it by an efficient copy of a Western substitute. Of course, we now know that even the best of Western substitutes might have proved a doubtful blessing – but that is another matter.

Two remarks must be made on the negative side. First, there was – after the early decades of Islam – absolutely no place whatsoever for women in public life. There was no modern-type male hypocrisy about this: it was declared and undisputed policy and philosophy. Women did have limited but guaranteed rights, and they could carry on various sorts of business by proxy. A few achieved fame as poets or mystics, or even as scholars; and many, at all levels of society, naturally played important and influential parts behind the scenes. But there was a sense in which they had no identity outside the family, belonging (so to speak) to some male or other, father, husband, brother, uncle, or whatever. Given some yardstick of happiness, one may well judge their lot generally better or worse than that of many women in the West, either at the time or nowadays; but if proper concern is with elusive abstractions like freedom and dignity, they were unquestionably the victims of serious injustices. Things have changed; but this is still one of the gravest problems facing Islamic social reformers, for there has lately even been a violent male backlash in many places against the slightest relaxation of what is felt to be divinely ordained practice.

Similarly with racial or religious minorities: these

had their limited but legally guaranteed rights, they often enjoyed great prosperity and influence, and actual persecution in the European sense was rare: but ultimately most Muslims looked on them as a sort of non-people. It is an attitude not notably worse than what often passes in our own society, but one still far from ideal.

At its best, however, the traditional Middle East social pattern was held together by a religiously based *social* sense far transcending its counterpart in the pre-modern West. In many ways Islam was as other-worldly and as prudish as some post-Augustinian Christianity, as preoccupied with drink and sex (or at least only extra-marital sex in the case of Islam) as being, in practice, most grievous sources of sin. But there was always powerful concern with the welfare of fellow-believers, if not with that of mankind in general. The most common bequests (outside the statutory family requirements) were for the care of orphans, the sick, travellers and scholars, and the upkeep of roads, bridges, colleges and so on.

Civilisatory achievements of the Middle East over the last 1300 years, and their legacy in the West

The Middle East has of course been, since the remotest past, the main source of *all* civilisation, and to it we owe such fundamental inventions as those listed in the opening paragraph of Chapter 11. However, it is not with these basics that we are concerned here, but with the subtler, smaller, less essential and less familiar, achievements and legacies of later times.

The Islamic Middle East was most active in all the arts, crafts and sciences of traditional, pre-modern civilisation, and in many of them it made permanent and unique contributions to the world stock. Some of these achievements were virtually original, many were obviously developments of earlier inventions or discoveries either made on the spot or imported from further to the east. Not all of them have left a permanent legacy within Islam itself, for that culture is in many ways only an attenuated version of what it once was; nor have they all affected the non-Muslim world, since some of them were so much a part of their own ambience as to be incapable of transmission.

Three aspects of the civilisation that are relatively poorly represented at the present day, and that could in the nature of the case hardly be transmitted to the non-Islamic world, were language, literature and the religious Law. But in their heyday these three fields of endeavour absorbed many of the best minds in the Middle East in the production of works of fantastic majesty and elaboration. An enormous amount, though still only a fraction, has been preserved and is studied by us in the West at the present time, particularly in comparative contexts. The essential point to be grasped here is that the traditional civilisation of the Middle East is in every sense what we might call classical – preoccupied with the niceties of linguistic and literary expression, and dedicated to the ordering of all sides of life by legal prescription. There is a close parallel here with Rome at its best, although intellectually the most important influences came from Greece.

Still in the realm of mind and spirit, the Islamic Middle East was long the home of a vigorous tradition of religious and philosophical speculation. Naturally, the religion and its spin-offs were transmitted directly by conversion over a wide area; but otherwise, interaction was virtually out of the question. If much Islamic theological speculation parallels that of Christianity, it is rather because essentially similar people were tackling similar problems with almost identical tools. The tools were derived from Greek and general Middle Eastern thought, but they were very certainly sharpened and developed by the thinkers of Islam before they were passed to the West in the 12th and 13th centuries. The West was eventually to use them with destructive effect on the whole medieval world-system, while in the Middle East itself they became blunted by repeated use in a mechanical fashion.

As a transition from the abstract to the concrete, we may instance science, medicine and mathematics. Here again, the ultimate source was Greek or general Middle Eastern, but the Islamic input is a very clear one; it might, indeed, have been overwhelmingly impressive if the medieval Muslims, like virtually all pre-modern thinkers, had not been handicapped by a deep reverence for the concept of absolute truth and for authority of all kinds, and by their own over-ingenious theories. In astronomy and chemistry their work went about as far as man could go without the telescope on the one hand, and a clearer grasp of chemical structure and of true scientific method on the other. In medicine the great achievements were in diagnosis, treatment with drugs and diets, and surgery of the eye: prejudice against dissection

This small Moroccan girl will be veiled by the age of puberty

hampered general surgical progress, as also did the lack of efficient anaesthetics and sterilisation. In mathematics the development of the decimal system of reckoning, though ultimately of enormous practical significance, was overshadowed by their brilliant work in algebra (the very word is Arabic) and in trigonometry. Virtually all the achievements in these three areas – science, medicine and mathematics – where known to the West at all (as sometimes through Spain), were taken over bodily and left unchanged for centuries. Many of those not known at the time (e.g. logarithms, fractions, work on optics, cholesterol control, and so on) were only discovered later, often much later, in the West by painfully long independent research. Many modern scientists and historians of science are quite unaware of this.

But the most enduring and memorable contributions of the Islamic Middle East to the West lie in material things, where the very names are so often themselves Arabic, Persian or Turkish in origin, however heavily disguised the modern forms may be. The channels of transmission for these were normally those of commerce or warfare. In architecture there were the dome, the alcove, and various types of arch; in military affairs, commanders-in-chief and arsenals (both betokening a new type of large-scale organisation), techniques of fortification, weapons, and various items of horse-harness and cavalry tactics; in commerce, large-scale warehousing, various textiles (cotton, muslin, satin, damask, fustian, taffeta), and administrative terms such as tariff, customs-house and tare; items of furniture (sofa, mattress, divan, ottoman); food and drink (sherbet, yoghurt, kebab, saffron, rice, jar, lemon, coffee, pilaf, halva, Turkish delight); plants, fruits and flowers of all kinds (oranges, apricots, tulips, lilacs, limes, dates, and so on). . . The list could be almost infinitely extended, even within these few arbitrary classes. Even so, it leaves out such major areas as carpets, music and ceramics, and odd items like chess, paper-making, windmills, and talc; to say nothing of the dozens of things easily identifiable by a specific (if sometimes inaccurate) Middle Eastern reference, such as Turkish tobacco, Turkish baths and towels, Morocco leather, Persian slippers, gum Arabic, Arabian horses, and so on and so forth. More will be said about all of these legacies in detail in Chapter 12.

The encounter of the Middle East with the West, and the contemporary situation

If the Middle East was so effective in the past, why is it in such difficulties now? There is no definitive, much less a simple, answer, as to why one society declines and another unexpectedly prospers, or why – in a long drawn-out struggle – one doubtful protagonist eventually overcomes what looks like a certain winner. At any rate, whatever the ultimate and enormous deficiencies of Western culture, and whatever the several (usually unsuspected) merits of the Middle East, the West has, over the last four centuries, gradually infiltrated, undermined and dominated the Middle East in a way virtually unparallelled in any other time or place. Even now, when direct political control is largely over, the U.S.A. and the U.S.S.R. still often call the tunes in Israel and Egypt, and economic manipulation and social destruction are as evident as ever.

The dynamic of Western penetration between about 1550 and 1800 was less political than commercial and technological; and the Middle East stood ready as an ideal, relatively settled theatre of operations because of the well-knit administrative machinery that controlled it – machinery that was ages-old but had been particularly highly developed by the Mongols and later the Ottoman Turks and others. This process of penetration had been going on for some time previously with the Venetians, the Genoese, and later the Portuguese: as one example, one may cite Marco Polo and his family, who had taken advantage of a well-organised but conservative East long before 1300. But from the mid-16th century on, everything was to happen on a vastly increased and constantly accelerating scale. For a long time, it was not at all clear that any sort of real or ultimate contest was in progress. The balance of forces may well have shifted conclusively by the early nineteenth century, but political and military trials of strength did not go consistently in favour of the West until well into the nineteenth. The Turks, it should be remembered, could still threaten Vienna as late as 1683, and Napoleon's Middle East campaign (which opened in 1798 and tailed off some three years later) was anything but a resoundingly clear success; the so-called Indian Mutiny and the Afghan and Sudanese wars caused Britain some bad times, even in the greatest days of Imperial power, and the Turks could still give bloody noses to the Allies during and

Morocco. Children playing in the sand outside one of the main gates of Fez

after the First World War. Moreover, as I have said already, the Middle East was still successfully busy about its own internal affairs as late as 1850.

If the secret behind the shift of dominance lies anywhere, it is certainly not in any of the easy explanations that are commonly advanced: an enervating climate, innate racial characteristics, the fatalism and rigidity of Islam as a religion, Mongol destructiveness, Turkish incompetence, corruption and crudity, and so on and so forth. What we have to try to understand, leaving aside some inevitable elements of chance, is why the commercial and technological dynamic developed in such a dramatic and self-sustaining fashion in the West, rather than in the East where the groundwork had been so well laid. A primary reason is certainly socio-political: society in the Middle East was, so to speak, too well integrated and uniform, working too smoothly for its own good. In the West society had developed a number of abrasive interests and counter-interests, of which obvious examples are church and state, monarchy and the free cities, monarchy and the landed, military aristocracy, the latter against the merchant bourgeoisie or the yeoman farmer, and so on. Not only did these multi-faceted confrontations interact with each other, but new forces were generated in the process: the corporations, for example – trade, academic, legal and medical – emerge in the West not as mere functional groups but as vigorous gadflies in society at large. All the new learning and the new skills were resisted by the same elements as opposed them in Islam, but there were in the West lively new champions prepared to press on, using force or persuasion, wherever, however far and however fast the new currents might be flowing.

If the East did not properly realise what was happening, neither did the West, but the West was favoured by a rising curve of circumstance and could afford its ignorance. The East, of course, was not simply penetrated, exploited, upset: it also reacted to the new things and methods the West was bringing, in some cases gladly accepting and copying, in others rejecting and forgetting. But even where it received and became proficient – in navigation, gunnery, smaller mechanical inventions, civil and military organisation, and so on – it failed until very recently to understand the essential spirit and drive that had led to these things, or what they themselves could lead to in terms of social and economic disintegration and servitude. The Middle Eastern modernisers and liberals have by now become almost as disenchanted with the West and its ways as were the original horrified conservatives who denounced firearms and printing as *bid'ah*, 'unlawful innovation', or black magic performed by infidel barbarians.

During the last 150 years several dramatic new factors have entered into this unsatisfactory relationship. From 1820 or so on, the Middle East became *strategically* important to the West as the latter's political and military interests now acquired worldwide scope. This importance grew sharply after 1850, and led to actual occupation and domination by various powers (chiefly Britain, France and Russia) on an increasing, and increasingly oppressive, scale. In such a situation, all sorts of institutions were taken over and consciously and drastically reformed – government, the civil service, the military, communications, education, and so on. Likewise, those countries (such as Iran and Turkey) that were not occupied, but strongly influenced, tried to reorganise their own institutions along similar lines. Various benefits undoubtedly accrued overall; but this was not the essential purpose of the exercise, and great harm was done too, especially since the process was in most ways external and irrelevant to the life of the people, or actually destructive of the very social machinery by which they operated from day to day. By 1900, even greater tensions were created by the West's discovery and need of the rich *oil deposits* in the area; and also by the *active disputing of Middle Eastern territory* among the various Western powers (Britain, France and Russia as before, with a powerful new Germany now added). By 1920, there had been added the rather large straw that was to break the Middle East's back: the problem that many, doubtless wrongly, assume to be the central, if not the only, one in the Middle East: Western sponsorship, in a muddled atmosphere of guile, ruthlessness, ignorance and idealism, of a *Jewish homeland*.

And so we arrive at the present-day situation, which we may characterise in a few brief final strokes. First, we are dealing with an area not generally rich or influential, but owing its importance to certain specialised strategic considerations and to stores of virtually only one commodity, oil, scattered rather widely and unevenly. Secondly, despite centuries of contact, this vast region is only partly and patchily westernised and industrialised, and generally unsympathetic to the West and the West's basic philo-

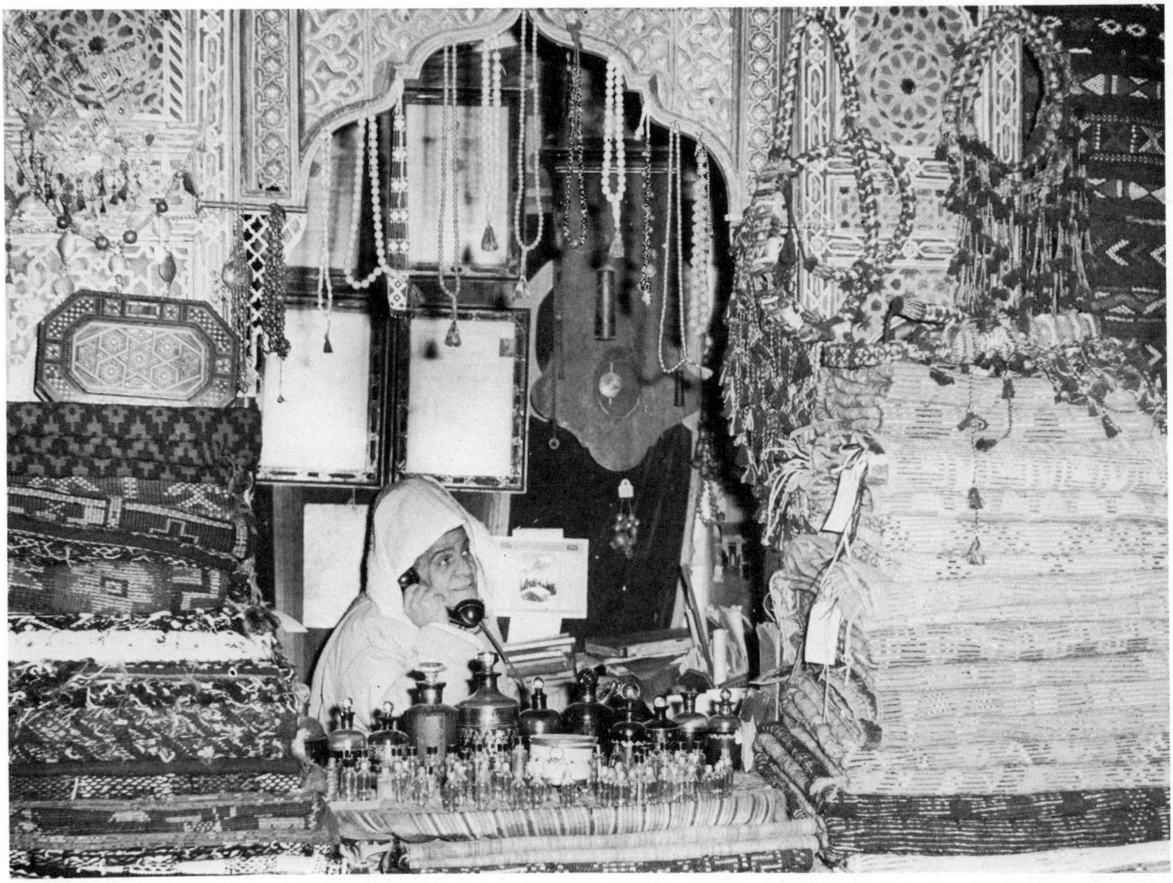

Morocco. A shop in the old quarter of Fez. The telephone adds a modern touch to the traditional display of carpets, jewelry, perfume and porcelain

sophies. Thirdly, a once proud and dominant culture has lost much of its own old identity and confidence, without being able to secure a real grasp on new ones, particularly in the modern corporate and industrial sense. (The West's own growing loss of identity and confidence will of course not help matters in the future.) Fourth, politically and economically, the area is broken up into (often quite artificial) fragments, which grow increasingly irreconcilable, despite desperate initiatives to the contrary. Fifth, beneath a show of at least nominal independence, the West (nowadays represented by the U.S.A. and the U.S.S.R.) still plays its power games, with Arabs and Israelis serving often as not much more than pawns.

As the past has shown, the people of the Middle East are just as clever as the Chinese, and just as tough and conscientious as the Japanese. What prevents them from showing such qualities at the present day, what drains their energies in the battle for existence or for futile and illusory ideals, is largely an accident – an accident first of history and then of social evolution along a road that made them easy victims for others. The present, with few exceptions, is squalid, and these unfortunately are days when few of those caught in squalidity have any longer much hope of triumphing over it. Individuals sometimes believe they see the way clear, but societies move slowly and reluctantly at this stage. If individuals cannot realise their goals, however, whether good or bad, this is certainly an age when – as the skyjackers and terrorists have shown – they can cause incalculable damage and suffering to themselves and others indiscriminately.

All the themes touched upon in this introductory chapter will now be taken up in detail in Chapters 2–17, and drawn together again in the final chapter.

North Africa. The Great Mosque at Qayrawān, built mainly between the ninth and thirteenth centuries

2

The historical background of Islamic civilisation

C. E. BOSWORTH

I

Seventh to thirteenth centuries: the rise of Islam and the age of the Caliphate

Islam begins with Arabia and the Arabs, and despite the brotherhood and equality of believers which Islam preaches, Arabdom has always retained special prestige within the Islamic world, a prestige buttressed by the religious respect accorded to the Arabic language as the 'tongue of the angels', the medium for God's Word manifested through Muḥammad in the Qur'ān.

In the Ancient World, the Arabian peninsula was a cultural and religious backwater, only marginally affected by such great civilisations as those of Egypt, Israel, Phoenicia, Mesopotamia and Persia. The Assyrians at times exercised suzerainty over the Aribi or proto-Arabs of northern Arabia from the eighth century B.C. onwards, and during the course of this millennium, petty kingdoms arose and flourished in South Arabia, including Sabā' or Sheba. These principalities had commercial and cultural links with the Levant and the eastern Mediterranean, and the whole region of South Arabia acquired a reputation amongst the ancients as a land of fabulous wealth, *Arabia Felix* ('fortunate Arabia') and *Arabia Odorifera* ('fragrant Arabia', from the frankincense and other aromatics obtained from or through there).

Yet paradoxically, Islam arose in the centre of Arabia, the most culturally isolated and economically backward region, in the towns of Mecca and Medina, the first of which depended for its modicum of prosperity on the caravan transit-trade across the peninsula. The Prophet's Meccan origin and his relative unawareness of the outside world – Muslim tradition heightens the wonder of the Qur'ān which he brought by referring to him as 'the unlettered prophet' – gave a specifically Arabian flavour to the new faith, even though much of the message of the Qur'ān clearly has Biblical antecedents and many of the Islamic cult practices are rooted in Christian and especially Jewish models.

The exact motivation for the appearance of the new religion remains obscure, but the personal faith of Muḥammad and the band of enthusiasts which he collected around himself, the Companions, obviously provided the catalyst for a mighty outpouring of the Arabs from the confines of the peninsula over much of the Mediterranean basin and southwest Asia. Within less than a century after Muḥammad's death in 632, Arab warriors reached the Atlantic in Morocco and the Indus River in what is now Pakistan. In 710 they had first crossed the Straits of Gibraltar into Spain, and Arab cavalrymen, attracted by the rich abbeys and monasteries of Merovingian Gaul, were soon raiding as far as the Loire and Rhône valleys; the place-name of the Côte des Maures ('Moorish Coast'), on the modern French Riviera, stands as a reminder of the presence of Muslim raiders. A century or so later, the Arabs had extensive footholds in the western Mediterranean, transiently in Apulia in Italy, and more lastingly, until the Norman reconquest of the later eleventh century, in Sicily. Thus, above all through Spain and Sicily, tentative cultural contacts were to become possible in the Middle Ages between the two largely closed and mutually suspicious worlds of Islam and Western Christendom.

But the most enduring and significant alterations in the political and religious map of the Mediterranean basin and the Near East resulted from the clash of the expanding Arabs with two old-established empires, both of which had aspired to

Turkey, Istanbul. The Byzantine Land Walls, near the Cannon Gate (Topkapı), breached by the Ottoman conquerors in 1453

dominate the ancient world, Byzantium and Sasanid Persia. Byzantium had been an imperial power controlling extensive non-Greek populations – Armenians in eastern Anatolia, Semitic-speaking peoples in Syria and Palestine, Copts in Egypt, Romance-speaking peoples in Sicily and Italy, etc. In addition to these ethnic differences, there were religious stresses within the Christian communities of the empire; the Hellenistic strain of Christianity seems to have been alien to certain older, local religious attitudes. Hence attempts by Constantinople to impose the doctrinal formulations of the official Greek Church on the churches of Armenia, Syria and Egypt provoked fierce resentments, so that the indigenous peoples were not unreceptive to the spread of Arab rule over their lands during the years 634–42.

Byzantium survived the loss of its Near Eastern and North African provinces to the Arabs and, thrown back upon the mountainous heartlands of Anatolia and the Balkans, was to endure for another eight centuries until the Ottoman Turks finally captured Constantinople in 1453 and Trebizond in 1461 (see below, p. 25). The initial impetus of the Arabs thrice brought them to the gates of the capital, but the prize of the Second Rome eluded them and, as remarked above, it was to be Turks and not Arabs who achieved this supreme goal of Muslim arms. Over the intervening centuries, a *modus vivendi* grew up between Greeks and Muslims. Byzantium was the one infidel power which the Muslims really respected, both for the artistic glories of Byzantine civilisation and because the Byzantines were rightly regarded as the repositories of wisdom in such fields as science, medicine, philosophy and music. A persistent tradition among later Muslim historians says that the Caliph al-Walīd I (705–15) obtained skilled craftsmen and materials from the Byzantine Emperor for the decoration of the Umayyad Mosque in Damascus and the Prophet's Mosque in Medina. Several works by Greek philosophers like Plato and Aristotle and the Neoplatonists, by mathematicians

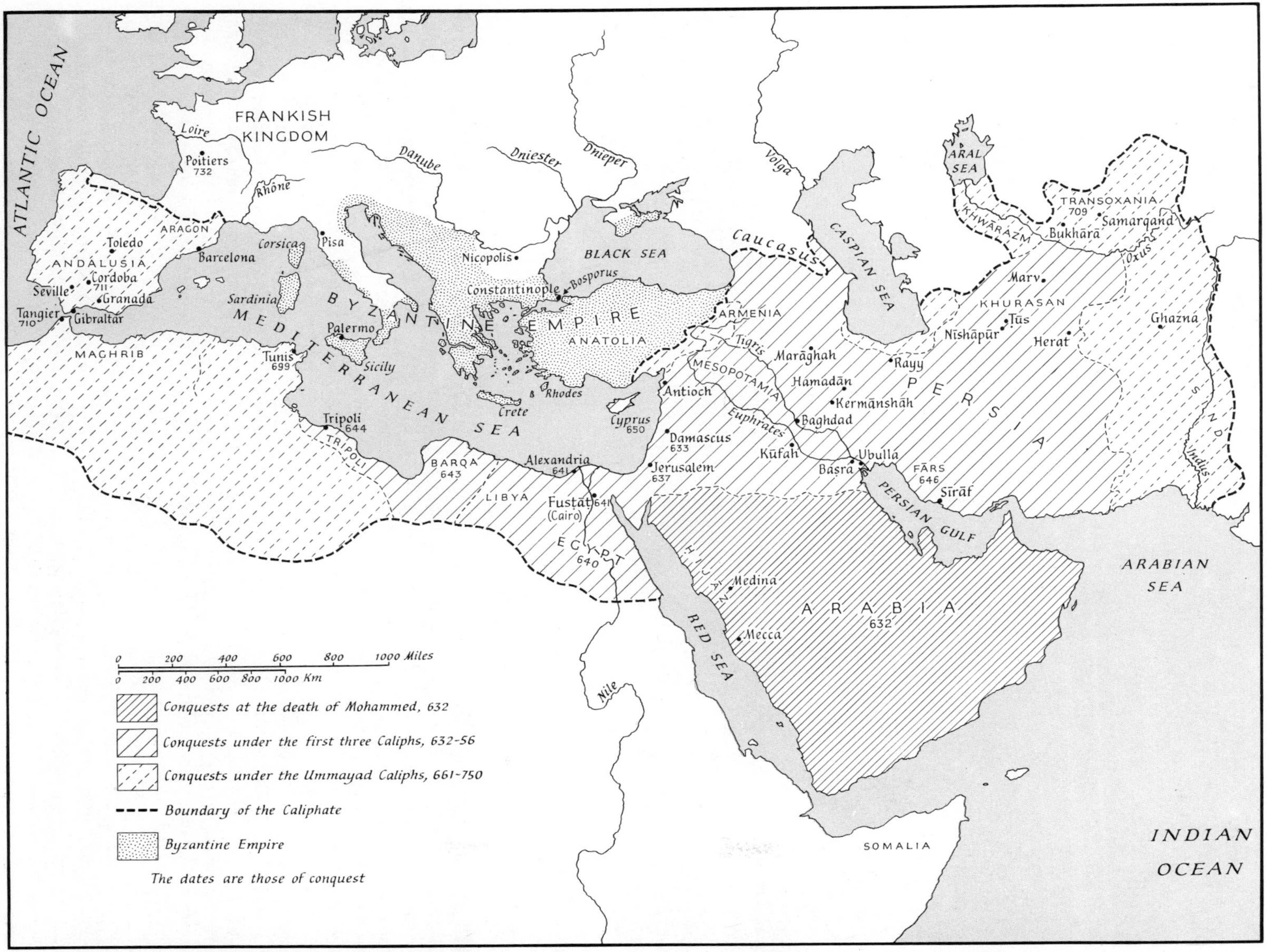

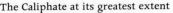

The Caliphate at its greatest extent

like Euclid and Archimedes, and by physicians like Galen and Hippocrates, were transmitted to the Arabs, usually *via* Syriac-speaking Christian scholars working under the Caliphs, especially in the eighth to tenth centuries. In this way, the Greek influence on early Islamic culture became a lasting one, and affected not only the disciplines just mentioned but also the development of Islamic theology.

The heritage of Byzantium was naturally felt most strongly west of the Euphrates–Tigris basin; east of the latter, the Arabs fell heirs to Sasanid Persia. In the former Byzantine lands, Christianity, secure on its sophisticated intellectual basis and in its tolerated (if inferior) status within the Islamic empire, survived and even at times flourished in a modest way (as is shown by the presence today of significant Christian communities in Egypt, Lebanon and Syria). In Persia, on the other hand, the Zoroastrian state church fell utterly with its secular partner, the Sasanid monarchy. The faith survived vestigially in remote parts of Persia for some three more centuries, but with scant manifestation of spiritual strength and intellectual prestige, and the modern, fossilised community of Zoroastrians in Persia seems doomed to die out shortly.

By 651 the last Sasanid Emperor, a fugitive on the fringes of Persia and Central Asia, was dead, and all but the most mountainous or otherwise inaccessible regions, such as the Caspian coastlands, were under some measure of Arab control. The Persian landowning class, the *dihqāns*, went over to the Arabs' faith and the Islamisation of Persia proceeded apace, although over the next two or three centuries the countryside suffered outbreaks of sectarian violence, often reflecting politico-social grievances as well as religious dissidence. In general sophistication of life, the Persians were in advance of the Arabs, with their desert background; hence post-classical Arabic (roughly speaking, the language of the ninth century onwards) contains a considerable number of Persian terms for topics like food and cooking, house furnishings, games and sports, and administration and warfare. But more significant for the future orientation of Islamic society as a whole was the adoption of Persian political practices and ethical concepts. In the primitive egalitarianism of Bedouin tribal society, the chief was only first among equals and held his onerous charge purely for his leadership qualities; this system survived to a large extent under the Umayyad dynasty of Arab Caliphs (661–750), who ruled from Damascus over a country which had known long-standing Arab immigration from the desert, and thus facilitated consolidation of their rule. Under the succeeding dynasty of 'Abbasid Caliphs (750–1258), the influence of Persian monarchical ideas, of court ceremonial and central administrative organisation, was to become perceptibly clearer. The purely Islamic religious and legal basis of secular authority was now diluted by these Persian imperial ideas, which involved the ruler's divine right of governing, the subject's duty of obedience, and the general practice of political expediency. Hence the appearance of characteristic dicta like 'better sixty years with an unjust ruler than one hour of civil strife', and the clear divergence of medieval Islam from Western Christendom in that the former, whilst possessing something like a divine right of kings, never developed the counter-doctrine of a right of resistance.

But this is to anticipate. After Muḥammad died in 632, it was not possible for anyone to claim the religious authority and charisma of the Prophet and assume command of the mass of believers (though the leaders of various heterodox factions did make such claims). The finality of Muḥammad's mission, the idea that he was the last of a long line of earlier prophets – popular lore numbered them at 140,000 – has always been a cardinal doctrine of Islam. Much of the historical development of the faith has revolved round the preservation of this doctrine against sectarian or heretical attenuation; in recent times it has been used to justify exclusion from the Islamic community of such deviationist religious movements as those of the Bābīs in nineteenth-century Persia (the forerunners of the modern Bahā'ī faith) and the Aḥmadīs in twentieth-century British India and then Pakistan. However, the infant Muslim community in 632 had to be provided with some leadership. The solution was a line of Caliphs or 'successors', who took over the political and military authority of Muḥammad but not his unique position as the Prophet of God. The exact definition of the Caliph's constitutional position and authority was to be disputed for centuries to come. One group within the community, the partisans of 'Alī (cousin, son-in-law and foster-brother of the Prophet, and Caliph 656–61), held that his descendants, the 'Alids, had an overriding, exclusive right to the Caliphal office by virtue of divine designation and the possession of an indwelling spiritual authority. This group constituted the Shī'ah, 'party' of 'Alī; and down to the present this has been the most important minority sect within Islam, being especially strong today in Persia, Lower Iraq, and parts of Arabia, Syria and India. The struggle between these Shī'īs and the upholders of mainstream orthodoxy, the Sunnīs ('partisans of the *Sunnah*, i.e. the 'example' of the Prophet), runs through much of Islamic history down to the nineteenth century, and its course has frequently been bloody. In the period between the tenth and twelfth centuries, the decay of the political authority of the orthodox, Sunnī Caliphs allowed Shī'ī-directed states to arise in various parts of the Islamic world, including North Africa, Egypt, Syria, Yemen and other parts of Arabia, Iraq and Persia. But orthodoxy showed great resilience and, helped by a fresh infusion of secular aid to the religious power, in the shape of various Turkish military dynasties, it reasserted itself and largely overcame these Shī'ī powers (see further below, p. 22). The great empires of later medieval Islam, those of the Mamlūks, the Mongols of Persia and South Russia, the Ottomans, and the Mughals of India, were strongly Sunnī in ethos; the exception was the empire of the Ṣafavids, the most successful of all the Shī'ī states, which within a few generations transformed virtually the whole of Persia into a bastion of Shī'īsm.

The Sunnī majority, however, held that the Caliphate was a constitutional necessity for the temporal welfare and protection of the community: the Caliph was there to ensure the safety and stability of the 'Abode of Islam', within which alone the good Muslim life could be led. In theory, the Caliph had to possess outstanding leadership qualities, and all but certain radical sectaries held that he should be from the Prophet's own Meccan tribe of Quraysh; since it had nurtured Muḥammad himself, Quraysh obviously possessed *par excellence* the qualifications for leading the community. The institution of the Caliphate began with the nomination on Muḥammad's death of his faithful follower Abū Bakr as the first Caliph (his successor in turn was to adopt the further title of 'Commander of the Believers'). This institution remained central (though in varying degrees at various times) to the solidarity of Islam down to the early twentieth century, when it was abolished by Kemal Atatürk, architect of the modern Turkish republic which arose out of the Ottoman Empire.

The 90 years of the Umayyad Caliphate were called by the nineteenth-century German orientalist Julius Wellhausen those of 'the Arab kingdom and its fall'. The state (to use a modern term) was basically the Arab military machine, extending its control over vast areas of the Old World. Clearly, there were not enough ethnically 'pure' Arabs in the military and governing class to go round for the everyday tasks of government and administration, predominant among which was that of tax-collecting. Furthermore, the mass of Bedouins were too destructive to be unleashed over ancient cultivated lands such as the Nile valley, the Fertile Crescent and Persia, where prosperity depended on the maintenance of a proper balance between pastoralism and agriculture, the latter often dependent on advanced systems of irrigation. The solution was to leave the existing Syrian, Greek, Coptic or Persian local officials in charge, and to let the agricultural population pay rent for their land to the Muslim state. The Arab warriors concentrated in garrison cities, usually new or virtually new foundations like Baṣra and Kūfah in Iraq, Fusṭāṭ or Old Cairo in Egypt, Qayrawān in Tunisia and Qazwīn in Persia. From these bases, warfare was carried into the 'Abode of Unbelief', i.e. the lands of the infidels. The expanding Umayyad Caliphate reached its peak in the early decades of the eighth century; thereafter, the expansion of Islam into peripheral regions like South Russia, Central Asia, black Africa, India and Indonesia was a much more gradual process, in which the pacific merchant or the religious devotee was often as influential as the militant fighter for the faith. In all the military raids, the capture of slaves was a prime aim. Medieval Islam was a slave-holding society, albeit the slave often enjoyed a better position than in other cultures. At first, slaves were used primarily for domestic purposes, but from the ninth century onwards there arose the peculiarly Islamic institution of military slavery (see below, p. 24); slaves were not much used for large-scale industrial or agricultural operations, except in such areas as Lower Iraq, where they were employed on great estates in the early 'Abbasid period for denitrifying and desalinating the topsoil.

After the 'Abbasid revolution of 747–50, the purely Arab element lost its exclusive political and military supremacy, though not its social, religious and cultural pre-eminence. In the immediate view, the 'Abbasid revolution was only an internal revolution amongst Quraysh, the replacement of one Meccan family by another; but the new dynasty came to power with a broad basis of support, including not only Arabs but also Persians and other ethnic elements, who had previously been able to enrol as *mawālī* or 'clients' of the Arab tribes, but who had suffered varying degrees of political and social discrimination. The 'brotherhood of Islam' was at this time still a limited concept, and the emphasis on piety rather than lineage developed only slowly. The transfer of the capital to Iraq, and its eventual establishment at Baghdad in 762, facilitated a perceptible orientalisation of the Caliphate. Iraq had been an integral part of the Sasanid empire, and a melting-pot of various peoples and beliefs; trade connections with the South Asian lands even brought colonies of Jhats from India and Malays to Ubulla and Baṣra at the head of the Persian Gulf. Persian officials made themselves administratively indispensable to the 'Abbasid Caliphs as secretaries and as holders of the newly-emergent office of *wazīr* or chief executive-minister. Imbued with the ancient traditions of their profession in pre-Islamic Persia, they promoted the image of the caliph as a remote figure enthroned above his subjects, his power divinely-buttressed. This exaltation of the despotic and religious aspects of the Caliphal office is seen in the generalisation under the 'Abbasids of hereditary father–son succession and the adoption of grandiloquent honorific titles expressing relationship to the deity, such as al-Muntaṣir billāh, 'He who is made victorious by God.' Thus evolved something like the popular Western view of the medieval Caliphate, as embodied in such works as the *Arabian Nights* or J. E. Flecker's *Hassan*: that of a cruel and capricious tyrant, wielding unfettered power and living in the luxury and vice of the harem. Naturally, there were in practice limits to this despotic power, for fears of assassination or revolt were ever-present, but there are certain elements of truth in this view.

Islam, no less than other civilisations, has not been free of the cyclical rise and fall of dynasties, or at least, of their rise as cultures and their subsequent degeneration or prolonged death-agonies. 'Abbasid culture and civilisation were at their most brilliant in the tenth–eleventh centuries. This was, for instance, the age of al-Mutanabbī, considered by many Arabs as their greatest poet, and of al-Fārābī, the philosopher dubbed 'the second master', i.e. second only to Aristotle himself. The Traditions of the Prophet had already been sifted and codified for legal use; and the scholastic theologian al-Ash'arī was laying the foundations of a subtle dogmatic theology which would take over certain features of Greek thought without compromising the essentially Islamic core of belief. Avicenna, by 1037, had accomplished his great work in philosophy and in medicine. Socially and economically, too, the Islamic world flourished. Urbanisation progressed, with such centres as Baghdad, Nīshāpūr, Cairo, Palermo and Cordoba standing out in dazzling contrast to the impoverished towns of Dark Ages Europe. Long-distance trading grew up, so that a prized delicacy like the edible (i.e. diatomaceous) earth of Khurasan was exported as far as Egypt and North Africa, whilst the superlative melons of Khwārazm (in what is now Soviet Central Asia) were transported in snow-packed, lead containers to the supreme centre of consumption, Baghdad.

Yet somewhat paradoxically, this was a period of political fragmentation and weakening central control in the Caliphate. The 'Abbasids retained their moral and spiritual leadership and were regarded by the Sunnī majority as the Imāms, 'religious leaders' or 'exemplars' of the community, but at the same time their political authority reached its nadir in the tenth century, being confined to central Iraq. The seeds of decay had been sown in the previous century, when the Caliphs had begun to recruit professional armies composed of military slaves (*ghulāms, mamlūks*), in the hope that these troops would give them undivided loyalty and prove more reliable than locally-recruited soldiers. Although slaves from nations like the Greeks, Armenians, Balkan and Russian Slavs, and Berbers were pressed into service, the favoured race was that of the Turks, prized for their steppe hardiness and valour in battle. Unfortunately for the Caliphs, it proved impossible to control these new troops, or rather, the military slaves were manipulated by unscrupulous contenders for power in the state. Hence provincial governors in regions like North Africa, Egypt, Persia and Central Asia asserted their political independence of Baghdad, whilst continuing to acknowledge the spiritual headship of the Caliphs (Muslim Spain had never given allegiance to the 'Abbasids, but soon came under a branch of the defeated Umayyad dynasty). Almost all of these local governors had their own praetorian guards, and the stage was set for the transition from political unity under the Caliphs to a states-system of territorial dynasties.

Not all of the new powers continued to pay even

Spain. The Great Mosque at Cordova, built eight to tenth centuries, perhaps the greatest surviving example of Moorish architecture

Egypt. The Mosque of Ibn Tūlūn in Cairo, built ninth century

lip-service to the ʿAbbasids. One aspect of the Shīʿī resurgence of the tenth century (see above, p. 19) is seen in the extremist, strongly anti-ʿAbbasid movement of the Ismāʿīlīs, whose partisans were known to the Crusaders as the Assassins (from their alleged hashish-eating proclivities), and who through their weapon of political 'assassination' achieved a notoriety disproportionate to their restricted numbers. Of more permanent significance was the Shīʿī Fatimid dynasty in North Africa and then in Egypt and Syria (909–1171), radical in origin but increasingly conservative as it settled down to the exercise of territorial power and its realities. Although internal enfeeblement and orthodox Sunnī reaction combined to destroy the Fatimids (who had claimed to be the rightful Caliphs, in rivalry with the ʿAbbasids), the cultural and intellectual heritage of Fatimid Egypt was outstanding, above all in the artistic and architectural spheres. The dynasty also wrought a major change in the cultural orientation of the Arab world. Their capital, Cairo, speedily eclipsed in splendour and vitality the ʿAbbasids' capital, Baghdad, whose earlier glories were later destroyed by the Mongol invasions; since then, Baghdad has been a provincial town, with Iraq on the margin of Arab culture, whilst Cairo has been the cultural focus for the Arab world.

The decentralisation of power from Iraq allowed nations other than the Arabs and the Arabised Persians to emerge and assume positions of power. Thus we have the rise of the recently-Islamised Persians and Turks to independent authority, and the development of their respective languages as modes of expression for Islamic literary and intellectual activity. On the Iranian plateau and in Iraq, there occurred in the tenth and eleventh centuries a curious, not yet adequately explained, upsurge of peoples from such remote parts of Persia as the Caspian region of Daylam and from Kurdistan, and these mountain folk established a network of principalities. Many of them were Shīʿī in ethos, and Shīʿism now began to appear as an expression of Persian national aspirations. The whole phenomenon of the Daylamī and Kurdish burgeoning marks a resurgence of the Persian spirit. Another aspect of this was the re-appearance of Persian as a fluent medium of expression, after nearly three centuries' existence as a virtually non-literary language; it was

archer to a position inferior to the infantryman and thus destroyed the whole basis of the state.

More than any other Muslim power of the late classical period, the Ottoman Turks struck terror into the hearts of Christian Europe, so that the Elizabethan historian of the Turks, Richard Knollys, described them as 'the present Terror of the World'. Backed by the Turkish military qualities of self-discipline and endurance, the Turkish invasions of Europe were indeed a potent threat, reaching on two occasions to Vienna itself. The Ottomans began as a group of *ghāzīs* (i.e. corps of mystically inspired warriors) in northwestern Anatolia, confronting the truncated Byzantine empire there, and eventually eclipsing other Turkish principalities by their superior *élan* and experience in war. In 1354 they crossed the Dardanelles into Europe, cutting off Constantinople in its rear, and expanded relentlessly into the Balkans. States like Serbia and Bulgaria were humbled, and for 500 years to come were to be nations without history. The Ottoman victory at Mohács in 1526 brought most of Hungary under Turkish rule for a century-and-a-half, providing a base from which to threaten Austria and the very heart of Christian Europe. The Balkan provinces came to form Rumelia, the European 'twin' of Anatolia. Turks were settled there, and there were also converts from the indigenous peoples, giving a strongly Islamic impress to much of the Balkans down to the nineteenth century and after; in 1939 one-third of the Yugoslavian province of Bosnia was still Muslim and about half of Albania. Ottoman authority in Anatolia received a setback from the invasion of the Tatar military conqueror Timur (or Tamerlane) at the opening of the fifteenth century. Half a century later, it revived under a series of outstanding Sultans: Mehemed the Conqueror, who attained the glittering prize of Constantinople in 1453; Selīm the Grim, conqueror of Syria and Egypt and humbler of the Ottomans' rivals to the east, the Ṣafavids of Persia; and Sulaymān the Magnificent (called by the Turks 'the Lawgiver'), conqueror of Hungary and Iraq. Ottoman fleets and their allies, the corsairs of Barbary (i.e. North Africa), operated in the Mediterranean and beyond, terrorising the Christians and carrying off captives from as far afield as Ireland and Iceland; and in the late seventeenth century, the Ottomans enjoyed their last major success by capturing Crete from the Venetians.

Much of this Ottoman vigour sprang from the use of a system of military slavery analogous to that of the Mamlūks. The Janissaries or 'New Troops', a crack corps of highly-trained soldiers and officials, were recruited from the Christian populations of the Balkans and later, from those of Anatolia, from the late fourteenth down to the early eighteenth centuries. Like the Arabs in the first stages of their expansion, the Turks themselves were a military class comparatively thinly spread over what had grown to be a vast empire. Utilisation of the subject population was a brilliant device for tapping the manpower of the Balkans. Moreover, the lengthy and arduous training of a Janissary in a thoroughly Islamic atmosphere conduced to his adopting a soldierly type of Islam. It was the discipline and fire-power of these troops (the Ottoman army made use of artillery and hand-guns from the mid-fifteenth century onwards) which did much to create in Europe the image of Ottoman ferocity and invincibility.

But Christian Europe rallied in the seventeenth century. The Treaty of Karlowitz in 1699 was dictated to a defeated Turkey, and soon afterwards the 'Sick Man of Europe' was born, to suffer a protracted decline of some two centuries. The Christian response to the Ottomans was really part of the new movement of western imperialism against an Islamic world more and more on the defensive. The Turks were pushed back through the Balkans; the Spanish and Portuguese attacked the North African coastlands; the Portuguese made incursions into the Indian Ocean and attacks on the allies of the Mamlūks and Ottomans there; and the Russians advanced against the Golden Horde's successor states and the Crimean Tatars, and eventually into the Caucasus. Yet in its heyday, the Ottoman empire was the most powerful and lasting state known to the Islamic world since the early Arab Caliphate. It gave autocratic, but often good government to lands which had previously suffered internal chaos and dislocation, and only towards the end, when the political and economic pressure of the West contributed to administrative breakdown and internal economic decline, did the quality of Ottoman rule deteriorate. In the present century, it has become customary for Arabs to attribute all ills of the Arab lands, from Egypt to Iraq, to the Turkish occupation – political repression, cultural stagnation, economic regression, etc. Yet this simplistic interpretation of the course of Arab history ignores the fact that such trends also affected

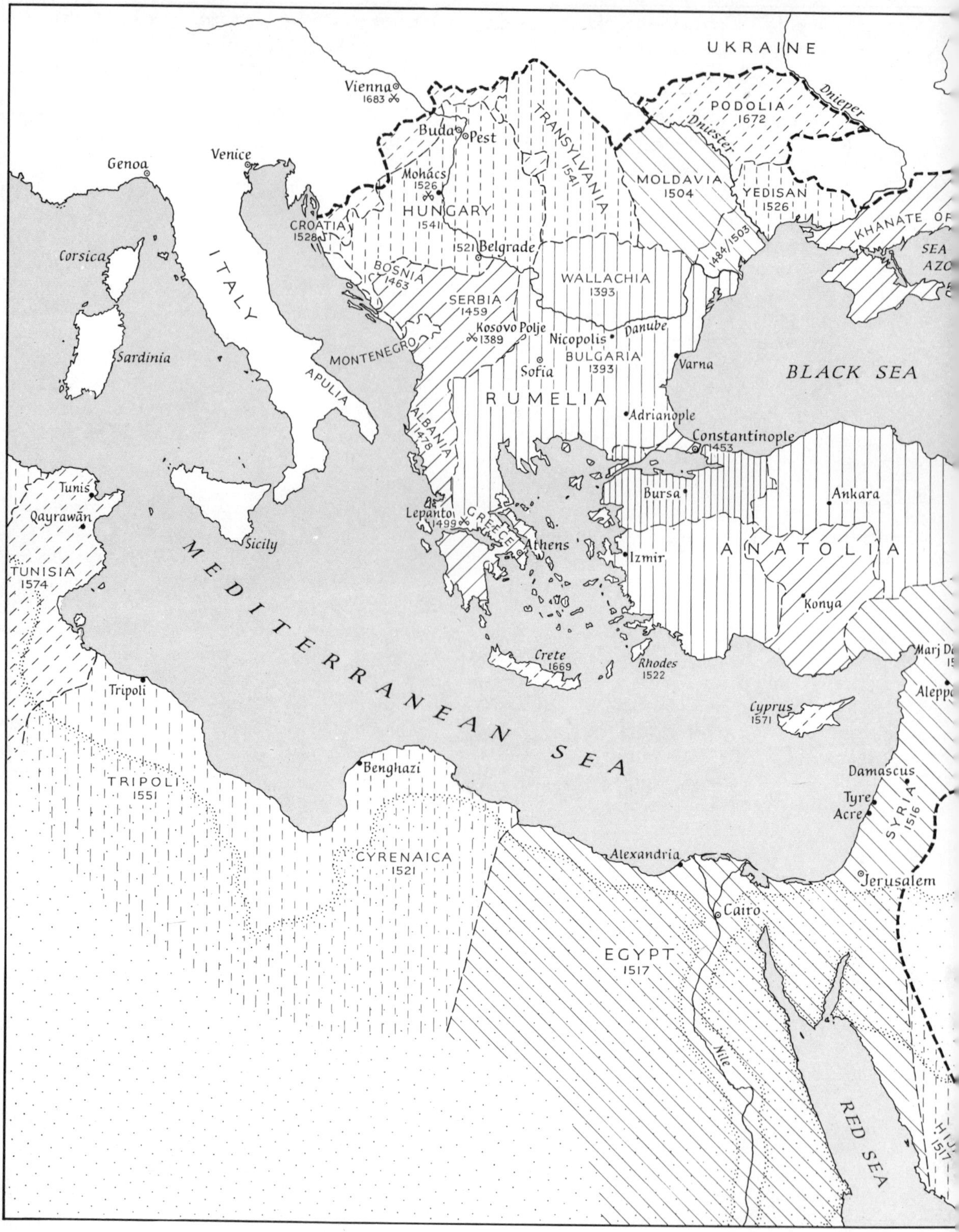

The Ottoman empire at its greatest extent

Donets
Don
Volga
ARAL SEA
Oxus
Samarqand
Bukhārā
CASPIAN SEA
DAGHESTAN
GEORGIA
Tiflis
Trebizond 1461
TREBIZOND
Chaldiran 1514
KARABAGH
ARMENIA
AZERBAIJAN
KURDISTAN
Tabriz
Qazvīn
Tigris
IRAQ
Euphrates
LURISTAN
PERSIA
Baghdad
Iṣfahān
Karbala
Baṣrah
PERSIAN GULF
Medina
0 100 200 300 Miles
0 100 200 300 Km
Ottoman Lands 1359
Ottoman Lands 1451
Conquests of Mehmet II 1451–81
Conquests of Selim the Grim 1512–20
Conquests of Sulayman the Magnificent 1520–66
Conquests 1566–1683
1521 Year of acquisition
Battle
Boundary of the Ottoman Empire in 1683
Approximate extent of desert
M. Verity

Sultan Sulaymān the Magnificent receiving the homage of John Sigismund Zápolyai, King of Hungary, 1566. From a sixteenth-century Turkish manuscript

other areas of the Islamic world, such as the Muslim West, Persia and India and were, indeed, possibly inherent within Islamic society. 'God knows best!' Certainly, there were no signs of anti-Turkish hostility amongst the Arabs of earlier times; the fourteenth-century North African historian Ibn Khaldūn saw in the almost universal hegemony of the Turks a sign of God's concern for the welfare of the Muslims, in that He had sent them, at a time when the Caliphate had become politically enfeebled, as the revivers and defenders of Islam against its enemies.

The Ṣafavids of Persia have already been mentioned as having established the one late medieval empire which was Shī'ī in faith. Somewhat remarkably, it arose from a local Azerbaijan Ṣūfī or dervish order which gradually became transformed into a militant Shī'ī propagandist movement. The Ṣafavids came to power in an area where the ground had been prepared for Shī'ī heterodoxy, and consciously adopted Shī'ism as an affirmation of the Persian national identity against the pressures of adjoining, hostile Sunnī powers like the Ottomans on the west and the Özbeg states of central Asia on the north-east. In the opening years of the sixteenth century, Shāh Ismā'īl Ṣafavī brought the whole of Persia under his control; later, the capital was moved first to Qazvīn and then to Iṣfahān, which was transformed into one of the finest cities of the Islamic world. The Ṣafavids maintained their power for over two centuries, till in the early eighteenth century they were overthrown by the Afghans. Shāh 'Abbās I (1588–1629) cultivated relations with European powers such as England and Holland in an effort to obtain allies against his enemies, the Ottomans and the Portuguese; and we owe many valuable accounts of seventeenth-century Persia to the western diplomats, travellers, missionaries and traders who visited 'the Grand Sophy'. The title 'Sophy' for the Shāhs almost certainly stems, of course, from Ṣūfī, and the Ṣafavid state began as a theocracy, with the Shāhs claiming semi-divine status as emanations of the Godhead, with infallibility as representatives on earth of the Hidden Imām; thus the Shāhs demanded spiritual as well as political allegiance from their Turkish troops, the Qïzïl-bāsh or 'Redheads' (from the red caps which they wore). In addition to these last, the Ṣafavids followed prevailing military fashion by forming regiments of slave troops (*ghulāms*), comparable with the Ottoman Janissaries. The *ghulāms* were mainly of Christian origin, from such peoples of the Caucasus region as the Georgians and Armenians; by contrast with the Ottoman system, they were not levied on a regular basis.

The remaining great Muslim empire arose in northern India, where the ubiquitous Turks and the Afghans founded military dynasties from the eleventh century onwards. Many of these stemmed from Turkish slave commanders, as the name of one dynasty of Delhi Sultans, the 'Slave Kings' (1206–90) shows. Muslim rule was extended as far as Bengal (early thirteenth century), Kashmir (fourteenth century) and into the Deccan or South India, where several local dynasties of considerable cultural splendour arose. All through its existence, the dominant feature of Indian Islam has been its minority position, numerically speaking, within a non-Islamic, predominantly Hindu environment; hence Muslim princes often ruled over extensive non-Muslim populations and relied on them as officials or soldiers. The comparative isolation of Islam in India meant a perpetual struggle to preserve the faith from syncretism and from the characteristic absorptive influence of Hindu religion; thus Indian Muslim rulers and the *'ulamā* usually identified themselves strongly with Sunnī Islam and the maintenance of orthodoxy.

The empire of the Mughals (this name being a form of 'Mongols') arose out of the successful efforts of Bābur, a Turkish prince from Central Asia, to carve out a principality for himself in northern India in the early sixteenth century. Under a series of remarkable Sultans in the sixteenth and seventeenth centuries the Mughal empire expanded over the greater part of the subcontinent. Akbar the Great, a contemporary of Elizabeth I of England, in a dramatic divergence from traditional Indian Islamic thought, attempted a rapprochement with his Hindu subjects, toying with a new, monotheistic creed of his own, 'the Divine Faith', which would transcend existing religions and bring about religious harmony in his dominions; such policies were, however, reversed by his successors, and Aurangzīb (d. 1707), the last great Mughal Emperor, reverted to strict enforcement of Muslim orthodoxy. A feature of these two centuries – one hardly noticed by the Muslim rulers of India, but portentous for the future – was the establishment of coastal trading stations or 'factories' by European merchants, such as the Portuguese, English and French. The English settlements formed the bases for subsequent territorial expansion in the eighteenth and nineteenth centuries, and it was the British who, in the aftermath of the Indian Mutiny, in 1858 deposed the last feeble representative of the Mughal line in Delhi.

III
The nineteenth and twentieth centuries: imperialism and independence

With the nineteenth century, the Islamic 'Middle Ages' draw to a close. As always with attempts to periodise history, it is hard to give clear-cut dates. In the Islamic world, we have in the background a long-term movement, whose significance has just been mentioned above, namely the extension of European political and economic influence over the fringes and later the heartlands of Islam. In addition to the areas mentioned above (p. 25), the Russians pushed across Siberia and, in the later nineteenth century, into Central Asia; the Dutch fastened their control upon Indonesia, a region which Islam had reached from India from the late thirteenth century onwards; the French extended their dominion over the local rulers of Morocco, Algiers and Tunis in the nineteenth and early twentieth centuries, and the Italians seized Libya. In the late nineteenth century, the 'scramble for Africa' brought extensive Muslim populations under French, British and German control.

The Islamic heartlands, from Turkey and Egypt to Persia, were inevitably threatened also. Once the peak of Ottoman power in the sixteenth century had passed, the technological gap between the West and Islam grew steadily wider, placing the Muslims at an increasing disadvantage in war. The medieval Islamic economy, once largely a closed economy except in respect of the supply of slaves and certain luxury goods, was now dislocated by the commercial imperialism of the West. Local crafts declined in the face of competition from European factories, and the demand for western imports accentuated the financial imbalance and the deficits already resulting from expenditure on defence (particularly the efforts to train modern-style armies with western weapons), and from a perceptible decline in administrative efficiency – the latter clearly visible in the Ottoman provinces. The birth of western-style nationalism in the wake of the French Revolution was a powerful solvent of the old order. Medieval Islam had never been without some social, religious and racial discrimination; Negro slaves had always been despised, and the lot of Christians and Jews had rarely been the sunny one depicted by some modern Muslim apologists. But the maintenance of the fabric of society had depended on a certain toleration of minorities (even if this was only the toleration of contempt for infidels) and on the compartmentalisation of social, religious and ethnic groups according to their functions in society; in the Ottoman empire this was exemplified in the formal *millet* system, by which various non-Muslim groups were assigned a considerable degree of internal autonomy.

All this was shattered by the onset of nationalism. After Napoleon's Egyptian expedition of 1799–1801, the Near East was never the same again. Reaction in Egypt led to the overthrow of the Mamlūk ruling class and the emergence of Muḥammad 'Alī in 1805 as governor of Egypt and founder of the 'Turkish' dynasty which was to rule there till 1953. Though still nominally subject to the Ottoman government (the 'Sublime Porte'), Muḥammad 'Alī behaved as an independent ruler, temporarily bringing parts of Syria and Arabia under his control, and embarking on attempts to westernise his country. His less forceful successors continued these latter policies, but brought the country into such a parlous financial state that it opened the door to powers like Britain and France to intervene, thus bringing about the British tutelage over Egypt which lasted, in varying degrees, till 1956. Egyptian attempts to extend southwards into the Sudan provoked a traditionalist reaction there, the Mahdist movement of 1881–96.

The Balkan provinces of the Ottoman empire were, not surprisingly, the first to be affected by the new European nationalism. The Greek Revolt of 1820 had already been foreshadowed by outbreaks in Serbia and Montenegro; in 1856 Moldavia and Wallachia became virtually independent as the nucleus of the later state of Rumania; after the Balkan War of 1877–8, Serbia and Montenegro became independent, and Austria occupied the strongly Muslim provinces of Bosnia and Herzegovina. The islands of Cyprus and Crete were lost, and after the Second Balkan War of 1912–13, the once-great Turkish province of Rumelia was reduced to eastern Thrace, the area around the capital Istanbul and Adrianople. The nationalist and sectarian hatreds during this period totally upset the delicate balance of Ottoman society; Russia set herself up as a protector of the Orthodox Christians of the Balkans, whilst the Armenians, once considered one of the most faithful elements in the Empire, came to be regarded as an internal 'fifth column' and were led along the tragic road of massacres and expulsions. Propped up by Western powers like Britain and France, the Ottoman Empire achieved something in the way of internal reform, including an abortive constitution conceded in 1876; but the First World War was as destructive for Turkey as for the Central Powers.

Active discontent amongst the Muslims of the Empire's Arab provinces hardly appeared before the opening years of the twentieth century, when the politics of the 'Young Turk' régime in Istanbul aroused Arab fears; but the Christians of Lebanon and Syria had suffered from Muslim fanaticism in the nineteenth century, in part provoked by western championship of Christian groups there. Arab national sentiment at this time expressed itself more in a revival of literary and cultural activities. The First World War saw the ending of Egypt's formal ties with Turkey, the Arab revolt in the Ḥijāz and the British campaigns in Palestine and Iraq. A vengeful attempt by the Allies to dismember even the Turkish heartland of Anatolia gave scope to the genius of Atatürk; eventually, by the Treaty of Lausanne in 1923, Turkey's present national boundaries were secured, with the capital now moved to Ankara. The Arab lands were detached from Turkey by the Treaty of Sèvres in 1920, but Arab hopes of complete independence were attenuated by the system of mandates and trusteeships: under these Britain controlled Palestine, Jordan and Iraq, while France ran the affairs of Syria and Lebanon. These arrangements were really consequent upon the secret Sykes–Picot Agreement of 1916, by which Britain and France were to divide most of the Arab lands of the Fertile Crescent into spheres of influence, with only the central portion as a fully-independent Arab emirate. In the Arabian peninsula alone were there fully-independent Arab states, chief amongst which was the Saudi kingdom based on Riyadh and

Cyprus. St Nicholas' Cathedral in Famagusta. Since the Turkish conquest in 1571 it has been a mosque, as indicated by the minaret

created by the expansionist policies of Ibn Sa'ūd. The 'Palestine problem' now emerged, for also during the War, Britain had in 1917 issued the Balfour Declaration in favour of a national home there for the Jews; in the following decades, Arab–Jewish hostility rose to a crescendo, culminating in the events of 1947–8 and the formation of the state of Israel.

Geographically, religiously and ethnically more homogeneous, Persia fared better than the Ottoman empire, but suffered also from external political and economic pressures. She too lost territory in the Caucasus to the advancing Russians, and throughout the nineteenth century was squeezed between Russian expansionism from the north and British efforts to preserve an influence in the Persian Gulf and free communications with India. Internally, Persia remained fairly peaceful during the nineteenth century, apart from some sectarian outbreaks like those of the Bābīs and Ismā'īlīs; but resentment grew against foreign political and economic interference and the autocracy of the Qājār dynasty. This resentment led to the constitutional movement in 1906, the temporary re-establishment of despotism, and eventually in 1925, to the overthrow of the Qājārs by a native Persian commander, Riẓā Shāh Pahlavī, father of the present Shāh of Iran.

Mecca and the Kaʻbah, from a sixteenth-century Persian tile

3

Islamic faith

CHARLES J. ADAMS

In every major religious community there exists a gap, more or less great, between the beliefs and practices of what may be called 'official' or 'orthodox' religion and the piety of common people. This is nowhere more true than in the Islamic case. While most Muslims are vaguely aware of the fundamental theological positions adopted by the community in the course of its development, only a small number, those who have had the privilege of advanced training in a traditional school of religious instruction, or *madrasah*, know these matters in detail from first-hand acquaintance with the works of the great religious leaders of the past. The Islamic community is second to none in the richness and depth of its intellectual heritage, and one of the areas where that legacy is the strongest is the field of religious speculation. There exist veritable macro-libraries of books dealing with Islamic theology, law, philosophy, mysticism and other subjects of religious relevance. In spite of its great extent the literature that survives to our time is only part of what existed in the past, many books of great interest having been lost, perhaps never to be recovered. Most of this treasury of writing and thought, however, is closed to the ordinary Muslim, not because he is in any way discouraged from the pursuit of learning, but because he does not have the training and background that would permit him to exploit it. Religious thought in the Islamic community has been brought to a high peak of refinement and subtlety, and the subject matter with which it deals is difficult and often abstruse. Those only can understand who have spent years of earnest study to prepare themselves. The religious sciences among Muslims, in other words, represent elaborately developed fields of specialised knowledge, that are as inaccessible to ordinary people as are the advanced theories of higher mathematics or of nuclear physics to an untrained layman. When one remembers also that the majority of Muslims are not Arabs and do not speak the Arabic language, whose classical form is difficult in the best of circumstances, while much of the religious heritage of Islam is preserved in lengthy and complex Arabic treatises, the nature and extent of the gap between the learned and the common people of the community will be even more apparent.

It may, therefore, with reason be claimed that there are two Islams, or more properly, two levels of Islamic life, that are of interest to one who wishes to know about the religion. On the one hand is the 'high Islam' of the learned and of the religious class, and on the other is the Islam of everyday life as it is appropriated and lived by the vast majority of members of the community. Both levels of religious expression are vital to an understanding of Islamic culture, the one showing the efforts of the community to be clear and firm about its spiritual foundations, and the other showing the way in which Islamic spiritual values affect the lives of people, what it means and how it feels actually to be a Muslim. Our purpose here is to describe something of the religious outlook of the common people of the Islamic countries. We wish to say something in broad terms about the ethos or the spirit of the Islamic faith. Islamic theology and law, aspects of 'high Islam', are discussed in Chapters 4 and 5. The task here is to indicate some of the perceptions and feelings of ordinary people who have little concern for theology and who, in fact, may be ignorant of even the simplest doctrinal formulations but who are, nonetheless, animated by an Islamic spirit and vision of the world. Not surprisingly, the faith of common people is often at variance with that of the religiously learned who sometimes consider their less fortunate fellows to be guilty of superstition which has no basis in the authentic sources of Islamic piety. Although some of their religious belief and practice may be unpalatable or seem inadequate to the strict and puritanical theologian, the common people of the Islamic world are, nevertheless, a pious folk who want to be true Muslims and who believe themselves to be so.

The reasons for the great difference between 'high Islam' and the religion of ordinary Muslims are to be found largely in the sophistication and complexity of Islamic religious thought in its higher levels of development and in the consequent loss of emotional content. At some time in the late third/ninth or the fourth/tenth centuries a turning point was reached in the community's religious evolution. As the arguments of theologians and lawyers became more subtle and difficult to follow, the common people were left behind. A fierce competition for status existed among the learned class, and each theologian strove by always more clever arguments to outdo his fellows. In consequence religious writings became more and more difficult to comprehend and ever farther removed from normal daily life. As specialists, the theologians wrote for other specialists, endeavouring to achieve more subtle distinctions and greater refinement of thought. There was very little religious guidance for ordinary people to be gained from discussions that they did not understand. Further, the intellectualism of the learned men, admirable as it was in its own terms, eventually became an end in itself without relation to pressing religious issues. When this happened, there seemed no longer anything vital at stake in what the theologians wrote or said. Their interests, which were largely professional, did not correspond to the religious needs of the populace who began to turn elsewhere for religious leadership. Especially important was the fact that theological discussion did not involve the emotions of ordinary people or bestow upon them that feeling of warmth, confidence and internal satisfaction that is so marked a feature of genuine religion. Although the class of men learned in the religious sciences has everywhere retained the respect of common people, the ordinary Muslim for many centuries now has found religious inspiration and leadership of a more immediate and relevant kind in the *murshid*s (spiritual guides) of the Ṣūfī (mystic) orders.

By the end of the third Islamic century the great theological problems that taxed the community in its early days had been largely solved, and the synthesis of ideas and convictions that made up the classical Islam of the 'Abbasid age had begun to emerge. By the middle of the fifth/eleventh centuries, virtually all creative thought in the area of theology had ceased, and from that time to our own the theological literature which has been produced consists largely of commentaries on some of the authoritative writings of earlier times or of manuals and compendia that rehearse over and over again the great issues of the formative age. The same period witnessed the rise of the Ṣūfī orders that eventually came to pervade the Islamic world. The congruence of dates is no coincidence. The success of the orders is due in large to their ability to fill the religious vacuum created by the increasing intellectualism and specialisation of theology and the religious law. To all practical intents and purposes a kind of Ṣufism, mediated through the orders, especially the cult of the saints and their tombs, has been the real religion of large numbers of Muslims for the past six or seven centuries.

Let us now consider some of the characteristics of the Islamic faith as it is held and exercised by the great body of Muslim believers.

The first point to be made is at once complex and simple. It is that the Muslim dwells in a universe where religion has the central place. In much of the rest of the world, affected by modernity and the growing secularity of our age, religion has lost its meaning and power to compel people. To some extent this is true also among a small segment of the Islamic populations, persons who have been much affected by modern trends, who have studied abroad, or who are influenced by secularist thought. It is not so, however, for the great majority of persons across the Islamic world upon whom religion retains a profound hold and who live out their lives firm in the conviction of being under the rule and the grace of a sovereign divine power. The consciousness remains, inchoate and vague though it may be, of a realm beyond the world of time and space where there dwell the powers that control events in this life and that determine human destiny in another world to come. The world in which we live is but a preparation for the other world, and life is to be lived in expectation of what follows it.

This lively sense of relation with a supernatural realm shows itself in many different ways. Perhaps the most evident is the operation of the religious law which has its basis in the will of the Sovereign Lord. The law determines the form of greeting that Muslims use toward one another, the types of food they eat or refuse, the manner of dress they adopt, the relations between the sexes, even so minor a thing as the method of cleansing the teeth. All of these aspects of culture, and many others beside, in addition to the specific obligations of worship, emerge from the religious teachings of the Islamic tradition, as mediated in the Qur'ān itself, in the example of the Prophet or, most important of all, in the established custom of the community in the past.

The role played by established custom or tradition among Muslims is particularly important but somewhat difficult to understand, for tradition has a clear religious meaning in Muslim minds. This is true even though custom differs markedly in the various regions of the Islamic world. There is no complete homogeneity or unity of social and religious practice among the various Muslim peoples. Indian Muslims and those of Negro Africa, for example, are sharply distinguished from one another in behaviour and even in some aspects of religious practice. In spite of their differences in attitude and behaviour, however, ordinary Muslims everywhere have a strong religious sense in common and hold the conviction that their way of life is an expression of *Islām*, that is to say submission to supernatural imperatives. In other words the most characteristic elements of daily life in the Islamic countries are seen by Muslims themselves to proceed out of their religion. These customs and mores are observed, and change is resisted, because ordinary people consider that in holding to their traditional mode of life they are acting in accord with the will of the power that controls the universe. The manner of living thus reflects a conception of human life under divine control and at the same time continuously reinforces that conception. Numerous facets of daily life actively symbolise the realm beyond and its significance in human affairs for the Muslim. It is often puzzling for foreigners to understand why ordinary Muslims cling so tenaciously to some features of their manner of life when other ways would appear more rational or more to their benefit. It is equally puzzling to comprehend why many admirable schemes for helping people through the introduction of new modes of behaviour have so abysmally failed. The cause of this unwillingness to change is often attributed simply to inherent conservatism. There is a more profound reason, however; it lies in the fact that the time-honoured customs of the Muslim peoples have their basis and their justification in religion. Although critically-minded intellectuals and reformers may find much in traditional Muslim life to disparage, in the understanding of common people the established way of living is the Islamic way. To change these things deliberately is not simply to give up what is familiar; it is also to forsake what is known to be right and true. There are few among ordinary Muslims, perhaps, who can articulate it, but it is somehow understood that to forsake the way of the fathers, the way that is well known, compromises and weakens the understanding of the world and of human life as an integral whole under the control of a divine power. Instinctively, the Muslim acts to preserve the spiritual foundation of his universe by clinging to the actions, attitudes and institutions that symbolise it.

For Muslims, the religious dimension of existence extends to encompass the whole of life and not only that small segment of activity concerned with specific acts of worship or the fulfilment of religious duties. For this reason all issues of social policy in Muslim countries are also religious questions requiring to be examined in the light of tradition and religious teaching. The continual appeal to religion in matters that others would consider secular and of no religious relevance is another often puzzling element in Islamic life for the uninitiated foreigner. What, for example, is achieved by adding the adjective 'Islamic' to the word 'socialism' in those Muslim countries where socialism has become an ideal? This and similar phenomena arise from the fact that religion has a central role in life for the Muslims and must be taken into account even at the level of state policy if leaders would count on the loyalty of the mass of people. The teachings of the religious tradition as they are mediated through the popular culture are the determinative and most important thing for the right conduct of human affairs in the eyes of ordinary men, and Muslims cannot be comfortable when the injunctions of religion are broken or ignored. If a social policy can somehow be shown to be in accord with Islamic conceptions and ideals, it is far more likely to gain public acceptance and support. Conversely, the most damning thing that can be said against a proposed policy or change in the status quo is that it endangers Islam. The immediate relevance of religion even in the political sphere explains the astonishing appeal and success of those political parties in various Muslim countries which hold a religious ideology. Such parties represent religious aspirations deeply rooted in the popular mind, and for that reason established régimes often have reason to fear them.

This vivid religious awareness has several accompanying characteristics that are worth noting. One of these is the strong sense of community that Muslims have felt throughout their history. Part of the reform effected by the Prophet Muḥammad was the creation of a band of followers, pledged to support one another as though they were kinsmen, but united only by their common religious faith. In the Qur'ān these obedient followers are called the 'best of communities'. They stood apart from the rest of mankind because of their common bond of faith, bore special responsibilities and had special privileges, and they had both a special destiny and a special mission. For these reasons, Muslims have always had a deep and personal love for the Prophet, his family and his early followers.

Even during the lifetime of the Prophet, his community was transformed into a kind of state with the Prophet as lawgiver, judge and commander-in-chief. After the Prophet's death, under the leadership of his Rightly Guided Successors, through military conquest the community founded an empire that quickly became the vehicle of one of the most brilliant civilisations of its time. Responding to the call of God through His Prophet meant gaining membership in a commonwealth of the faithful, where all were equal, and all were charged with upholding a common cause. This cause was nothing less than subjecting the world to the dominion of God by striving for the hegemony of the community of the faithful. The task of the community under the leadership of the *Khalīfah* (Caliph) or Successor to the Prophet of God was to order human affairs according to the *sharī'ah* or religious law that represented the specific formulation of the divine will for human life. Muslims thus had a sense of mission as a kind of chosen people, a Messianic community, who were to bring a new era of well-being to mankind by ensuring a social order that reflected the intentions of the Creator.

The sense of community is very much alive among Muslims today. It cuts across regional, national and linguistic barriers to create a great brotherhood that stretches from the shores of the Atlantic in Morocco to the Philippines. Within this brotherhood, though there are both those who are wealthy and those who are poor, those who are educated and those who remain unlettered, there is a vivid awareness of common ties, outlook and purpose. The equality before God and common purpose of Muslims are symbolised dramatically in such religious ceremonies as the daily prayers, where rich and poor prostrate themselves side by side in the identical ritual of obeisance to the common Creator of all. They may be seen again in the great rites of the annual pilgrimage to Mecca, where thousands of the faithful from every Muslim land gather in solemn congregation to celebrate the most revered of the Muslim's religious duties. Their equality is symbolised by all laying aside their normal clothing and putting on the seamless garment of the pilgrim, the outward marks of status and position being left behind as the pious pilgrims enter the sacred territory, circumambulate the Ka'bah, stand in the presence of God at 'Arafāt, or perform the other parts of the complex pilgrimage rite. Wherever Muslims gather together, if one leaves aside some divisions caused by sectarianism, there is a sense of kinship and warmth. In a mosque, in the performance of his prayers in some other place, or even in social contact with other Muslims, the faithful Muslim feels himself to be among his own as he cannot do with those outside the community.

Even so corrosive and powerful a force as modern nationalism has not always been able to override the Muslim sense of community. Indeed, in much of the Islamic world, nationalism has been forced to adapt itself to this awareness on the part of Muslims of constituting a group apart because of common religious faith. It is of the utmost significance, as W. C. Smith has written[1], that no Muslim people anywhere in the world has been able truly to include non-Muslims in its concept of the nation. Even in Turkey where a secularist ideology has been professed since before the time of Mustafa Kemal, the non-Muslim Greeks, Armenians and others are regarded as citizens of Turkey, but never as 'Turks'. A 'Turk' is regarded by definition as a Muslim of Turkish speech. The situation is generally similar for Jews and Christians in Islamic Iran, for the minority groups of Pakistan, and for Christian Arabs, although in the former Transjordan one had a patriarchal agrarian society in which the family or clan system

[1] Wilfred Cantwell Smith, *Islam in Modern History* (New York, Mentor Books, 1959) p. 83.

was paramount, so that within one grouping one could find both Muslim and Christian families; in present-day Jordan, too, there exists a substantial middle-class population of Christian Arabs who are very influential and 'Jordanian' in a nationalist sense. When the question is posed, 'Who are you?', the Muslim may reply in terms of family, regional associations or even national identity, but he will find a place also for his 'Muslimness'. In the past his identity as a Muslim would likely have loomed foremost in his mind. Today, in many parts of the Arab World, the situation is more fluid; for instance the new Palestinian ideology seeks a secular state. Nevertheless, the Muslim awareness of belonging to a special community that is set apart from others persists as a powerful factor in both individual and social life.

The force of this community feeling may also be seen at the level of international relations. Although Muslim nations do come into sharp conflict with one another from time to time, there still persists a fellow feeling which predisposes them toward mutual support. Especially in those cases where a Muslim people is attacked or threatened by a non-Muslim power, there is usually solidarity of feeling and support for the Muslim brother in spite of linguistic and ethnic differences and separation in space. Again the affirmative attitude toward other Muslims is almost instinctive, for religion and tradition have taught that Muslims are an *ummah* or community different from all others. Members of the *ummah* must be brothers to one another in adversity and difficulty in order that the cause of right will not suffer. However, the ambivalent attitude of Turkey and Iran in regard to the Arab–Israeli dispute should be noted.

Another characteristic of Muslim piety related to the feeling of community oneness is the great sense of confidence that being Muslim instils in the breasts of the faithful. There is an essential optimism in the Islamic outlook, both for the individual and for the community. This confidence grows out of the conviction that Islam is a divinely ordained path for men, the very will of God for human life, which in His mercy He sent down for men's guidance through the Prophet. When a man feels certain that his values, ideals and way of living are those which the Creator Himself has decreed, what greater assurance can he have or desire? The Muslim can go forward in life confirmed in the rectitude of his way, knowing that he is fulfilling a pattern based on the very nature of things. For most Muslims, therefore, it is inconceivable that a man could be anything but a Muslim. Someone who is acquainted with Islamic teachings or the contents of the Qur'ān and who still does not see the light must be wrong-headed or evil. Not to be religious at all, borders on the indecent in the common Muslim understanding. For the Muslim himself there is neither doubt nor hesitation about the rightness of his perception of reality and of man's duty. The revelation guarantees, and the experience of the community testifies, to the absolute rectitude of a way of life in which one may feel certainty and also pride.

Much of the strength of Muslim certainty stems from the fact also that Muslims feel themselves part of a sacred history stretching back to the very foundation of the created world. The Prophet of Islam with his Revelation of Guidance to a generation that had gone astray was only the last in a long series of divine spokesmen who had appeared among different nations in different epochs, one for each people addressing it in its own language. The Islamic community, thus, repeats an ageless history and continues the established mode of God's dealing with mankind. Islam has nothing of the character of innovation or of accident; it is not the peculiar invention of Muḥammad in response to his own limited experience. Rather it is the eternal truth, the one right religion that was the religion of Adam and of Abraham and of Jesus, as well as Muḥammad, the religion that God has established for all men. In resolving to follow the straight path of Islam one sets one's feet upon a way trodden by countless others, prophets, saints, heroes, pious and learned men from the very beginning of the world. The effect of a man's submission to God's ordained way is to renew his contact with the eternal well-springs of being.

The assurance that Islam holds out to the faithful comprehends not only the eventual destiny of mankind in another world to come but has meaning in this world, as well. The way of the Muslim is the best way of life, necessarily so, because it reflects an ageless divinely ordained pattern. It follows, therefore, that it must also be a successful mode of life for those who follow it truly. As people who cooperate, as it were, with the creative forces of the universe, Muslims may reasonably expect to enjoy well-being here and now in addition to bliss in the hereafter. Such was certainly the experience of the early Muslim community, a fact that is much celebrated in the countless stories of the Prophet, his Companions and

Turkey, Konya. Tomb of the thirteenth-century Persian mystic poet Jalāl al-Dīn Rūmī, and mosque of the Mevlevīya Order ('Whirling Dervishes') founded by him

the heroes of the early and classical ages, so often repeated and so fondly loved. The early community swept all before it. In seeking to carry out its mission it founded an empire that was crowned with all the evidences of worldly success. In addition to sheer power and military glory, there was prosperity and cultural creativity of the highest order. All of these in the Muslim understanding are a manifestation of Islam and the result of the faithful Muslims' having accepted their special and Messianic role in the world. Although the ordinary Muslim may know very little of this past history and be even less capable of analysing the attitudes deriving from it, he nonetheless shares in the confident optimism about the Muslim's destiny. One cannot do better, either individually or socially, than to live in an Islamic way; everything works together to bolster the Muslim's self-assurance and expectation.

This philosophy of history, which translates itself into feelings of confidence and rectitude, has been subjected to strains in modern times as the mundane fortunes of individual Muslims and the major Islamic countries alike have suffered decline. For intellectuals there is much soul-searching to understand what has gone amiss, and among more ordinary folk there is a malaise often amounting to despair. The very existence of these elements in contemporary Muslim life, however, testifies to the hold of Islamic conceptions upon the mass of people. The present moment may be confused, but whether explicitly expressed or only instinctively felt, the majority of Muslims retain the profound inner feeling that all will come right for the 'best of communities'. History is, after all, in the hand of God, and things must work for the best for His people, even if the fulfilment of their expectations be deferred to the coming of the *Mahdī* or the Day of Judgment. In spite of the appalling social and economic difficulties that beset the lower classes in many Muslim countries, life continues to be possible and meaningful, and religious faith continues to inspire confidence.

It is time now to consider the broad outlines of

the Muslim feeling about man's place in the world; we may in this way come to have some appreciation of the ethos of Islam. We shall attempt to describe how Muslims in general, both the élite and the ordinary people, view their religion and the human situation. Two questions may help to make the discussion clearer. The first is to ask: 'What is the fundamental human problem as Muslims apprehend it?'; and the second is to inquire: 'How is that problem solved?'.

In response to the first query, the simplest and most basic answer is that man is a creature. In thinking of themselves and the meaning of life, the matter uppermost in Muslim minds is the fact that human beings, like everything else in the universe, are created by forces which they neither understand nor control; men come into being and pass away, not from their own choice, but at the whim of overwhelming powers beyond their ken. Men, even in comparison with some of the animals, are relatively weak and incapable. The body is subject to disease, weakness, and eventual dissolution in the awesome finality of death, without men being able to predict these things or to release themselves from the inexorable round of birth, old age and death. Weakness of the physical frame is matched also by weakness of mental capacity. Men do not know whence they came, where they are going, what they are to do while here, how the universe operates, or, indeed, why it exists at all. Men have a degree of intelligence, but it is flawed. Nothing in their native endowment will permit them to rise to an understanding of these profound mysteries, for their capacities are only those of creatures. The most telling aspect of creaturehood is, therefore, its limitation. Correspondingly, the most challenging problem for mankind caught in this limitation is somehow to escape the fumbling, suffering and meaninglessness that are its consequences.

The limitation of creaturehood, as said above, applies to the intelligence. In these terms the human problem is that we do not know how to live. Since in the nature of things we cannot penetrate into the creative mysteries of the universe, it is impossible for a mere man by his unassisted faculties to find out how he should best lead his life. More fundamentally, it is impossible even to know what is right and what is wrong. Essential as this information may be for ordering human affairs, it lies beyond the capacity of the human mind to achieve through its own powers. Something more is required for men to lead proper lives, and that something must come from beyond the creaturely human sphere. In one sense, therefore, the problem of the human situation is ignorance (*jahl*). *Jahl*, which at one time referred primarily to the hot-headedness, foolhardiness and *hubris* of the pre-Islamic Arabs, came to be understood as 'ignorance', in the sense of the lack of sufficient and reliable information that would enable human beings to live fulfilled and proper lives.

It is to be emphasised that there is no element of guilt in this Muslim understanding of man's place in the world. Human beings are in difficulty, not because they have done something wrong for which they must incur punishment, but simply because they are what they are. Neither do Muslims have any sense that men are cut off from life-sustaining truth because human nature has been corrupted. The Muslim feeling is rather one of dire disability, of helplessness in the face of the unknown, and of dependence upon powers above for one's well-being. These inadequacies arise from human nature itself, for a man is a limited creature.

The response to our second question may also be put in a word; it is 'guidance'. Given our native disability, what we men require is to be told in detail and with authority how we ought to live. We require to have guidance for the proper conduct of our lives and in order to distinguish between right and wrong. What the Muslim wants and what he expects above all else from his religion is guidance in respect to the myriad situations of life. Guidance, then, is perhaps the most basic word in the entire Muslim religious vocabulary. And it is guidance that Islam offers in abundance. The Revelation in the Qur'ān is the divine method of letting men know what they need to know in order to live properly. Even with the Revelation men may not understand the mysteries of being or have insight into the character of God, but they know enough in order to please God, to live successful lives in this earthly existence and to attain paradise in another. This knowledge is all that men, as creatures, need. The Revelation is a definitive statement of what God expects from the human race. Thus, the ignorance inherent in creaturehood and the consequences that it may breed are overcome by a divine act of mercy, and men, while still being men, can live rightly and anticipate happiness. The ebullient assurance Muslims feel in the superiority and rightness of their religious attitudes springs

Iran, Iṣfahān. Muslims performing obligatory ritual ablutions before prayer

from the knowledge that the community possesses a divinely ordered map of the right kind of life.

Further, the guidance that Muslims have received in the Book (the Qur'ān) and the example of the Prophet is practical, simple and clear. The Muslim knows exactly what he is expected to do, and not to do. Religious teachings contain a number of explicitly stated prohibitions. There are also certain fundamental duties incumbent upon the Muslims, the so-called Pillars of Islam: confession of faith, the five daily prayers, alms-giving, fasting in the month of Ramaḍān, and the pilgrimage to Mecca at least once in a lifetime if at all possible. None of these has any hidden element, and none, except perhaps the last, is beyond the capacity of every man. A Muslim may thus fully and perfectly fulfil the religious duties required of him, living up in every way to the divine pattern ordained for his life. Nothing more is expected or needed; there remains no striving toward an unattainable ideal, no demand for perfection, no requirement that men should be like God. Content in the soundness of the guidance given him and in the knowledge that it is within his grasp to do what is required, the Muslim can feel himself a good man without qualification and find happiness in doing so.

Muslim prostrating himself at prayer

All of this is quite in contrast to the brooding and guilt-ridden outlook of the type of Christian who is obsessed with his own sinfulness and his inability ever to be that which his vision of man demands. Hence arises the vital role of the saviour in Christian religious thinking as a power who does on behalf of men what they cannot do for themselves. There is no corresponding figure and no corresponding function in orthodox Sunnī Islam. In Shī'ī Islam, the Mahdī has at least some of the attributes of the Saviour. Comparatively, the Muslim outlook is at once simpler, more optimistic and more reassuring; men know what they must do, and they have the power to do it.

What most needs to be appreciated here in speaking of these Muslim attitudes is that one is not dealing merely with an intellectual construction, with an idea that Muslims may have learned from a book or a teacher, but with the way that Muslims actually feel. It is the Muslim's personal experience of life that produces his religious response. The religious attitude has, of course, contributed fundamentally to the formation of Islamic culture as a whole, which in turn reinforces the typical Islamic perception of man, his nature, and his place in the scheme of things. At bottom, however, is the religious experience of man's helpless creaturehood and his need for guidance that are matched by the assurance held out in the revelation.

Along with the feelings of confidence and assurance there is another element in the Muslim's basic religious response. It is the feeling of obligation that is accompanied on the one hand with the threat of punishment and on the other with the promise of reward. Islam, it has been said many times, is essentially a religion of law. The basic content of its religious teaching is a series of commands and prohibitions, *dos* and *don'ts*, that form the substance of the way a Muslim is to follow. The proper attitude toward these divinely ordained rules and their divine author should be *Islām*, obedience, submission, or commitment, which is the sense in Arabic of the name of the religion itself. Muslims thus perceive the character of ultimate reality and of human life as being a series of demands. There impinges upon every man the will of the Creator to whom each individual is personally answerable. Men know what is required of them, for the Prophet has made the religious duties plain in the Revelation, and the responsibility to obey is an awesome one. In addition to assurance, therefore, the Muslim's religious experience is one of judgment, of being held accountable to a power in the unseen realm of the supernatural. Thus, both the confidence in the rightness of the way and the awareness of being under judgment serve to strengthen the Islamic sense of dependence upon the powers beyond that have created and ordered this world.

To this point our discussion has dealt with what might be called standard or 'orthodox' Islam; the time has now come to explore some other factors in the Islamic religious picture. The first matter to be noted is that the supernatural or unseen realm plays a role in Muslim consciousness in ways that are not always reflected in 'orthodox' religious thought or that may even be contrary to it. In the belief of common people in particular the universe is inhabited by a host of supra-human, normally invisible, beings, some of them beneficent but the greater majority dangerous to mankind. The Qur'ān and Islamic theology generally recognise several of these types of super-terrestrial beings, for example, the angels, the *shayṭān*s or devils, and *jinn*. The angels function as the servitors and messengers of God; they also directly affect the lives of men, for it was an angel who brought the Revelation to Muḥammad; it is an angel who keeps the record book of human deeds; it is the two angels, Munkar and Nakīr, who, in the tomb immediately after death, subject men to the fearsome questioning about their faith; it is an angel who holds the Balance on the Day of Judgment, and it is an angel who executes the divine decree of death at the appointed hour. All of these, however, are actions in obedience to divine decrees; the angels do not act capriciously at will to afflict men. The purpose of their creation is good, to act as protectors and overseers of men.

Not so, however, with the devils, or *shayṭāns*, a numerous breed of malevolent spirits who whisper into men's ears to lead them astray, who deliberately ensnare men to mislead them by crafty means, only then to abandon them to their fate. These devils are the force in the universe that opposes the will of God, and in the popular understanding every man is attended by both an angel and a *shayṭān*, the one urging him to good and the other attempting to lead him astray. The devils are very numerous, are ugly in appearance with hooved feet, and the better known of them have names. Their weapons against men include in particular disease, and they are able to appear in human form at will without betraying their nature or their evil intent. Even the prophets, such as John the Baptist, have had their *shayṭān*s but were too morally upright to listen to their evil counsel. With this host of wily and malevolent beings on every hand, the world has a dark and fearful side for the Muslim, in spite of the divine will that men should attain bliss. One of the *shayṭān*s stands out above the others as The Devil or the chief of the devils. He is Iblīs, originally an angel, who refused to obey the decree of God that the angels should make obeisance to Adam, and who, because of his rebellion, fell from favour to become the arch-enemy of God.

Yet another class of supernatural beings, familiar to every reader of the *Arabian Nights*, are the *jinn* or genies. These beings are also normally invisible and have the power to take on many forms. Like men, but unlike the devils, the *jinn* may achieve eternal bliss if they follow the guidance sent in the Revelation, and many have done so. There are several different classes or types of *jinn*, the most powerful and most evil being the *'afārīt* who may do violent harm to any whom they choose. The *'afārīt* are sometimes identified with the souls of men who have died a violent death and who remain in this world to haunt and torment the living. Both popular folklore and Islamic literature in a variety of languages abound in stories of the *jinn* and their relations with men. It is commonly believed that men may and do contract marriages with the *jinn*, and there is a highly developed lore among Muslims about the means that men may employ to have communication with the *jinn* and enlist these supernatural powers as their servants. A madman is considered to be possessed by a *jinn* (i.e. to be *majnūn* or 'jinned'); a *jinn*, or possibly a devil, is often the inspiration of a poet or writer, and a *jinn* may be the helper of a magician that makes his otherwise unnatural actions possible. An extensive literature in popular Islam shows Solomon as taming the *jinn* and using them (though they occasionally rebel against him) as a work-force in order to perform his many wonders. The belief in these spirits is all but universal among the generality of Muslims in our own day, and the art of seeking communication with the *jinn* is very much alive in many parts of the Islamic world.

Communication with the unseen or supernatural realm is carried out in a variety of different ways. There exist soothsayers who through familiarity with a *jinn*, demon or spirit, or through manipulation of certain materials, are able to see into the future, to divine the causes and cures of disease, to find lost objects and the like. One of the most important of the windows into the supernatural is the science of astrology, which is widely accepted as an authentic way of seeing into the future. The same purpose is served by types of geomancy, using arrangements of dots drawn on paper or in the dust, or by calculations from the alleged mystical significance of numbers. Belief in the efficacy of magic is also widespread. If the magic proceeds on the basis of the wizard's knowledge of secret lore, then it is nothing more than a manipulation of the elements of the world in skilled fashion, but it often also operates through the intermediary of a helper, a *jinn* or a devil, whom the magician controls through a talisman to do his will. The acts of a magician in every way resemble a miracle, the only difference being that miracles are done by holy men, saints and prophets for good purposes while magicians act with evil intent. Muslims know and believe in a great number of miracles, and again both literature and even learned religious writing are filled with stories of the miracles done by Muḥammad, by the heroes of early times, by other prophets, and by the saints who always live in the world. Everyone who has ever visited the East is also familiar with the Evil Eye, a power which some people possess to do harm, though perhaps unconsciously, to others whom they envy and which must be guarded against with great care. In sum, the supernatural is very near to the Muslim mind; it presses in on every side in a variety of ways to remind the Muslim of his creaturehood and of his subjection and dependence upon powers that reside in a higher and mysterious realm. One of the commonest Qur'anic phrases on the lips of the average Muslim, designed to protect himself from the devil and all works of darkness, is 'I seek Thy protection from Satan the Accursed'. In spite of all this, however, the ordinary Muslim is not an animist or a polytheist, living in terror of a multitude of forces that may overwhelm him and do him ill. For above all these demons, ghosts, and spirits there stands the sovereign God whose decree is supreme in the universe. The ultimate protection and well-being of a Muslim in this world teeming with spiritual beings are guaranteed by the power of God if only he follows the guidance offered in the Revelation. In spite of the darker and fearful side of popular belief and superstition, on balance Islam retains its spirit of assurance.

Sufism is one of the most important channels for the impingement of the supernatural upon the Muslim and therefore one of the fundamental factors in popular religion. In many respects Sufism, in both its higher expressions and its popular forms, stands in sharp contrast to 'orthodox' Islam. The aim of the Ṣūfī devotee is to draw nigh to God, to experience directly and immediately something of the divine nature, even to attain union with God. This goal is much higher and more difficult to achieve than that of obedience to exoteric rules that are clearly formulated. It also implies a radically different view of the nature of man and of human possibilities. The Ṣūfī wants to know the mystery of God, to enter into the very nature of the Divine, and to do this he must forsake worldly life, overcome his own personality, and strive through an arduous discipline to be wholly transformed into that Other which is his aim. In the process he must traverse many mystical states and stages before achieving the culminating ecstasy of extinction or *fanā'* in the reality of God. The major motif of the Ṣūfī endeavour is thus that of the soul yearning for God, the spiritual element in man longing to return to its source in the all-encompassing Divine reality, the lover seeking the ecstasy of merging with his beloved. This motif is repeatedly symbolised in the literature of the Muslim peoples whose poetry is dominated by the theme of an all-consuming but unfulfilled love. The hero of this literature is the lover driven to distraction by his passion, eternally seeking the beloved but never able to possess her. For perhaps a fleeting second the frustrated lovers may have contact, only to lose one another again and be plunged back into the throbbing yearning. Erotic though the theme may appear at the superficial level, it is at the same time a description of the human situation and the human goal, for the lover is the soul, and the beloved whom he so ardently and unceasingly seeks is the Divine. Such is the religious outlook so often and so lovingly reiterated in familiar stories such as Laylā and Majnūn (the youth driven mad by love), which are known to every Muslim, literate and illiterate, lowly or exalted.

The contact of common people with the Ṣūfī element in the Islamic religious heritage has come in largest part through the great Ṣūfī orders or brotherhoods which spread all over the Islamic world after the twelfth century and retained their significance until the present. These brotherhoods with their mystical doctrine and their organised centres (*khānaqāh, zāwiyah* or *tekke*), resembling monasteries, served many purposes for the common folk of the Islamic world. The Ṣūfī teachers were immediately accessible sources of counsel, guidance, spiritual instruction and succour. The *khānaqāhs* were often the agencies of stability and order in a local region, Ṣūfī orders in several cases having become the holders of temporal power and their heads the founders of dynasties. The Ṣūfī centres also supplied material assistance to those in need, medical care for the indigent, hospitality for travellers, and many other services. Through the association of the orders and certain mystical doctrines with chivalrous organisations and the craft guilds which controlled the work of the artisan class, the orders also served an important function of social integration and identification. It may even be claimed that the orders had a vital role in the stability of the polity as a whole, for they became one of the channels of communication between common people and their rulers. With the passage of time, not only the lower classes but the orthodox *'ulamā*, the learned men of religion, as well, were attracted to the orders. Since the *'ulamā* were trained in state-supported religious schools and found their employment in the judiciary or the bureaucracy of the state, they were able to act as a link between the orders and the mass of the population whose religious needs were served by the orders. In short the Ṣūfī orders were one of the most important features of Islamic society in the medieval and pre-modern periods, both in a religious sense and socially. Though less visible, they retain an importance even today, especially in the rural areas of the Islamic world, but they have come under severe criticism by reformers and secularised intellectuals. In the case of Turkey the orders were forbidden after the Turkish Revolution of the 1920s, and their *tekkes* in that country were forcibly closed (1925). Even under this pressure, however, Sufism and the orders have begun a slow but certain revival, and Sufism continues to thrive vigorously if somewhat covertly on Turkish soil.

The element in Ṣūfī teaching that holds the greatest attraction for the common people of the Islamic world is the doctrine of the saints or *awliyā'* (the friends of God). A Ṣūfī saint is an individual with outstanding spiritual gifts, one who has himself successfully journeyed along the Pilgrim's Progress of the Right Way to the goal of immediate contact with the Divine. His success in penetrating to the very secret of Reality is to be accounted for by his having secured an esoteric knowledge of the methods of spiritual discipline from another great spiritual figure, also a saint, who was his teacher and preceptor in a relation of great and special intimacy. Thus the Ṣūfī saint stands in the line of a succession of spiritual teachers who stretch back at least to the Prophet, Muḥammad, and who through him or his son-in-law 'Alī have direct access to the divine mysteries and the divine power. Every saint in consequence has about him the aura of holiness. He carries an element of the very Divine Being in himself and is the locus of a peculiar power or blessedness known as *barakah*. Even to be in the presence of such a man or to touch his garment is to capture something of this blessing for oneself, and the common people of the Islamic world pay the highest reverence to the men who are reputed to be among the friends of God. A saint possesses also, by the grace of God, the capacity to perform miracles. In his spiritual evolution he has passed the stage where all the secrets of nature and of being are known to him; it lies, therefore, within his ability to interfere with the normal course of things in miraculous ways, though the true saint will never do so for his own advantage or in conspicuous fashion. This miraculous power, however, may be used to benefit those who seek the assistance of the saint, and the ordinary folk of Islam come in their thousands to these spiritual leaders seeking ways out of their difficulties. Even in death the saint retains his sanctity and his power, so that his tomb will be a centre of pilgrimage for his devotees. Scattered throughout the Islamic world there are thousands of such tomb shrines, some magnificently decorated and adorned but others so humble that the name of the saint buried there may have long since been forgotten. The tomb shrines of such famous Ṣūfīs as Jalāl al-Dīn Rūmī (located in Konya), 'Abd al-Qādir al-Jīlānī (located in Baghdad) or al-Hujwīrī, known as Dātā Ganj Bakhsh (located in Lahore), annually attract hundreds of thousands of faithful devotees especially at the time of the annual celebration or *'urs* (a sort of wedding feast) in honour of the saint. The pious come to circumambulate the shrine or sit in meditation near it, to touch or to kiss the tomb, to rub the dust of its environs on their foreheads (and even their eyes), to offer a humble gift, and to present their prayers and petitions to the saint. The shrines are the places of resort of all those with grief or trouble. More importantly, for the common understanding the Islamic saints are the links with that unseen world where human destiny is formed and controlled. They are the mediators of divine power in the world, the channel by which reality flows into all things and through which all things are sustained. The saints, their power and their shrines are the heart of religion for a vast number of Muslims, even though much of the religious practice connected with this cult goes sharply against the teachings of 'high Islam'. Much to the scandal of the puritanically minded, there have not been lacking Ṣūfīs who made explicit the implications of common piety by declaring roundly the superiority and priority of the saints over even the prophets.

The stories of the saints, their austerities, their piety, and their miracles in circulation among the Muslim peoples are legion. Especial favourites are tales of the miracles of saintly men, some of whom could raise themselves into the air without visible means of support ('levitation'), others who could be simultaneously in two places at once, and still others who possessed information of events in far places or those still to come in the future, or were capable of 'thought' reading from looking at people (*firāsah*). None of this is difficult for the ordinary Muslim to accept, for, as we have said, the supernatural and unseen realm looms very near in his mind and is likely to break through into the events of history at any moment. The cult of saints once again adds strength to the Muslim sense of being in the hands of powers beyond himself, powers that he may contact and know in order to assure his own access to truth and beatitude.

It is apparent after this long discussion that the religious outlook of Muslims contains a number of different elements that are not easily describable in a single formula. Even so, nothing has been said of the piety and spiritual experience of very large numbers of Muslims, such as the Shī'a, of whom there has been no space here to treat. The reality of Islamic religious life is a great richness, an effulgent diversity that seeks always new forms of expression. As a living religion Islam has been a constantly changing spiritual perspective on human life that through more than 1300 years of existence has shown itself capable of meeting the religious needs of a major segment of mankind.

Mecca, the pilgrimage to the Sacred Mosque and the circumambulation of the Ka'bah

4

God and his creation: two medieval Islamic views

MICHAEL E. MARMURA

I. Introduction

The Qur'ān is an ardent reaffirmation of monotheism. It declares that the world and all that there is in it is created by God, omnipotent, omniscient, merciful and just. The creation is a 'sign', a manifestation of His power and wisdom. It is also a manifestation of His bounty and goodness; for He has created things for man's benefit. Men are enjoined to consider God's handiwork, to reflect on the wonders of His creation.

Medieval Islamic thinkers, however, differed in interpreting Qur'ānic statements about the divine creative acts. By the eleventh (Christian) century, two very divergent views of God and His creation emerged, one voiced by the speculative theologians, *al-mutakallimūn*, more specifically, those belonging to the school of al-Ash'arī; the other by certain of the leading philosophers. The Ash'arites adopted and elaborated a doctrine of creation *ex nihilo*. They held, that is, that at some moment in the very distant past, God created the universe out of nothing. They supported this interpretation by elaborating an atomic theory of matter, maintaining that the physical world is composed of indivisible particles which God creates out of nothing. Since all parts composing the natural world are created out of nothing, the world, the sum of these parts, is created out of nothing. To deny the doctrine of creation *ex nihilo*, these theologians argued, is to deny the God of revelation, infinite in power and wisdom.

The majority of the medieval Islamic philosophers opposed this doctrine. God, they argued, is the supreme cause of all existence (other than His own); but this does not mean that He created the world out of nothing at some remote moment in the past. It cannot mean this, they argued, because such a view leads to a number of impossible consequences. To give but one of their examples, God's act of initiating the world at a finite moment in time means that an eternity must have preceded this act. If, for the sake of argument, we admit the possibility of this eternal time in which there was no world, God's act of initiating the world after this infinite lapse of time must involve a change of state in His nature; an impossibility, since the divine nature by definition is changeless. They further pointed out that the Qur'ān does not state that the world was created *ex nihilo*. Hence, they argued, some other interpretation must be given to the scriptural language referring to the divine act of creating the world. Since God is eternal actuality, they continued, He is eternally active. The world, which is the effect of His eternal activity, must be eternal.

Clearly, these are two radically different interpretations. They involved different conceptions of the divine nature, attributes, agency, the material and spiritual worlds God creates, natural causation, man's freedom of the will, the nature of the human soul, reward and punishment in the hereafter. They involved, in other words, two differently thought out views of God and His creation, each claiming for itself sole accord with revelation. This at once raises a fundamental question. What is it that renders one of these two views 'theological', the other 'philosophical?' What differentiates the Islamic speculative theologian (*al-mutakallim*) from the philosopher (*al-faylasūf*)?

The difference, as we see it, is basically one of motive and starting point. The Islamic theologians began by accepting revelation. They then applied reason to interpret, defend, justify and solve problems arising from its assertions. The starting point of the philosophers, on the other hand, was reason and experience. They believed that their empirical and rational investigations led to the demonstrative certainty of the existence of the one God, the ground of all being. Having arrived through rational proof at God's existence, they accepted revelation as affirming the same thing, but in symbolic, pictorial language. This, however, was the very point the Ash'arite theologians contested, rejecting the philosophers' claim that the God they arrived at through demonstration is the God of revelation. In so challenging the philosophers, they made it clear that the issue between them was not the question of the existence of God, but the nature of the godhead.

II. The Ash'arite theologians' view

It is generally recognised that Islamic speculative theology (*kalām*) developed under the impact of Greek thought. This, however, does not mean that its motive was philosophical or scientific. Its primary concern was with understanding and interpreting the revealed word. Moreover, its origins were quite local and sprang from early political and religious controversy. Thus the impetus to theological argument was probably first brought about by dissident groups known as *al-Khawārij*, or 'Seceders', so named because they trace their origin to a group that seceded from the army of the fourth Caliph, 'Alī (d. 661), in his civil war against Mu'āwiyah. These groups raised the question of defining true Islamic belief and developed extremely puritanical doctrines regarding the nature of the Islamic community.

At the same time, however, Greek thought began to exercise an influence on Islamic theological thinking at quite an early period, certainly during the last fifty years of the Umayyad Caliphate, between 700 and 750. Most of this influence was probably indirect, through encounter with Christian theology. In this period we already have in Islam definite positions on the question of man's freedom of the will, some theologians staunchly advocating such freedom, others vehemently denying it. We have also reports of criticisms by Islamic theologians of the Aristotelian theory that bodies consist of substances and accidents inhering in them.

It was, however, early in the ninth century, under the sponsorship of the 'Abbasid Caliphs, that a vigorous programme of translating Greek philosophy and science was undertaken. The first half of the ninth century also saw the rise to political power of the most important of the early schools of *kalām*, the Mu'tazilite, a school that originated in Umayyad times. Three successive 'Abbasid Caliphs who ruled from 817 to 847 gave it official support and strove to impose one of its dogmas on all Muslims. A reaction set in, however, and the Caliph al-Mutawakkil (d. 861) reversed the policy of his three predecessors; the Mu'tazilites were persecuted and lost their political power. Despite this, for over two centuries, they continued active and creative as theologians, though gradually losing their position as the leaders of *kalām* to the Ash'arites.

Al-Ash'arī himself, who died around 935, began his theological career as a member of the Mu'tazilite school, but rebelled against it. It is hence not surprising to find Mu'tazilite elements in the Ash'arite view of God and the world. Thus, for example, the Ash'arites took over from the Mu'tazilites and developed the doctrine that material bodies are composed of indivisible atoms and accidents inhering in these atoms. Moreover, Ash'arite causal theory, so central to their theology, had been held totally or in part in some Mu'tazilite circles. On the other hand, Ash'arite theology is essentially a repudiation and reversal of the two cardinal principles of Mu'tazilism, namely, the principles of divine oneness and of divine justice. This does not mean that the Ash'arites denied God's unity and His justice. It only means that they interpreted these concepts very differently from the Mu'tazilites.

Some of the attributes of God the Qur'ān speaks of, such as the attributes of Life, Power and Knowledge, were regarded as eternal by the Mu'tazilites. Are such eternal attributes to be considered as distinct from the divine essence, as something 'additional' to the essence? To so consider them, the Mu'tazilites maintained, would constitute a denial of God's oneness. For God then would consist, as it were, of the divine essence and of eternal attributes distinct from it. Some of the Mu'tazilites hence simply identified the eternal attributes with the eternal essence. Others adopted a doctrine of negative attributes whereby to state, for example, that God is a Knower, is not to state anything positive of Him, but simply to deny that He is ignorant. Some also resorted to the enigmatic statement that the eternal attribute is neither God nor is it anything other than God.

The Ash'arites opposed this doctrine, maintaining that the eternal attributes are 'additional' to the divine essence and that this does not violate God's oneness. The Mu'tazilite denial of the distinction between essence and eternal attribute is in effect a denial of the attributes altogether and a distortion of the intent of the scriptural language when it mentions such attributes. Moreover, the Ash'arites argued, if the eternal attributes are not separated from the divine essence, then the divine act ceases to be a voluntary act. For then God would be acting through His very essence or nature. But what does this mean? It means that action proceeds from Him in the way it is said to proceed from a natural inanimate object; fire, for example, warms by its very nature and has no option not to produce warmth. The Mu'tazilites were aware of and sensitive about this criticism which they anticipated and attempted to meet. Thus some of them argued that the divine will itself is created by God and is not eternal. This answer, however, was vulnerable to very telling criticism by the Ash'arites.

Turning to the Mu'tazilite principle of divine justice, it affirmed, among other things, that when God judges men in the hereafter, rewarding the righteous and punishing the wicked, He judges them only for those acts they have freely chosen and initiated or 'created'. In other words, the Mu'tazilites held that man is the 'creator' of those acts for which he is morally responsible. A second aspect of this doctrine is the theory that the moral value of an act is an objective property or state of that act. Thus evil is an objective attribute of the act of lying; goodness an objective attribute of the act of helping others. When God commands the performance of a good act, He does so because the act is in itself good. The act is not good simply because God commands it. Relating to this is the theory that reason unaided by revelation can discern the moral value of an act. The gift of reason entails moral responsibility.

Another aspect of this doctrine of justice is that God always acts for the good of men. The Mu'tazilites were what one might call philosophical optimists. This does not mean that they closed their eyes to physical and moral evil. Far from it. They struggled to the utmost seeking an explanation for this. They were particularly concerned with the problem of the suffering of the innocent, of children, of the insane and also of animals. Their belief in life after death gave them an avenue for offering solutions to this problem. Thus, some maintained that children who die are given a permanent place in paradise. They are given this either as an act of divine benevolence, as compensation for suffering, or both. It is not given as a reward, however. The place or station of rewards in paradise is the highest and is reserved only for individuals who have attained the age of discretion, who are morally responsible for their acts and have chosen to act righteously.

This solution to the problem of evil did not satisfy the Ash'arites. They pointed out that a child who dies young is still denied the opportunity to attain the highest station in paradise and that, given the Mu'tazilite definition of justice as an objective value, this is unjust. They further argued that since God is omniscient and foresees that certain individuals will be doomed to eternal punishment, He could not be acting for their welfare in allowing them to attain the age of discretion, becoming thereby responsible for the sins He knew they would commit. At the root of this dilemma, the Ash'arites argued, is the Mu'tazilite objectivist theory of moral acts. Apart from its failure to solve the question of evil, it restricts divine action. This manifests itself in the divine acts of reward and punishment. These acts become conditioned by the inherent and objective merit or demerit of the human acts. A consequence of this, the Ash'arites argued, is the Mu'tazilite dogma – never very popular in Islam – that those who commit the great sin and die without repenting are eternally damned in the hereafter and cannot be forgiven. Such a doctrine, the Ash'arites pointed out, denies not only divine omnipotence, but also God's infinite compassion and bounty.

The Ash'arites thus reversed the Mu'tazilite doctrine of moral acts. They maintained that an act is good simply because God either performs or commands it; bad, because He prohibits it. If we examine any act, we will not discern any intrinsic moral qualities in it. The theory that reason can attain knowledge of the objective moral attributes of acts is simply false because no such objective moral values exist. Outside the commands and prohibitions of the religious law, what people regard as moral judgments are subjective and stem usually from conflicting motives of mundane self-interest.

Man, the Ash'arites further maintained, does not 'create' his own acts, all human acts (like all other events in the world), being the direct creation of God. This does not mean, they continued, that there is no distinction between an involuntary human act, a spasmodic bodily movement, for example, and the deliberate act. For while the first act is simply created by God, the second is created with another event, the power we experience when performing those acts we class as deliberate.

Now the Ash'arite analysis of involuntary and deliberate human action has been differently understood; to many it remains enigmatic. A common criticism of it is that it remains a deterministic theory. Whether or not this is the case, their analysis certainly reflects a main theological concern, namely, to defend what they conceived to be the Qur'ānic concept of divine omnipotence and omniscience. This concern manifests itself in their atomism and causal doctrine. The Ash'arites rejected the Aristotelian doctrine that matter is in principle infinitely divisible. In this they followed most of the Mu'tazilites who had advocated an atomic view, influenced by Greek, possibly also by Indian, atomism. This doctrine of atoms was partly adopted to safeguard the concept of divine omniscience as expressed by the Qur'ānic statement that God knows the determinate number of all things. It was also adopted to ensure the concept of God's direct control of all His creation. Bodies, the Ash'arites maintained, are composed of atoms and accidents inhering in them. Atoms and accidents are created by God out of nothing. They are also constantly being annihilated and recreated by God. They do not causally interact with each other. What we erroneously believe to be causal interaction in nature is in reality nothing but sequences of concomitant events whose uniformity is arbitrarily decreed by God. There is no inherent necessity in the order of nature; God can thus discrupt it at will as indeed He does when miracles take place.

The Ash'arites adopted the occasionalist view that causal efficacy resides only with God. The divine act, however, is a voluntary act. It proceeds, not from His essence or nature, but from the attributes of Power and Will. That the divine will is eternal, they maintained, does not entail that the divine enactment of the world is eternal. God can eternally will a finite event in time. Indeed, the world which is nothing but a series of such finite events, was created *ex nihilo* at a finite moment in the distant past. An eternal world, if possible at all, could only be the consequence of a God who acts by the necessity of His nature, by a being devoid of the attribute of Will, nay, of Life.

III. The philosophers' view

Islamic philosophy belongs to the tradition of philosophy as we know it in the West. It is rooted in Greek philosophy and is by and large a continuation and development of it. The cultural context in which it developed was of course different. To say, however, that it was rooted in Greek philosophy, does not mean that Islamic philosophy simply repeated what the Greek philosophers had said. Repetition there was. But there was also extensive critical comment, refinement, a rethinking of concepts and in general a remoulding of ancient philosophy that gave Islamic philosophy a distinctive stamp of its own.

Space does not permit us to go into the history of the movement of translating Greek philosophy to Arabic. Suffice it to say that without it Islamic philosophy as we know it would not have emerged; hence its great debt to Christian scholars of the Eastern churches who undertook the translations. Nor can we discuss the types of Greek philosophical works that were translated, except to note that they included a body of writings belonging to the Christian era. Nonetheless, the major influences were three. These were Plato (d. 347 B.C.), Aristotle (d. 322 B.C.) and Plotinus (d. *ca.* A.D. 270), whose influence on Islamic (as well as Christian and Jewish) thought was immense. Now, the writings of these three philosophers offered the Islamic philosophers three different ways of viewing the relation of God to the world. All three ways were alternatives to the doctrine of the world's creation *ex nihilo*.

The first of these views, that of Plato as understood in medieval Islam, was the closest to the doctrine of creation advocated by the Islamic theologians. It maintained that the world was created by God at a moment of time, but not out of nothing. There was, to begin with, some kind of formless chaotic matter. The act of creation at a moment of time consisted in bringing order to, not in producing, the very stuff on which this order was imposed. This view, accepted, as we shall see, by one important Islamic philosopher, al-Rāzī, was rejected by most. In general, Plato's immense influence on Islamic philosophy lay in the realm of political thought.

Aristotle's view of the relation of God to the world was more influential. According to this view the world is eternal. There is an eternal and constant rotation of the heavens; and in this earth of ours, the world of generation and corruption, a constant rotation of forms over matter. This eternal process of movement and change is caused by the eternal God. God is the first mover in the sense that He is the final cause, the aim to which everything tends and desires. God moves the world by attraction, as it were. God is an intellectual principle, thought thinking thought, remote from the individual concerns of men. This view had a special appeal to the Islamic philosophers, although they combined it with the third view, that of Plotinus and his followers. This was not entirely deliberate. Due to an error, they mistook some Plotinian doctrine for Aristotle's.

For Plotinus, the source of all existence is what he normally refers to as 'the One'. The One is totally other than all else, transcending Aristotle's concept of God. Moreover, the One is not simply the cause (whether directly or indirectly) that keeps the world in perpetual motion. All existents are emanations, an overflow from the One. The simile of the sun and its light is perhaps the most apt to give an idea of Plotinus' meaning: existence emanates from the One as light emanates from the sun. From the One, an intellect or mind first emanates, followed by a world soul. The universe emanates from the world soul. This creative process is an eternal one. Islamic philosophers, later on, identified the One of Plotinus with the God of Aristotle and argued that this is the same as the God of the monotheistic religions. They found Plotinus' doctrine of emanation particularly attractive. They thought it helped explain how God, declared in the Qur'ān to be totally dissimilar to His creation, could yet create something that does not resemble Him in any manner.

Turning then to the medieval Islamic philosophers themselves, they did not hold one identical view. What is perhaps more accurate is to say that there emerged among certain of these philosophers a view of God and the world that became very influential and, in its general outline, the most representative of medieval Islamic philosophy. The first two major Islamic philosophers, however, were exceptions that prove the rule. In their views of God and His creation, they not only differed from each other, but from later, more typical Islamic philosophers. These two were al-Kindī (d. *ca.* 860) and the physician-philosopher, al-Rāzī (d. either 923 or 932).

Al-Kindī adopted the doctrine that the world emanates from the One, which he identified with the God of the Qur'ān. In a lengthy argument he offered a proof to demonstrate both God's existence and oneness. Unless there is a being who is utterly one, devoid of all multiplicity, there can be no variety and multiplicity in the world. But, al-Kindī argued, multiplicity and variety in the world is a fact which we experience and cannot dismiss. Hence, the being who is utterly one, namely God, must exist. But the most astonishing thing about al-Kindī is that he was the only major medieval Islamic philosopher who, without any equivocation, upheld the doctrine of the world's creation *ex nihilo*, giving lengthy arguments to show that an eternal world is impossible. Hence although al-Kindī adopted the Plotinian doctrine of emanation, he rejected the doctrine that this emanation is an eternal process.

Al-Rāzī, one of the most important physicians of medieval Islam, was also a philosopher of note and independence of mind. He was greatly influenced by Plato's Timaeus, and was the major Islamic philosopher to adopt the Platonic view that the world was created at a moment of time, but not out of nothing. On the other hand, he was less sympathetic to the Platonic view held by most of the Islamic philosophers, namely that philosophy should be confined to the few, an élite. He is further noted for his criticism of prophecy, maintaining that reason is sufficient to guide us in the moral life.

It was, however, Alfarabi (al-Fārābī) (d. 950) and Avicenna (Ibn Sīnā) (d. 1037), who more than any one else, shaped the general character of Islamic philosophy. It is difficult to exaggerate the influence of Alfarabi on the course of Islamic philosophy. Perhaps the first thing to note about him was that he was a professional: there is no amateurishness about him. He commented extensively on Aristotle's works and was largely responsible for putting the study of logic in medieval Islam on a sound basis. In the Islamic world he was referred to as The Second Teacher, the first being Aristotle.

Now, for medieval man, the earth was the centre of the universe, that is, the centre in the physical sense, not necessarily in importance or value. In the order of existence it was the most remote from God and hence, in order of value, lowest. But within our earth, by virtue of being endowed with reason, man stood highest in the scale of value. Around the earth revolved the heavenly spheres. The closest was the sphere of the Moon, then the spheres of Mercury, Venus, the Sun, Mars, Jupiter and Saturn, respectively. Beyond Saturn was the sphere of the fixed stars; finally, an outermost sphere without stars which most of the medieval Islamic astronomers assumed. Now Aristotle had maintained that the eternal movements of the spheres are caused by intelligences or minds, numbering some fifty-four, apart from the prime mover, God. But Aristotle had never made quite clear the relationship of these intelligences to God.

Alfarabi, first of all, identified Aristotle's God with the One of Plotinus, maintaining that his is the same as the God of revelation. Secondly, he limited the number of intelligences to the number of the spheres, making both these intelligences and spheres emanations from God, explaining the emanative process as follows: God, being pure intellect, undergoes an act of self-knowledge. This is a creative act which results in the emanation from God of a first intelligence. This first intelligence, in turn, undergoes an act of knowing God and this act results in the emanation from this first intelligence of two things: a second intelligence and the outermost sphere of the world. The second intelligence then undergoes the act of knowing God, resulting in the emanation from this second intelligence of a third intelligence and the sphere of the fixed stars. The process is repeated by the third intelligence and so on down to the sphere of the moon. The last of the intelligences, the Active Intellect, produces our earth, the world of generation and corruption. This entire emanative process, it must be remembered, is for Alfarabi an eternal one.

The universe for Alfarabi is an orderly, rational one, emanating in degrees from a supreme mind, God. Man, on this earth, being endowed with voluntary action, must order his own life and society to be in tune with the rational, harmonious order of the universe. Only thus can man attain happiness. Just as the universe is ordered by a supreme rational being, God, and each heavenly sphere is governed by an intelligence, so man, a small universe in his own right, ought to govern himself by his reason. The same holds for human society. The state should be organised in such a way that each level of society performs its proper function, all acting as a harmonious whole. Following Plato, Alfarabi maintained that this is achieved only when the ruler is a philosopher-king. Certain philosopher-kings are also lawgivers. Alfarabi identified the philosopher-lawgiver with the prophet who receives revelation from the celestial intelligences as emanations. Revelation gives the same truths as philosophy, but in the language of imagery and symbols which everyone can understand. Only the very few are endowed with the capacity to become philosophers and only the philosophers are entitled to interpret scriptural language philosophically.

If Alfarabi laid down the foundations of a philosophy that more than anything else was to typify the Islamic strand of philosophy, his successor, Avicenna, developed it into one of the most comprehensive of systems. Adopting Alfarabi's emanative scheme, he refined it, or perhaps made explicit ideas that were implicitly there. What proceeds from the first intelligence emanating from God, Avicenna held, is not simply another intelligence and a bodily sphere, but also a celestial soul. In other words, we have thereafter a series of triads, each consisting of an intelligence, a soul and a body. We cannot go into the various reasons why Avicenna insisted on this refinement, except to note that it allowed him a fuller explanation of prophetic revelation.

Avicenna's philosophy is noted for its doctrine of essence. Considered in itself, a nature or an essence is neither universal nor particular, neither one nor many. In itself, 'horseness', Avicenna tells us is simply 'horseness'. Furthermore, scrutiny of an essence will not yield the knowledge of whether such an essence exists or does not exist. From what a thing is we cannot infer that it exists. Thus, considered in itself, any of the species we encounter around us, is only possible: it can exist or not exist. The fact of its existence has to be explained in terms of something extraneous to it, namely its immediate cause. This cause necessitates its existence. Thus while in itself it is only possible, it is necessary through another. The same applies to the cause. In itself it is only possible, but necessary through another cause, and so on. But a chain of such causes cannot go on indefinitely,[1] Avicenna argued, and must terminate in a being who is not necessitated by anything else. This is God, the Necessary Being, whose essence and existence are one and the same. Since God is eternal, the universe, the necessitated consequence of the divine essence, must be eternal. This, as we shall see, was one of the main bones of contention between the Ash'arites and Avicenna.

Another of Avicenna's basic theories is that of the human soul. An emanation from the active intellect, the human rational soul is an immaterial substance that becomes individuated when it joins the material

[1] Involved here is Avicenna's theory of essential causality where cause and effect coexist in time. Such a chain of essential causes is impossible. Causes that precede their effects in time Avicenna terms 'accidental causes'. Only the infinity of accidental causes, he argued, is possible.

body at birth. Avicenna strove to prove both the individuality and immateriality of this soul. He further held that the individual soul is immortal and retains its individuality after bodily death. Good souls live in eternal bliss, contemplating the celestial intelligences and God. Bad souls, tarnished during their earthly existence by their succumbing to bodily, animal appetites, live in eternal misery, ever desiring contemplation of God and the intelligences but never attaining it. On this earth, some souls have the capacity to attain direct knowledge from the celestial intelligences. These are the souls of prophets. But this knowledge is transmitted by the prophet in the language of metaphor and symbol which everyone can understand. Avicenna endorsed Alfarabi's theory of prophecy, refining and elaborating it.

It should also be added that Avicenna identified the celestial souls and intelligences in his emanative scheme with the angels of the scriptures. He thus upheld the oneness of God, the existence of angels, prophetic revelation and a doctrine of individual immortality, giving all these a philosophical explanation. Yet, in medieval Islam, Avicenna never attained a position comparable to a St Augustine or a St Thomas Aquinas in Christendom. On the contrary, he was denounced as an infidel by the Ash'arite theologians and others. Why?

The reason for this is not difficult to see and we have already hinted at it. The Ash'arites did not denounce Avicenna because he did not believe in God, immortality, and prophecy, but because he had what they firmly believed to be the wrong conceptions of this one God, of immorality and prophecy. This was the very point of Avicenna's arch-critic, the lawyer, Ash'arite theologian, and mystic, al-Ghazālī (d. 1111). In his *The Incoherence of the Philosophers*, he subjected Avicenna's metaphysical theories to incisive logical criticism. After arguing that, contrary to Avicena's claims, these theories have not been demonstrated, he pronounced seventeen of them as innovatory deviations from true Islamic belief, three as being outright irreligious.

That the first doctrine denounced by al-Ghazālī as irreligious was that of the world's eternity is hardly surprising. Al-Ghazālī pointed out repeatedly that this doctrine rests on the premise that God acts by the necessity of His nature and hence denies the divine attribute of Will. The second was Avicenna's doctrine that God knows particulars 'in a universal way'. According to this doctrine, God does not know individual men but only the universal qualities of man in the abstract. Such a God, al-Ghazālī pointed out, cannot be the God of the Qur'ān, very much concerned with the destinies of individual men. The third doctrine was that of the soul's immortality. Avicenna's denial of bodily resurrection, al-Ghazālī argued, is a denial of the divine power capable of such resurrecting of men.

Now this denunciation of these theories was voiced in legal terms and raised the question of whether Islamic religious law allows the study of philosophy. There was therefore need for the philosophers to answer al-Ghazālī, not only on the philosophical level, but also on the legal. The man who answered al-Ghazālī on both these levels was none other than the great Averroes (Ibn Rushd) (d. 1198) of Muslim Spain, the most Aristotelian of the Islamic philosophers, and an Islamic lawyer in his own right.

In a relatively short legal work, Averroes first argued that philosophy is nothing more than the systematic investigation of the wonders of creation that reveal God's wisdom and might. As such, the revealed law commands the study of philosophy. This command, however, is restricted to those who have had the native ability to pursue philosophy and the actual philosophical training. To all others, philosophy is prohibited. In this Averroes was restating Alfarabi's principle that philosophy must be confined to the few. Averroes also endorsed and refined Alfarabi's doctrine that the philosophical demonstrative method led to the same truth revealed by scripture, but that scripture expresses this truth in imaged, symbolic language that the non-philosopher majority can understand. Averroes, however, worked out a sophisticated theory of scriptural interpretation in terms of which he argued that even if the philosophers condemned by al-Ghazālī had erred in their interpretations of the scriptures, their error is permissible. This is not to say that he conceded that they did err.

On the more philosophical plane, he answered al-Ghazālī's *Incoherence of the Philosophers* by a work entitled, *The Incoherence of 'The Incoherence'*. In it he replied point by point to al-Ghazālī's criticisms, sometimes criticising Avicenna as well, particularly when the latter deviated from Aristotle. It would be too much to claim that Averroes met all of al-Ghazālī's objections to the philosophers. On the other hand, he pointed out weaknesses in al-Ghazālī's criticisms, clarifying the philosophers' positions, often showing them to be more convincing than the Ash'arites'. To al-Ghazālī's charge that the philosophers have denied God His attributes of Life and Will, Averroes responded by insisting on the analogical use of the language of attribution. In his turn, he charged that the Ash'arites have misused this language, succumbing to anthropomorphism, and have made of God 'an eternal man'.

To adjudicate between Ash'arite and Islamic philosopher, however, is not our purpose here. Nor does space allow discussion of parallel conflicts in Christian and Judaic intellectual history. Our main concern has been to show the contrast between the world views of the Ash'arites and the Islamic philosophers, indicating thereby some of the issues that belong to the main stream of medieval Islamic thought.

5

Law and traditional society

R. M. SAVORY

In the eyes of a Muslim, the law is an integral part of his religion; in Islam, law is more important even than theology, which has frequently taken on the character of defensive apologetics rather than that of a doctrine of God. The late Joseph Schacht, one of the world's greatest authorities on Islamic law, stated categorically that 'it is impossible to understand Islam without understanding Islamic law'. In the Muslim view, the law is virtually as much the revealed will of God as is the Qur'ān itself. In Western tradition, the law derives its authority from the reason and will of man, and from his moral nature. It represents and seeks to uphold the norms of behaviour and conduct which are approved by society at large, and these norms, of course, change as the opinions of society change. In Islam, the religious law or *sharī'ah* (literally, 'the straight path'), theoretically governs the life of every Muslim in all its aspects. Since the *sharī'ah* constitutes the will of God, any Muslim who violates it not only commits a crime, but also a sin. In other words, law and morals are aspects of religion, and jurisprudence is not only based on theology but has subsumed numerous elements which, from a western viewpoint, would belong to theology rather than to law. For these reasons, Islamic law has had a far greater influence on Muslim society than Western law has had on Western society.

Muslim law lays down one's duties to both God and man; but, since one's duties to one's fellow men are also laid down by God, either explicitly or implicitly, there is no real distinction between them. The law is concerned with the external manifestations of a man's faith – that is, his actions. It is also concerned with his social life, since this inevitably involves relations with other men – in such matters as matrimony, inheritance, the functions of money, the division of labour, and so on. But all his dealings with other men are seen in terms of his duties toward God, and are regarded as affecting his 'standing', so to speak, in the eyes of God. *Fiqh*, the Arabic word for the science of law, jurisprudence, means 'knowledge', or 'understanding', of these duties. It was defined by one school of law as follows: 'the science of law is the knowledge of the rights and duties whereby man is enabled to observe right conduct in this world, and to prepare himself for the future life'.

It will be readily apparent that such a definition restricted the law largely to the domain of 'private law', and that the field of 'public law', which has to do with the relations of the citizen with the state, and problems in which the public interest is involved, was not covered by this definition. This may, indeed, be said to be a fundamental weakness of Islamic law. There were whole areas of law, constitutional law, criminal law, law governing land tenure, and so on, where the *sharī'ah* either did not apply, or applied only in theory, the law administered in the courts being based primarily on customary law.

The basis of pre-Islamic society in Arabia was the tribe. Ancient Arabian social structure was founded on kinship, on blood relationship. The tribe was merely an extension of the family. The tribe was a group of people, claiming descent from a common ancestor, who joined together for mutual defence. The law of the tribe was customary law – that is, the body of unwritten rules which had evolved as the tribe evolved. The individual had no legal rights as such – these were vested in the family and in the tribe. The family (and hence the tribe) represented the individual in legal matters; it claimed his rights, avenged his wrongs, inherited his property, and answered for his crimes.

Islam changed this picture entirely, and shaped and moulded Islamic society into something totally different from pre-Islamic society. First, the blood-tie, which was the basis of pre-Islamic tribal society, was abandoned, and replaced by loyalty to the *ummah*, to the Muslim community as a whole. When a person became a Muslim, he severed his connection with his kith and kin, unless they too became Muslims. This is not to say that the Arabs abandoned their pride in race, or their passion for constructing genealogies to prove the purity and distinction of the stock from which they sprang. But their primary loyalty was transferred from the family and the tribe to the far larger unit, the Muslim community. Second, the concept of the equality of all Muslims in the sight of God, and among themselves, replaced the aristocratic structure of society at Mecca and Medina. Muslim 'A' was superior to Muslim 'B' only because Muslim 'A' had embraced Islam at an earlier date, or because he was stricter in religious observance. The basis of the new social order was the Islamic faith, and, through the personal commitment of every Muslim to God, the personal life of the individual emerged – even though, in certain respects, the community assumed legal and social rights which were formerly vested in the tribe.

What were the bases on which the law of the new Islamic community was built? First and foremost, there was the Qur'ān, the word of God as revealed to His Prophet, Muḥammad. Only a small portion of the Qur'ān, however, takes the form of legal prescriptions – some six hundred verses in all, and of this number only about eighty can be considered legislation in the strict sense. The remainder deal with religious duties, with the rituals of fasting, prayer and pilgrimage, and so on. Much of the so-called Qur'anic 'legislation' consists of general ethical principles: for instance, the Qur'an urges compassion toward the weaker members of society, and calls for good faith in commercial transactions, and for upright conduct in the administration of justice. The Qur'ān also gives evidence of a desire to upgrade the status of women.

Clearly, a system of law could not be built on such scanty material, and there was the further difficulty that the legal implications of the precepts contained in the Qur'ān were not always self-evident. For instance, a man was permitted to have up to four legal wives, *but* he was also enjoined to treat them all equally. The question arose, was this a legal requirement, or was it to be left merely to the conscience of the husband? There was also the problem of what to do with those areas of customary law which were neither abrogated nor modified by the Qur'ān. The Sunnī, orthodox, answer was that customary law continued in force unless explicitly amended by the Qur'ān. The Shī'īs, or non-orthodox Muslims, took the exactly opposite view. In their opinion, customary law was abrogated unless it was specifically endorsed by the Qur'ān.

The early Muslim community was thus faced by the fundamental problem of how to obtain legal rulings which would be accepted by the whole community, on points on which the Qur'ān was either silent or unclear, or was susceptible of more than one interpretation. As long as Muḥammad was alive, of course, there was no problem. Matters in dispute were referred to him for a ruling, and Muḥammad, as the *de facto* arbiter or supreme judge, made a decision which related to the particular case in question. After Muḥammad's death, the Caliphs, as his successors, endeavoured to implement the Qur'anic legislation in the spirit of the Prophet. But as the Arab armies swept across Iraq, Syria, Iran and Egypt, the legal problems of a vast and diverse empire could no longer be dealt with in this way. The Umayyad Caliphs in Damascus created the office of *qāḍī*, or religious judge, as an answer to the problem. The *qāḍīs* were entitled to give judgement on the basis of their *ra'y*, or legal opinion, which was arrived at on the basis of whatever precedents there were, plus common sense.

This *ad hoc* solution gave rise to considerable latitude and variation in the administration of the law, particularly in those considerable areas of law in which customary law was still valid. As the Islamic empire absorbed more and more people of different cultures and customs, naturally the *qāḍīs* had to cope with even wider variations in customary law. Up to the end of the seventh century A.D., and well on into the eighth, the Islamic state did not possess a formal legal system, or a code of law, or anything remotely resembling it. All it had was a practical system of legal administration; decisions in the courts were made on a purely pragmatic basis, and cases were judged more or less on their merits, without reference to any formal body of laws. That formidable body of religious law, the *sharī'ah*, which in theory regulated every aspect of the life of a

Muslim, was not developed until the eighth and ninth centuries A.D.

The 'Abbasids, in the course of their propaganda campaign aimed at overthrowing the Umayyads, criticized *inter alia* the Umayyad legal administration which, said the 'Abbasids, had failed to put into practice the spirit of the Qur'anic legislation. Stung by this criticism, the Umayyads, during the last decades of their rule, tried to put their house in order, and the first schools of law made their appearance. The Umayyads were too late, however, to stave off the 'Abbasid revolution, and the 'Abbasids came to power in A.D. 750, on what has shrewdly been called an 'Islamic state and society' platform. The 'Abbasids set about instituting a legal system based on strict Qur'anic principles, and their starting point was rigorous analysis of Umayyad legal practice. Under the impetus of this policy, the schools of law developed rapidly. The first two were the schools at Medina in Arabia and Kūfah in Iraq: from the beginning, these schools reflected respectively the conservatism of the Medinan scholars, and the more cosmopolitan, and hence more tolerant, atmosphere of the newly-formed society at Kūfah.

Islamic jurisprudence thus came into being as a conscious attempt to formulate a system of law which would embody the spirit of the general ethical principles enunciated in the Qur'ān. It inevitably found itself to a considerable extent in opposition to legal practice as currently administered in the courts. The jurists therefore had to decide whether to accept or reject Umayyad practice in any given case. The criteria they adopted for this purpose were threefold: first, the consensus among the jurists of a particular school. This was known as the *sunnah*, or 'ideal doctrine' of that particular school (this use of *sunnah* should not be confused with its use in the sense of the 'customary practice' of the Prophet, etc); second, *qiyās*, or reasoning on the basis of analogy in order to determine which of two or more possibilities was closer to the spirit of the Qur'anic legislation. The use of *qiyās* gradually superseded the use of *ra'y*, or the expression of legal opinion, which had been the method used by the Umayyad *qāḍīs*. Third, the authority of the *ḥadīth*, or Traditions of the Prophet. These were reports of words spoken by the Prophet, transmitted orally by a person who had heard Muḥammad utter them, or eye-witness accounts of the acts of the Prophet. The authenticity of these Traditions was vouched for by an uninterrupted line (known as an *isnād*) of trustworthy persons.

Traditionists, as the men who collected and sifted these *ḥadīth* were called, disliked the methods used by the scholars of the legal schools, namely, human reasoning by analogy and personal opinion, and preferred to base their legal rulings on the precedents of the actual words and acts of the Prophet, so far as these could be determined.

Just as the work of the jurists of the various schools of law was a reaction against the pragmatic approach of the Umayyad lawyers, so the work of the Traditionists was a reaction against the use of human reasoning by the jurists; it represented an attempt to subordinate all legal subject-matter to the religious and moral principles expressed in the Traditions of the Prophet.

By the end of their first fifty years in power, the 'Abbasids had not made much progress toward their goal of producing a systematic codification of the law. A number of schools of law were in existence, but each of these had its own *sunnah* or ideal concept of the religious law, and all of them were engaged in argument, individually and collectively, with the Traditionists.

The man who brought order out of chaos, al-Shāfi'ī, made his great contribution to the development of Islamic law at the beginning of the ninth century A.D. Faced with a situation in which, for instance, jurists of the Mālikī school of law at Medina ignored even Traditions of the Prophet if these happened to conflict with the 'ideal doctrine' of their own school, al-Shāfi'ī decided on drastic remedies. In essence, he decided to go back for guidance to the source of divine revelation, the Qur'ān itself. He admitted that the substantive legal material in the Qur'ān was scanty but, he argued, the Qur'ān *did* indicate how this material could be supplemented and interpreted. One frequently recurring text from the Qur'ān formed the cornerstone on which al-Shāfi'ī built the whole edifice of Islamic law: 'Obey God and His Prophet.' This text clearly indicated, said al-Shāfi'ī, that the Traditions of the Prophet were to be considered a source of law second only to the word of God itself. If the Traditions of the Prophet reflected the divine will, obviously they could no longer be rejected at the whim of jurists. By this means, al-Shāfi'ī sought to unify Islamic law; instead of each school of law having its own *sunnah*, or accepted doctrine of that school, there was henceforth to be one *sunnah* and one *sunnah* only, namely, the practice followed by the Prophet and the precedents set by him. Al-Shāfi'ī's rationalisation of Islamic law, while marking a great step forward, constituted a victory for the Traditionists over the jurists, to the extent that from then on the *ḥadīth*, that is, reports of the words and actions of Muḥammad, assumed paramount importance. The function of human reasoning became subsidiary and complementary.

As a result, from the ninth century onwards, there was an enormous growth in the science of *ḥadīth*-criticism, as scholars sought ways of resolving conflicting, or even contradictory, Traditions on the same subject. One method of resolving conflicts was by subjecting the *isnād*, or chain of authorities for a particular *ḥadīth*, to the closest scrutiny. Another method was by declaring that Tradition 'A' was stronger than Tradition 'B' because more people had reported it; the weakest *ḥadīths* were those which had been reported by a single individual only.

As the great mass of *ḥadīth* was subjected to rigorous criticism and analysis, there evolved a more systematic classification of those Traditions judged to be sound, and the ninth century A.D. saw the compilation of the first of the great manuals of *ḥadīth*. The vast majority of the *ḥadīth* attributed to the Prophet are apocryphal, in the sense that they rarely, if ever, represent the actual words of Muḥammad. In the opinion of modern scholars they represent a projection backwards into the past on the part of the jurists. Often the subject matter of a Tradition will show whether it is genuine or false. For instance, if a *ḥadīth* deals with problems which cannot have faced the Muslim community until well after the death of Muḥammad, then clearly it is not genuine. But the *substance* of many Traditions, especially those which deal with day-to-day problems arising out of the Qur'anic 'legislation', may, in fact, enshrine some decision of Muḥammad which had been preserved by oral tradition.

Al-Shāfi'ī brought order and system into Islamic law, and deserves his title of 'the father of Islamic jurisprudence'. He enunciated four *uṣūl*, or principles, as the basis of jurisprudence: the Qur'ān; the *sunnah* of the Prophet; *ijmā'*, the consensus of the Islamic community; and *qiyās*, or analogical reasoning. Of these, the first two were the all-important ones. The concept of the consensus of the Islamic community was introduced by al-Shāfi'ī so that, if necessary, the consensus of the scholars of a particular school of law could be overridden; in practice, this principle was applied only within narrow limits. He based this doctrine on a Tradition of the Prophet: 'My community will never agree upon an error.'

The role of *qiyās*, or reasoning by analogy, was also severely restricted by al-Shāfi'ī; it could never be used to contradict a rule established by any of the first three principles. The four principles of al-Shāfi'ī were never seriously challenged after him. Two important new schools of law came into being as a result of al-Shāfi'ī's work. One of these, the Shāfi'ī school, accepted his doctrines; another, the Ḥanbalī school, weakened al-Shāfi'ī's doctrine of *qiyās* even further, and adopted the extreme position that human reasoning was not valid in any form as a source of law. The Ḥanbalīs insisted that every legal ruling must be based on the authority of either the Qur'ān or the *sunnah* of Muḥammad.

Al-Shāfi'ī, by playing down the principle of human reasoning and personal judgment in the formulation of law, and by placing primary emphasis on the law as deriving from the Qur'ān, the revealed word of God, and from the *sunnah* of Muḥammad, which he invested with the authority of the divine will, virtually put an end to speculative inquiry by the jurists. As a result, the legal system became more rigid, and less responsive to the needs of society as it changed. To the degree that it became less responsive to the needs of society, it became divorced from reality, a body of legal theory which was not observed in practice.

The claim of Islamic law to be based on divine authority meant that its own authority could not be questioned. By the beginning of the tenth century A.D., jurists of all schools felt that all essential questions had been thoroughly discussed and final answers to all problems reached. The consensus of the Islamic community, once arrived at, was considered infallible and was unlikely to be amended by a succeeding generation of scholars. The jurists therefore felt that in future, no independent reasoning was necessary, and they confined their activities to interpretation and explanation of the law as it had been finally established. As they put it, 'the door of *ijtihād* (independent inquiry) was closed'. Henceforth, scholars could proceed only on the basis of 'imitation'. Inevitably, this meant the over-elaboration of rules, the piling of gloss upon gloss, and the growth of casuistry.

It would, however, be an over-simplification to assert that the 'closing of the door of independent inquiry' resulted in the complete stagnation of the law. For one thing, al-Shāfi'ī's efforts to unify the law were only partially successful. Some schools, notably the Mālikī and Ḥanafī, resisted his attempt to make the *sunnah* of Muḥammad the supreme authority, superior to the *sunnah* or 'accepted doctrine' of the individual schools. The Mālikī and Ḥanafī schools also subtly reintroduced, in different forms and under different names, the principle of human reasoning and personal judgment. In other words, they brought back precisely those elements of the legal method of the schools in the seventh and eighth centuries which al-Shāfi'ī had tried to eliminate. In this way, diversity of opinion between the various schools not only continued to exist, even though in theory the 'door of independent reasoning had been closed', but the differences between the views of school 'A' and school 'B' were much greater than some authorities have been prepared to admit.

How far was the classical theory of law, as developed by the jurists, put into practice and administered in the courts? As we saw earlier, *sharī'ah* law was always more or less limited to private law, and had very little to do with public law. Consequently, although the Umayyad Caliphs appointed *qāḍīs* to administer *sharī'ah* law in the courts, they made it very clear that the supreme judicial authority resided in themselves, and *qāḍīs* who gave judgements which displeased the secular authorities were peremptorily dismissed. This accounts for the extreme reluctance shown by some jurists to accept appointment as *qāḍīs*. The *qāḍīs* could not reasonably resent the fact that the political authority restricted the scope of their jurisdiction, since there were large areas of law which were not covered by the *sharī'ah*. For instance, in criminal law, the only crimes which could be judged according to *sharī'ah* law were those for which specific penalties were laid down in the Qur'ān. These were six in number: unlawful sexual relations; false accusations of unchastity; theft; wine-drinking; armed robbery; and apostasy. Even in judging these crimes, the *sharī'ah* courts were often ineffective, because of the rigid rules of evidence in force in these courts. Written evidence was not acceptable (although some written documents later came to be accepted), nor was circumstantial evidence. Only the oral testimony of two Muslims of unquestioned moral and religious probity was allowed, and no cross-examination was permitted.

The Muslim community, in order to deal with cases not covered by the religious law, permitted the development of a system of courts, known as *maẓālim* ('complaints') courts, which was parallel to, but separate from, the *sharī'ah* courts. The *maẓālim* courts came into being, certainly by early 'Abbasid times, possibly under the late Umayyads. The Persian kings of the Sasanian dynasty had set up courts of this type, and had presided over them in person in order to investigate complaints made against government officials. The Caliphs adopted this practice, and within a short time the *maẓālim* courts were instituted on a formal basis, and many cases concerning property, land tenure, criminal justice, taxation, and all cases involving the police, were heard as a matter of course by the *maẓālim* courts.

By the Middle Ages the Islamic world thus found itself with a double system for the administration of justice. Instead of an all-embracing system of canon law based on the Qur'ān and the *sunnah* of the Prophet, it had a system of religious law much reduced in scope and authority, and side by side with this, a system of secular law administered by the political authorities on the basis of customary law, on the basis of equity, and sometimes on no other basis than the arbitrary decision of the ruler.

Not unnaturally, the lawyers were distressed by the way in which secular courts had usurped the authority of the *sharī'ah* courts, and they tried to rationalise what had happened by evolving the theory of 'policy in accordance with the *sharī'ah*'. This theory acknowledged the *de facto* authority of the secular ruler in matters in which the interests of the state, or the public interest in the widest sense, were involved. The jurists thus made the best of a bad job, by maintaining the fiction that the sovereign, even when giving judgment in the *maẓālim* courts, was exercising his authority within the limits permitted by the *sharī'ah*. In reality, the relative status of the *maẓālim* and the *sharī'ah* courts varied considerably with time and place.

In Egypt and Syria in Mamlūk times, for instance, the political authority exercised a jurisdiction which was virtually independent of the *sharī'ah* courts. In those parts of the Islamic world where the bulk of the population was non-Arab, the *sharī'ah* courts were obliged to make concessions to customary law, particularly in the field of family law.

In the important area of commercial law, the *sharī'ah* was hampered by what at first sight appears to be an insurmountable handicap. I refer, of course, to the Qur'anic prohibition, which is quite specific, on the taking of interest (*ribā*). Such a prohibition would appear to be totally divorced from the realities of trade and commerce in a free society. Yet the classical theory of Islamic law, as developed by the jurists, far from affording any relaxation of this ban, made it even more rigid. The jurists evolved the doctrine that any speculative transaction, any transaction which resulted in the 'unjustified enrichment' of one party, was forbidden. If a profit were made, it should be given to the poor. This doctrine was derived from the Qur'anic phrase 'God will abolish interest and cause charity to increase.' In the case of barter deals there were two principles involved, according to the jurists: first, the two amounts to be traded must be equal in weight or quantity; second, there must be no time lag in the completion of the transaction, because during the interval the value of one commodity might fluctuate, and this would permit one party or the other to make a speculative gain. As N. J. Coulson has caustically observed: 'It is difficult to see any point or purpose in a transaction where 'Umar takes 20 lb of Zayd's wheat in exchange for 20 lb of his own wheat in the same session.'[1]

Since the whole principle of usury was so expressly prohibited in the Qur'ān, people were naturally reluctant openly to act in defiance of the Qur'anic injunction. On the other hand, trade was vitally important to the medieval Islamic world, and so the jurists developed a whole series of complicated 'stratagems' or 'devices', known as *ḥiyal*, (for example, partnerships, etc.) to enable people to get around the law.

Another important area of law in which there was discrepancy between theory and practice, was that of constitutional law. The successors of the Prophet Muḥammad as the political leaders of the Islamic community were called caliphs, or *imāms*. As the supreme ruler and administrator, the caliph-*imām* also had overall responsibility for the administration of the law. According to the classical doctrine of Islamic law, as developed by the jurists, the caliph-*imām* could and should be disobeyed if he issued orders which were contrary to the *sharī'ah*, and could ultimately be deposed if he acted contrary to the dictates of the religious law. If the caliphs behaved like tyrants, did the ordinary Muslim have an obligation to obey them? 'Yes', said the jurists, basing their argument on the Qur'anic text: 'Obey God, His Prophet, and those in charge of your affairs.' In view of this, they argued, a Muslim was obliged to obey the caliph-*imām* because God had willed that the latter should hold office. Even if the ruler behaved like a tyrant, tyranny was preferable to anarchy. From the tenth century A.D. onwards, however, the political power of the caliphs was progressively usurped by *amīrs*, *sulṭāns* and other purely secular rulers, who made no claim to be successors of the Prophet but ruled by virtue of their military strength. Confronted by this political reality, the jurists gradually extended the argument mentioned above to justify the power wielded by *amīrs* and *sulṭāns*. Once more, the jurists were forced to rationalise in order to make theory correspond a little more closely to practice.

It should be noted in passing that the development of Twelver Shī'ī political theory, and in particular the Twelver Shī'ī theory of the imamate, produced a concept of law which was fundamentally different from that of the Sunnīs. For the Sunnī, the caliph-*imām* was simply the political and administrative leader of the Muslim community, and the defender of the faith. For the Twelver Shī'ī, the *imām* was the infallible interpreter of divine revelation, and the sole repository of all truth and knowledge. This doctrine had important effects on the approach of Shi'ite jurists to Islamic law. In judging the authenticity of Traditions of the Prophet, they attached less importance to the general validity of the *isnād*, or chain of transmitters, than to whether or not the Tradition was transmitted by a Shi'ite *imām*. Because the Shi'ite *imām* was infallible, Shī'ī jurists rejected human reasoning and personal judgment *in any form* as criteria for the formulation of legal rulings. Similarly, Shi'ites rejected the role of *ijmā'*, or the consensus of the Islamic community. But, just as Sunnī legal practice differed from Sunnī legal theory, so did Shī'ī legal practice differ from Shī'ī legal theory. In practice, the Shī'ī jurists found themselves forced to give a place to human reason, and to acknowledge the authority of the *mujtahid*s (eminent Shi'ite theologians and jurists, selected by the acclamation of the community, who have through the ages acted as the representatives on earth of the twelfth and last Shi'ite *imām*, who disappeared in A.D. 874).

[1] *A History of Islamic Law*, Edinburgh 1964, p. 42.

To sum up, then, it would be true to say that classical legal doctrine, as formulated by the Islamic lawyers, was substantially modified and supplemented in practice by elements of customary law, by considerations of equity, and by the arbitrary decisions of secular rulers. It is also true that Islamic lawyers were concerned much more with what the law ought to be, than with what it was in practice. The reason for this attitude was that the *sharī'ah* was a sacred code of law, reflecting and deriving its authority from the will of God. In other words, the *sharī'ah* was and is not just a code of law but also a code of behaviour and ethics. It is a combination of law and morality. As Schacht has put it: 'each institution, transaction or obligation is measured by the standards of religious and moral rules'. The *sharī'ah* was formulated under the impetus of religious and ethical ideas and not solely of practical considerations, and this is the fundamental reason for the many contrasts between legal theory and practice in traditional Islamic society.

6

Arabic literature: a living heritage

ELLA MARMURA

What picture if any, does the term Arabic Literature conjure up in the mind of the Western reader? Probably no more than those tales of adventure and romance known in the West as The Arabian Nights. To the Arabs, however, these tales are only a strand in the many and diverse strands that make up the whole pattern of Arabic literature. It is therefore safe to say that apart from the work done in some universities and by a few individuals, Arabic literature is an undiscovered world to the vast majority of western readers.

An idea of the scope and range of Arabic literature is perhaps best conveyed by indicating its dimensions, first in terms of time and space and later in terms of content and artistic excellence. From the sixth century A.D. to the present day, there has been a continuous tradition of literary achievement in Arabic – the continuity partly being in the language itself, which in the twentieth century is structurally the same as it was in the sixth. As to space, this literature originated in pre-Islamic Arabia. With the coming and spread of Islam, it became the literature of all the regions that comprised the Islamic World, irrespective of native tongue or race. For many centuries it was the literature on which were nurtured all the peoples living in the area between Arab Spain in the west and central Asia in the east. Naturally in due course some of the native languages asserted or reasserted themselves, as was the case with Persian. In Spain it disappeared with the disappearance of the Arabs, though the influence of Arabic remained for a long time. (Apart from place names, there remains a sizable component of Arabic common words in the Spanish of today.) But for more than three centuries it was the literature of the whole Islamic World, Arab and non-Arab contributing to it and taking pride in its excellence.

As with many literatures, poetry appeared before prose, and by the sixth century there flourished in pre-Islamic Arabia a corpus of poetry highly developed linguistically, metrically and artistically. It set standards of excellence which in later generations many poets, Arabs and non-Arabs, strove to emulate. The most striking thing about this poetry is that it was lyric poetry, descriptive and highly individualised, reflecting the bedouin's[1] ideals and attitudes towards life. This is perhaps best illustrated in the *qaṣīdah*, conventionally translated as 'ode', of the young poet Ṭarafah (d. *ca.* 564) where he tells those who censure his way of life that since they cannot make him live for ever, he should be allowed to squander his youth and substance on the battlefield and the pursuit of pleasures – these being wine, knight-errantry and dalliance, thus summing up much of the pre-Islamic temper with its admixture of hedonism, idealism and a certain pessimism:

> Canst thou make me immortal, O thou that blamest me so
> For haunting the battle and loving the pleasures that fly?
> If thou hast not the power to ward me from Death, let me go
> To meet him and scatter the wealth in my hand, ere I die.
>
> (trans. R. A. Nicholson).

Ṭarafah was a composer of one of the much celebrated Seven Odes – sometimes counted as ten, known as the *mu'allaqāt* (sing. *mu'allaqah*) – of which several translations have been made into English. Space does not permit an analysis of any of these odes

[1] Not all the inhabitants of pre-Islamic Arabia were nomads. Settled communities engaged in trade and agriculture existed in various parts.

but they all follow certain patterns and conventions. They usually begin with the poet halting at the deserted encampment of his mistress where he recalls his love and its agonies, to be followed by a description of his mount, his journey across the desert and the hardships he endures. Finally he comes to the topic of his poem which could be panegyric praise or defence of his tribe or himself, satire or virtually any other theme. Throughout, despite the conventions, the individuality of the poet emerges strongly.

Reading these odes or any other poetry of the period in the original, one is struck by the powerful language, the sophisticated metres and the perfect rhyme schemes – for Arabic poetry employed the monorhyme. But even in translation the reader cannot but be impressed by its vivid imagery. No Wordsworths, these poets gave a factual, yet often dramatic picture of nature with its stark beauty and terror, and the reader is conscious of movement and vitality. This is particularly evident in the ode of Imru' al-Qays (d. *ca.* 540) with its vivid descriptions of a horse charging through the wilderness, a desert storm and the freshness of the dawn after the rain, when birds sing as if drunk with spiced wine. The special relationship, almost human, to animals is likewise effectively portrayed in this poetry.

Religious sentiment played little part in the poetry of the bedouin. Instead there were the ideals of manliness and a belief in Fate – not a surrender to it but an acceptance of the unpredictable and inevitable. As heroic poetry, it glorified feats of courage, fostered the tribal spirit and fanned the fires of feuds. But not always. In one of the odes – that of Zuhayr – one hears an impassioned appeal for peace. In images piled upon each other, the poet likens war to an all-devouring conflagration, to a grindstone crushing men like grain, to a fruitful she-camel bearing ill-omened twins, and to the rich land of Iraq giving abundant yield but of evil and destruction:

> War ye have known and war have tasted: not by
> hearsay are ye wise.
> Raise no more the hideous monster! If ye let her raven,
> she cries
> Ravenously for blood and crushes, like a mill-stone,
> all below,
> And from her twin-conceiving womb she brings
> forth woe on woe.
>
> (trans. R. A. Nicholson).

Archaic though some of the idioms of this poetry are, many of its phrases have been assimilated into the language, enriching its repository of imagery. The image of a dimsighted she-camel trampling at random, by which the poet Zuhayr described the Fates, is still echoed in the speech of the Arabs. Yet the significance of this poetry is not merely in its language or in its being a commentary on the life of the time; it remains a truly human reaction to situations, particularised as they may be in time and place, and an expression of a genuine poetic experience.

Between A.D. 610 and 632, the Qur'ān, the sacred book of Islam, was revealed to the Prophet Muḥammad and proclaimed by him to the people of Arabia. It called on them to believe in One God:

> God
> there is no god but He, the Living,
> the Everlasting.
> Slumber seizes Him not, neither
> sleep;
> To Him belongs
> all that is in heaven and the earth.
> (trans. A. J. Arberry).

It told them of His omnipotence, His goodness, His justice and His mercy and directing them to a new way of life and a belief in the hereafter. This new religion, Islam, and its sacred book, the Qur'ān, were to change the whole history of the Arabs.

For the Muslims, the Qur'ān is the word of God revealed to His messenger Muḥammad and is inimitable. Besides being a religious testament, the Qur'ān is the finest achievement of the Arabic language, expressed in a distinctive genre of prose all its own. No translation can adequately convey the magnificence and originality of its language, its rhythmical patterns, its assonances, its vivid imagery, the dramatic quality of some of its narratives or the overall grandeur of its style. The Arabs consider it unsurpassed in literary eloquence.

The Qur'ān has had far-reaching influence on Arabic literature by way of ideas and modes of expression. In addition, the study of the Qur'ān gave rise not only to religious, legal, historical and other studies, but also to a variety of literary, lexical and linguistic disciplines. But far more important, it consolidated classical Arabic, made of it a world language and safeguarded and preserved it through the ages.

As a result of the Arab conquests and the spread of Islam, Arabic, as was mentioned earlier, became a universal language. Two processes were now at work at a gradual, non-uniform pace, Islamisation and Arabisation. In time the latter took permanent

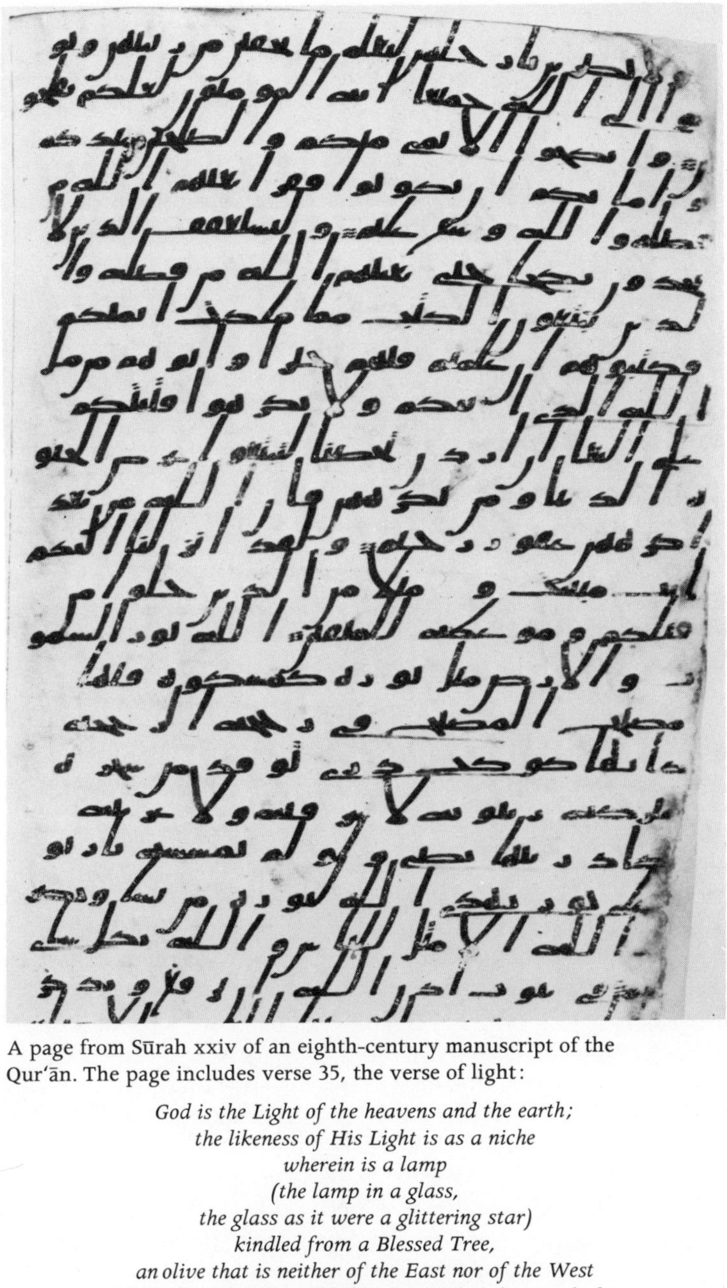

A page from Sūrah xxiv of an eighth-century manuscript of the Qur'ān. The page includes verse 35, the verse of light:

God is the Light of the heavens and the earth;
the likeness of His Light is as a niche
wherein is a lamp
(the lamp in a glass,
the glass as it were a glittering star)
kindled from a Blessed Tree,
an olive that is neither of the East nor of the West
Whose oil wellnigh would shine, even if no fire touched it;
Light upon Light;
(God guides to His Light whom He will.)
(And God strikes similitudes for men,
and God has knowledge of everything.)
in temples God has allowed to be raised up,
and His Name to be commemorated therein;
therein glorifying Him, in the mornings and the evenings
(trans. A. J. Arberry)

Qur'ān, colophon stating that it was copied in 1568 for the second Sharīfī Sulṭān of Morocco

root among the inhabitants of what is known today as the Arab World. The indigenous population of these lands, descendants of every race and nation that lived or occupied the area from time immemorial, mingled with their conquerers. The vast majority accepted Islam, but all became Arab in speech and culture. They are the people who have carried on and maintained the Arabic literary heritage to this day. Another result of this expansion was that Arabic, emerging from its semi-isolation in Arabia, encountered new areas of knowledge hitherto unknown to it. Yet the language had the vitality and flexibility to accommodate the new ideas and later to make its own original contributions in these new fields of knowledge opened to it.

Returning to poetry, we find a kind of lull in poetic activity during the Prophet's lifetime and the reign of the Orthodox Caliphs (632–661) who followed him. There were several reasons for this, one being that the Prophet regarded the poets as exponents of the pagan ideals and way of life which were contrary to the teachings of Islam. But no sooner had the Umayyads (661–750) assumed power in Damascus than we witness an upsurge of poetic creativity which spread to the cities as well. This poetry expressed itself in the main in two areas: satire – political, tribal and personal – and love poetry (the *ghazal*).

The former flourished mostly in Iraq, and to an extent in Syria. The Umayyads, with their more secular approach to affairs, encouraged poetry, mainly to uphold and defend their rule. In a society where the mass media as we understand them today were non-existent, poetry was an effective weapon and the enemies of the Umayyads employed it in the same manner. The satire was witty, often vicious, yet had popular appeal. The satirical poetry of the period is associated with three major poets – al-Akhṭal, al-Farazdaq and Jarīr.

Ghazal found its habitat in the cities and deserts of Arabia. Hitherto, love poetry, generally speaking, represented but one strand in the multi-thematic ode, but now we have poetry wholly devoted to the love theme. This poetry found expression in two different genres. One was gay, light-hearted and urbane, and this grew in the cities of Mecca and Medina. Both were now cities of affluence but shorn of political power. Many of the young Muslim aristocrats excluded from public office, frittered away their wealth in the pursuit of pleasure. Schools of singing had sprung up and a number of the love lyrics were set to music. The leader of this school of poetry was 'Umar ibn 'Abī Rabī'ah, (d. *ca.* 720) a Meccan aristocrat who wrote charming verse in light metres and simple, unaffected language, often heightening the effect by dialogue. The following lines from a poem translated by W. G. Palgrave capture some of the spirit of his verse:

> Gently she moved in the calmness of beauty,
> Moved as the bough to the light breeze of morning.
> Dazzled my eyes as they gazed, till before me
> All was a mist and confusion of figures.
> Ne'er had I sought her, and ne'er she sought me;
> Fated the hour, and the love and the meeting.

The second genre of *ghazal* flourished mostly among the bedouin, portraying an intensity of feeling and depicting all the anguish and despair of tragic love. Although often chaste, it was not 'idealised' love, but sprang from the depth of a shared human experience. Its two most characteristic themes are the faithfulness of the lover and the hopelessness of the quest, expressed simply and unpretentiously. When one poet says that as the fingers are immutably attached to the hands, so rooted in his being is his love for his mistress, one is touched by the utter sincerity and directness of the image. The leader of this school was Jamīl (d. 701) of the tribe of 'Udhrah,[2] who sang of his star-crossed love for Buthaynah. There were more than one pair of unfortunate lovers round whose lives whole love narratives – many fictitious – appeared. One of the best known is that of Majnūn[3] and Laylā, which has also found its way into the romances of Persian and Turkish. The *ghazal* of this period is some of the most poignant in Arabic literature and, in the opinion of many, is Arabic love poetry at its best.

The Umayyads were followed by the 'Abbasids, who reigned from 750 to 1258. Their capital, Baghdad, one of the most magnificent cities of the medieval world, became the centre of learning and every kind of intellectual activity. The earlier years witnessed a period of intensive translation by which the philosophy and sciences of the Hellenistic world were introduced to the Muslims. This stimulated scientific, philosophical and other studies, to which Arabic made significant, original and lasting contributions. Arabic had become the vehicle of a world civilisation. On the other hand, the Arabs, having their own well-developed literature, did not feel the need or urge to translate other literatures, and thus did not come to know the literary treasures of Greece and Rome. It could well be that the intellectual climate of the post-Hellenistic world had also something to do with this omission. Arabic literature therefore followed its own course, though not unaffected by the new intellectual climate around it. This is particularly evident in the field of prose.

The new rulers in Baghdad had now become the patrons of poetry and the arts. During the first hundred years when 'Abbasid power was at its height, poets flocked to Baghdad seeking court patronage. Baghdad was a truly cosmopolitan city where one found Arabs and non-Arabs composing eloquent poetry in Arabic – the blind poet Bashshār (d. 784) being the first important non-Arab poet. Though the old themes of poetry: panegyric, elegy, satire, *ghazal* and so on were not abandoned, the new poetry was primarily urban, reflecting much of the material prosperity and sophistication of life in Baghdad. Many of the poets sought to express themselves in the new idiom of the day, freeing themselves of many conventions. The practice of starting a poem by halting at the deserted encampment, carried over from pre-Islamic poetry, was ridiculed by the poet Abū Nuwās (d. *ca.* 813), a contemporary of Harūn al-Rashīd. What mattered to him was the life of the tavern, not the desert, though he did resort to this prelude in his eulogies. Abū Nuwās was a wit, a libertine and a fine lyricist who composed poetry on all the known poetic themes and even wrote religious poetry at the end of his life. But the theme he excelled in was wine-poetry, specially in his portrayal of carousing parties and the pleasure and abandon of wine.

Among the outstanding poets of the period were Abū al-'Atāhiyah (d. 826), who wrote poetry in a religious vein; Abū Tammām (d. 846) whose poetic gifts and intellectual abilities were submerged in his use of rhetorical devices, but who will always be remembered for his fine anthology of the shorter

[2] 'Udhrite' love became a term to describe chivalrous love.
[3] Majnūn means the 'possessed' or 'madman' and was the nickname given to the poet Qays ibn al-Mulawwaḥ.

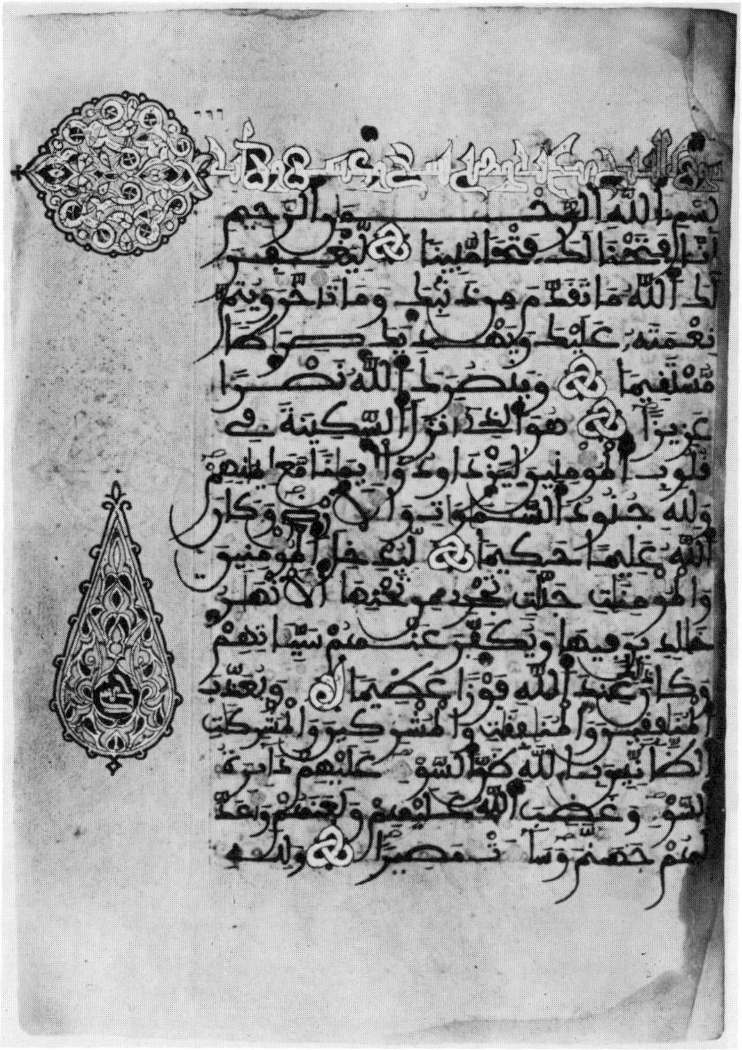

The beginning of Sūrah xlviii from a sixteenth-century Moroccan copy of the Qur'ān

pre-Islamic and early Islamic poetry known as *al-Ḥamāsah*; and the poet al-Buḥturī (d. 897), who compiled a similar anthology. Al-Buḥturī excelled in descriptive poetry, particularly of architectural monuments. In a poem describing a visit to the deserted palace of Ctesiphon, a moment of history, frozen in time and in a mural, is recreated by al-Buḥturī in an imaginative poetic mood. Ibn al-Rūmī (d. 896) was noted for his fine portrayals of nature and his introspectiveness.

Yet, because of their dependence on court patronage, it was to panegyric that the poets directed most of their attention. This tended to limit their scope and poets had to resort to rhetorical devices and far-fetched similes, often using old imagery in a new garb. In time literary embellishments began to play an important part in literary composition, thus depriving poetry of some of its spontaneity. This in a sense was contrary to the nature of Arabic which, based in a system of root notions with elaborate derivations, invites a conciseness and economy of words that can be most effective.

The above should not imply that no great or significant poetry was being written, though this was no longer confined to Baghdad. With the decentralisation of 'Abbasid power in the tenth century we find a flowering of literary activity in the various parts of the Islamic world. The court of the tenth-century Ḥamdānid prince, Sayf al-Dawlah, attracted men of letters, philosophers and poets to his capital at Aleppo in northern Syria. Among them was al-Mutanabbī (d. 965), perhaps the most quoted poet in Arabic. It was to Sayf al-Dawlah and his wars against Byzantium that the poet dedicated some of his greater odes. Al-Mutanabbī, denounced by some, while regarded by many as one of the greatest poets in Arabic, has been on the whole difficult for some western scholars to appreciate. To explain him briefly, there is on the adverse side his arrogance, boastfulness and bombast, a certain pettiness and vindictiveness in his satire, an utter lack of humour and his sometimes strained imagery. On the other hand, al-Mutanabbī, steeped in the purity of the Arabic tongue and its literary traditions, instilled a new life and vigour into poetic diction and the ode. In no other poetry is the individuality, the ego of the poet, so apparent. The ideals his poetry portrays – manliness, ambition, self-pride, continuous striving and searching, and a refusal to be cowed – have a heroic quality. His was the poetry of self-assertion. His turbulent life and many wanderings gained him an insight into human nature and a worldly wisdom which he was able to sum up in concise, memorable lines.

Also in northern Syria, but later, another great poet and writer was to appear. He was Abū al-ʻAlā' al-Maʻarrī (d. 1057), the philosopher-poet of Arabic. Blind from childhood, he became an ascetic, never married and is said to have left on his grave an epitaph that may be translated freely as follows:

> This is my father's sin against me,
> Which I've committed against no one.

His compassion for animals and their young made him a vegetarian in later life. A man of great learning, dignity and deep humanity, al-Maʻarrī pondered on all the important issues of life and of society in his day. There is a pessimistic strain in his poetry which attains a certain meditative dignity and philosophical calm, particularly in his later poems. A questioning spirit, he often uttered unorthodox ideas; a social critic, he attacked the sham and the hypocritical. Yet he was highly respected in his community and students came to him from far and wide. The note of pessimism in his poetry may be seen in the following paraphrase of lines from a youthful elegy:

> Friend, behold our graves that fill the space. What of the graves from the time of ʻĀd?[4]
> Tread gently for I do not think the earth's crust is anything but the remains of men.
> Unworthy it would be of us to slight our forbears, separated by distant time though we may be.
> Perhaps the self-same grave has become a grave many a time, laughing at the crowding of opposites
> And the buried upon the buried in the long run of the ages.

Unlike al-Mutanabbī, whom he admired, al-Maʻarrī had the ability to laugh, which he displayed in some of his prose works, the best known of which is *The Epistle of Forgiveness*. In this work he imagines that a friend of his visits the other world to find that some of the pre-Islamic pagan poets had been forgiven and allowed entry into paradise. He has some lively discussions with the residents of the other world and finds that many of the poets have not mended their ways, still engaging in literary squabbles as they had done on earth. The work is to an extent an exercise in philological erudition, underlined with irony and wit. The excessive pedantry renders it abstruse at times, but it remains an originally conceived piece of writing.

Now that we have stepped into the realm of prose, we must consider briefly some of the major contributions in this field and a few of its outstanding figures. Apart from the Qur'ān which stands in a category by itself and the Ḥadīth, i.e. the traditions and sayings of the Prophet, there was little 'literary' prose in the early days of Islam except for oratory. 'Brevity is the soul of eloquence', say the Arabs, and this has characterised much of their early prose. But it was not until the eighth and ninth centuries that prose emerged as a distinctive literary genre, which rather than poetry was to become the true expression of the age. Since space does not allow a full discussion of its development, we have to be selective, focusing in the main on one aspect, story-telling. In this connection, it should be noted that the Qur'ān contains some of the best narrative prose in Arabic, the story of Joseph being a case in point.

In secular literature we should first mention Ibn al-Muqaffaʻ (d. 759), who translated the Pahlavī version of the Sanskrit fables of Bidpai, known in Arabic as *Kalīlah wa Dimnah*. These celebrated animal stories, perhaps more in the spirit of an Orwell than an Aesop, are noted for their unaffected

[4] An extinct Arabian tribe mentioned in the Qur'ān.

style. But it was the ninth century writer al-Jāḥiẓ, ('the goggle-eyed'), who was to become the 'Abbasid *littérateur par excellence.* A versatile, witty and original writer, al-Jāḥiẓ had imbibed to the full the Arabic literary traditions, as well as the intellectual climate of the Baṣra and Baghdad of his day. This is reflected in his numerous and diversified writings, which are both intellectually rewarding and entertaining. His style was characterised by assonances, balanced phrasing and a tendency to digress. He loved to tell a story, and his books are interspersed with anecdotes and character sketches. These gifts are skilfully displayed in his widely-acclaimed book, *The Misers,* which also shows his keen appreciation of the life around him. In an episode in the book al-Jāḥiẓ speaks of a quarrel between a landlord and a tenant with such humour and realism that it could be true not only of ninth-century Baghdad, but of any age and clime.

While in the *The Misers* al-Jāḥiẓ was telling stories mostly about his contemporaries, in the *Book of Songs,* Abū al-Faraj al-Iṣfahānī, (d. 967), a descendant of the Umayyad ruling house, was deriving his material from the past as well as the present. In over twenty large volumes he compiled a monumental collection of the biographies and poetry of all known poets, singers and musicians. More than that, as scene after scene (in no historical sequence) unfolds, we find depicted every facet of Arab life in pre-Islamic and Islamic times. Ibn Khaldūn[5] aptly called it 'the book of the Arabs and their register', while a modern scholar[6] has said that the immense panorama it presents is probably unequalled in any literature down to modern times. Invaluable as a source book, it is a delight to read for its lucid style and wealth of human stories.

Story-telling was to find another outlet in the *maqāmah,* translated as the *Assembly* or *Séance,* which made its first appearance in the tenth century. Its two most celebrated exponents were al-Hamadhānī (d. 1008) and al-Ḥarīrī (d. 1112). The *maqāmah,* which comes nearest to the short-story, is one of a series of dramatic episodes, unrelated but having the same hero throughout. The hero, a witty and rather unscrupulous adventurer, wanders from place to place and manages by sheer wit and literary skill to survive and survive well. He is provided by the author with a narrator who relates his adventures and literary compositions. By this time rhetorical devices and literary adornments had found their way into prose, and the *maqāmas* were written in highly polished *saj'* (rhymed prose) and embellished with verse, serving as a medium wherein the writer could display his learning and verbal virtuosity. Nevertheless, they make entertaining reading as tales of adventure and roguishness, revealing as well many aspects of society and the life-style of the time.

On a different level, there were the popular romances and folk tales which, originating in medieval times, have been going strong for centuries and are still very much part of folk-culture in the Middle East – many of them being heard in coffee houses, market places or village gatherings. The romance of 'Antar is one of these and is based on the exploits of the black pre-Islamic poet and composer of a *mu'allaqah* who is known in history as 'Antarah. His chivalry and his love for 'Ablah have captured and fired the imagination of successive generations, who made of him the idealised hero of love and adventure. The stories woven around him have been described as the nearest thing to the epic in Arabic. In the West, the best known of the popular romances is the *Thousand and One Nights,* also known as the Arabian Nights. Its leading figures – Scheherezade, Sindbad the Sailor, Aladdin, Ali Baba and others – are all familiar and need no introduction. Although they represent different traditions and time periods (Indian, Sasanid Persian, Baghdadi, Cairene, for example), these tales have acquired a distinctively Islamic stamp – the sea stories among them having affinities with the vast travel literature of the medieval Arabic geographers.

One must also mention here a work which, though not strictly literature, comes nearest to the novel in its composition and structure. This is the philosophical romance, *Ḥayy ibn Yaqẓān,* written by the Spanish–Arab philosopher, Ibn Ṭufayl (d. 1185). The child Ḥayy grows up alone on a desert island, and the story traces his self-education from the most elementary knowledge to the highest levels of philosophical attainment and knowledge of God. At the end of the story Ḥayy has a brief encounter with society, but recognising that his teachings and way of life are not for the masses, he withdraws (accompanied by a kindred spirit who shares his beliefs) to his desert island to end his days in contemplation and worship. The story is written with skill and

[5] An eminent historian of the fourteenth century who will be mentioned later.

[6] H. A. R. Gibb, *Arabic literature,* 2nd ed. Oxford 1963, p. 97.

finesse: the language simple, yet evocative. Reading it is a rewarding experience even for the layman. It may be worth noting that the earliest translation of this treatise into English was made in 1710.

With Ibn Ṭufayl we have moved to the western regions of the medieval Arab world. The contribution of Andalus, as the Arabs called Spain, to philosophy and the sciences are discussed in other chapters of this volume. In poetry the Andalusian poets had at first modelled their compositions after the eastern poets, but by the end of the tenth century a new strophic form had appeared called the *muwashshaḥ*, 'the girdled'. Using the lighter metres and having a refrain suggestive of its origin as song, it broke with the monorhyme and developed varied rhyme schemes of its own. The themes of a *muwashshaḥ* were usually love and descriptions of nature. This genre became very popular and remains so. Today one can hear a *muwashshaḥ* anywhere in the Arab world sung to haunting traditional melodies. Another strophic form was to appear later in the West, the *zajal*, i.e. melody, expressed mostly in the vernacular. The *muwashshaḥ*, popular as it was, did not replace the traditional forms of poetry. Ibn Zaydūn of Cordoba (d. 1071), considered the greatest Andalusian poet, used mostly the latter, particularly in his beautiful and tender love poems to the Spanish Umayyad princess, Wallādah.

The western regions included also North Africa and Sicily, and both contributed to Arabic poetry and letters, the latter even after its re-conquest by the Normans. North Africa was to produce one of the greatest historians of all time, the fourteenth century Ibn Khaldūn. We mention him here because his philosophy, which probes in an unprecedented manner the forces that work and shape societies and civilisations, includes pertinent remarks about Arabic literature and its place in the social scheme of things.

Turning again to literature proper, a great deal has been written about the influences which Andalusian poetry may have had on medieval European poetry, particularly the poetry of Provence. This, however, is not within the province of this essay. A treatise on love, written by the theologian Ibn Ḥazm of Cordoba (d. 1064), called *The Dove's Neckring*, seems to have had considerable influence on the concepts of medieval love in Europe and still has great appeal. Another Andalusian figure said to have influenced some medieval Christian writers is the Ṣūfī (Islamic mystic), Ibn 'Arabī (d. 1240). His greatest influence, however, was on Islamic mysticism, and his thought had a determining effect, particularly on subsequent Persian mystic poets and philosophers.

Ibn 'Arabī was a writer who also composed mystical poetry using the *muwashshaḥ* form. But the greatest Arabic mystical poet was Ibn al-Fāriḍ of Cairo (d. 1235). In his poetry Ibn al-Fāriḍ expressed the love of the Divine in the language and imagery of traditional love- and wine-poetry. The desert journey of the ancient poet becomes the mystical journey; the poet's haltings and wanderings become landmarks in the quest for mystical experience. As a religious spirit he also rendered the physical pilgrimage to Mecca and its hallowed haunts as symbolic of man's journey to God. In a way, his poetry is a synthesis of the love themes of Arabic poetry within a mystical mould. It is also a euphonic medley of sounds giving it a musical dimension all its own. It may be worth noting in this connection that this mystical strain had started much earlier in the east. As early as the eight century, we have the woman mystic Rābi'ah of Baṣra (d. 801) expressing her love of God in the following verses:

> Two ways I love Thee: selfishly,
> And next, as worthy is of Thee.
> 'Tis selfish love that I do nought
> Save think on Thee with every thought;
> 'Tis purest love when thou dost raise
> The veil to my adoring gaze.
> Not mine the praise in that or this
> Thine is the praise in both I wis.
>
> (trans. R. A. Nicholson).

Thus far we have highlighted aspects of the medieval Arabic literary achievement. But the story does not end here. Another chapter must be added – that of modern Arabic literature. Here, however, we can give no more than a brief indication of the changes in direction that this literature is taking.

After a period of decline in literary activity, particularly in the sixteenth, seventeenth and eighteenth centuries, the Arab World witnessed at the beginning of the nineteenth what has been termed a renaissance. It is usual to date this from the Napoleonic expedition to Egypt in 1798. In literature this renaissance manifested itself in two ways, both working together and acting as stimuli. One was a revival of interest in the language and literature of the classic period, to which the Christian Arabs of Lebanon contributed significantly; the other an opening up to Western literary influences. The appearance of newspapers and magazines was particularly important in fostering the movement and helping it spread.

In a totally different context, the Arabic-speaking world had a second encounter with a foreign culture (the first being with Hellenism in the medieval period), this time taking full cognisance of its literature, resulting in a period of intensive translation from French and later English and other languages, and in experiments with new literary forms and concepts.

The full measure of this two-sided movement was felt in the latter part of the nineteenth and in the twentieth centuries. The area in which it exerted greatest influence was the national movement, being responsible to a large extent for the awakening of the Arab national consciousness. The twentieth century has been crucial in the life of the Arabic-speaking world. The thrust of the West, the struggle for independence, the tragedy of Palestine with its traumatic effects, the political, economic, social and cultural changes and the interaction of the old and the new have all been reflected and echoed in the literary movement. Out of it a new literature has emerged, drawing on its past heritage and adapting to new concepts.

An interesting aspect of this literature has been the appearance of a new literary scholarship. With the new tools of research, Arab scholars are now studying their literature critically and appreciatively and their work is invaluable both as research and in directing the literary tastes and critical sensibilities of the rising generations and of Western specialists.

It is perhaps in poetry that contemporary literature has been most adventurous. In the earlier part of the century some very good poetry – lyrical, patriotic and descriptive – was written in the traditional manner, while in the New World of the Americas Arab immigrants were producing, amongst other things, poetry that was freer in style and content. But new types of poetry were emerging, coming into full force in the last thirty years or so, employing new poetic forms, different rhythmical and rhyme patterns and experimenting with the language. This poetry was both inward-looking and outward-reaching, creating new images and symbols to translate the poetic experience. Though greatly influenced by modern Western poetry it is an indigenous art.

Drama, the newest literary genre in Arabic, passed through stages of translation, imitation, adaptation and experimentation. Then in the hands of skilful writers there was a breakthrough. Several of the plays that have appeared are very satisfying, both artistically and intellectually. In a country like Egypt the theatre has become part of the social and cultural pattern of city life.

What has been said about the drama is more or less true of the novel and short-story where success has been perhaps greater. Some very significant and original contributions of intrinsic literary merit have been made, many of which have found their way into English and other languages. The autobiographical genre of the novel has also been effectively developed. the most notable example being Dr Ṭāhā Ḥusayn's *The Days*, recording (in Part 1 of the novel) with sensitivity and masterly simplicity a blind boy's inner experiences and responses to life around him in an Egyptian village at the turn of the century.

This brief statement is hardly intended as a critical assessment of modern Arabic literature. It serves simply to say that, rooted in and fed by its great heritage and responding to new stimuli, Arabic literature is coming into its own. In its endeavour to accommodate the needs of its particular world, it is also seeking to identify with the world at large.

7

Persian literature: an affirmation of identity

G. M. WICKENS

One of the themes in this book touches the enormous, and even unique, importance of the Iranian element in Middle Eastern culture, particularly during the Islamic period. It was an importance that manifested itself in two ways. First, the Iranian component maintained its own distinct identity in a manner and a degree infinitely beyond any of the other cultural areas covered by the rapid spread of early Arab Islam. Secondly, it persuasively permeated the new Islamic society in all spheres of life – in civil and military administration, in religious ideas and feelings, in art and architecture and the crafts, in manners and dress and cuisine, in short in all the major refinements of civilised living. Of course, many other non-Arab cultures contributed substantially here as well, e.g. the Byzantine, and the several survivals of all the earlier civilisations, but to nothing like the same extent as the Persian. The Iranians, it must be remembered, were in a few years nominally conquered and absorbed by the Arabs, their religion and their culture; but, given their stability, their independence of outlook, their patience, and their subtlety, this very situation enabled them to work, like a catalyst, *from within* the new culture in a way not open to an external society like Byzantium. As history has demonstrated, moreover, it was at the same time an option not open to any of the other *conquered* societies: the Iranian achievement is all the more remarkable when one considers how Arabic and the Arab way of life irreversibly came to dominate, for example, the Graeco-Egyptian world of the Copts and the Graeco-Aramaic civilisation of Syria. In no sphere of life was Iranian apartness, with its concomitant feeling of superiority, more evident than in Persian literature of the classical period (*ca.* 900–*ca.* 1500). Often it displays itself overtly, even aggressively, but most commonly it is implicit in the very existence and distinctiveness of the literature as such.

Persian writing goes back to at least 600 years before the Christian era, to the age of the great Achaemenian dynasty that eventually succumbed to Alexander the Great. We meet it again, in considerable quantity, in the period *ca.* A.D. 200–*ca.*650, the era of the Sasanian dynasty that so long menaced the Eastern Roman Empire. The surviving writing of these early periods, however, is less literary than monumental, religious and documentary. Of literature in the specialised sense, we still know little that is certain before the Islamic period. Almost as vague are the years A.D. 650–*ca.*900, though lack of enough hard facts should not inhibit certain fairly obvious inferences. All through the period of Arab and Arabic domination, Persian clearly never ceased to be spoken generally, and even recited and sung at a popular or ritual level. In the relatively simple and unstructured world of which we are speaking, any revival of the language from scratch at a later date (as with Modern Hebrew in Israel) would be quite out of the question. Under the early Arab domination, moreover, for perhaps as long as a century, Persian continued to some extent to be written, even for official purposes. Then, at least as regards preserved records, it more or less disappears until about A.D. 900. At that time, according to the latest discoveries, it emerges in a new form, much simplified grammatically, with a considerable admixture of Arabic vocabulary, and written in the Arabic script. Typically though, from the very beginning, Persian chooses its Arabic vocabulary discriminatingly and moulds both vocabulary and script, as well as morphology, to its own ways and its own purposes. (In the simplification of grammar and the adoption of vocabulary, there is an interesting parallel with what happened to Old English after the Norman Conquest.)

Even before this new emergence, Persian men-of-letters had not been lacking. During the two centuries from 700 to 900 scores of Persians were already writing highly esteemed prose and verse, *but in Arabic*, at that time still very much the sole prestige-language of culture in the Islamic world. So highly rated were their literary and scholarly productions that many people, including Arabs both then and now, speak of them as though they were in fact Arabs, native writers and speakers of the language they used to such effect. From 900 onwards, these writers could once again use Persian as a vehicle of literary expression, and they did so increasingly. Within a century, virtually all Iranian-produced literature (in the specialised sense) is once more in Persian. Even the quasi-literary writings (on, say, philosophy, science, history and religion) increasingly switch, in Iran and the Iranian orbit, from Arabic to Persian. Eventually, by about 1300, Arabic becomes a rarity in these regions for virtually all purposes; like Latin and Greek in later Western Europe, however, it remained a constant, if somewhat artificial, element in Iranian education; and it even underwent a revival in the sixteenth to seventeenth centuries when the Ṣafavid dynasty (paradoxically, for 'nationalistic' reasons) brought eminent Shi'ite scholars from Syria. By the present day, both through natural attrition and by nationalist policy, Arabic as such is virtually dead in Iran, and Modern Standard Persian reigns supreme over all other minor languages and dialects.

The re-emergence of Persian as a literary vehicle in about 900 took place in a particular political and social setting that gave it great force and at the same time set definite limits to its potentialities. The ninth century saw the initial break-up of the universal Caliphate, both from weakness at the centre and because of the powerful surge of more or less 'nationalistic' movements around the periphery. This was partly the case in Spain and Egypt, but nowhere more so than in Iran and those areas of Northern India and Central Asia that fell within the Iranian orbit. Here, although the spearhead of attack was nearly always dynastic ambition, there were behind it deep thrusts of national and linguistic feeling, with a romantic confidence in past greatness to inspire future achievements. In such a political and social framework it was doubtless inevitable that the first compositions should be either historical prose or verse-sagas: both had great propaganda value, and the poetry in particular offered incalculable inspirational force. In later ages, these factors became, if not unimportant, at least less self-conscious and more diversified. But one social and economic fact, present from the beginning, could never be entirely shaken off: the overwhelming bulk of Persian literature, until modern times, was composed under dynastic or noble patronage, and this had two unfortunate consequences. In the first place, it led to much commissioned work, uninspired stuff deliberately designed to flatter the patron. Secondly, taste tended to be markedly 'courtly' – artificial, lush, over-ingenious; and there was a natural disinclination in such an atmosphere for the writer to risk liberties and innovations, especially if these too obviously suggested the natural and the real. Nevertheless, Persian writers – at least the greatest of them – were marvellously successful in working within these constrictions, and from time to time they even managed to break or circumvent them – with varying consequences to themselves.

In poetry, one of the most ingenious devices to escape from the boundaries of social convention and taste was the use of a mystical setting and mystical imagery. This is not to say by any means that the thing was done in every case deliberately or hypocritically. Many poets undoubtedly had genuine mystical yearnings; others toyed with mysticism as being in the air, rather as an uncommitted modern poet might at least toy with the ideas of the New Left; still others were obviously delighted by the technical challenge of working against a mystical background, whether assumed or genuinely felt. In any case, mysticism had in itself been one of the (perhaps only partly conscious) Persian ways of 'fighting back' against an originally stark and unsophisticated Faith; and it was accordingly only natural that it should come to be an integral part of that other instrument of self-affirmation, Persian poetry. In the long run, this was to affect at least some Arabic poetry; and in the still longer run, it was itself to become a frozen, conservative element along with all the others in Persian literature up to modern times. But before this happened, prodigious things were accomplished. Perhaps the most striking phenomenon is that in innumerable Persian poems it is quite impossible to distinguish the patron from the beloved, or the earthly beloved from God: all three are yearned towards and complained of, and favours are sought from all. Sometimes, even when they can be distinguished, they are associated in the one poem in a way that the West usually tends to find incongruous and distasteful.

We can touch here on only a few of the major writers, and we must deliberately limit discussion of them in favour of direct presentation of their own words in translation. The first really great Persian poet, and the author of the outstanding national epic, is Firdawsī (d. *ca.* 1020). His poem runs to some 60,000 double-lines, dealing with the story of Iran from the creation until the Islamic conquest. Written in a style markedly low in Arabic elements, it is a frank call to the good old days and ways, full of battles and marvels, but also of touching passages of charity and tenderness shown equally to friend and foe. Firdawsī laboured for 30 years for a royal patron, but was sharply disappointed in his expectations. One of his stories has already passed into English literature in the adaptation made in 1853 by Matthew Arnold, *Sohrab and Rustum*. We shall look here at two lesser known passages, both famous in their own right in the original. Here is a piece in which an early Persian 'freedom-fighter', a blacksmith, raises his apron as a standard in his campaign against a quasi-Arab tyrant named Ẓaḥḥāk and in favour of the legitimate heir to the throne, Farīdūn:

Now as Kāvah left the forecourt of the Shah,
  The market-quarter gathered round him.
He cried aloud and called for retribution,
  Called for justice for the universe entire;
And that leather-apron the blacksmiths wear
  Across their legs when striking with the hammer,
Kāvah raised aloft upon a lance
  As dust rose up from all the market-place.
Crying aloud and lance in hand, he went:
  'Men of renown, worshippers of God!
'Any whose heart's with Farīdūn,
  'And who withdraws his head from Ẓaḥḥāk's bonds!
'Bestir yourselves, for this leader's the Devil himself,
  'An enemy to the World-creator in his heart.'
And so by that worthless, unworthy hide he used,
  The cry of friend from enemy was known;
That man heroic went ahead,
  And no small army gathered round him;
Alone he knew where Farīdūn would be,
  Set off and went straight thither.
And so to the new chieftain's forecourt he came,
  And when they saw him there a tumult rose.
The Prince saw that hide up high upon the lance,
  And drew conclusion for a favourable star;
With Grecian brocade he decked it out,
  Placing a frame of jewels upon it made of native gold;
He placed it at his own head as though around a moon
  (For that Emperor took it as a fortunate omen);
Streamers he hung from it – red, yellow, violet –
  And called it The Kavahian Standard.

In contrast, we offer a tenderer episode from the same work. Here two lovers, spending the night together illicitly, complain that they must separate at dawn. Romantically, the girl had offered to raise and lower the hero at her tower by her hair! From their union will spring the great Iranian Hercules of tragic destiny, Rustam:

Their love increased with every moment; good sense was far, desire was to the fore.
Thus till the white of dawn rose up and a drum-roll arose from the camp,
Then Zāl said farewell to that one, moon-bright, their bodies entwined like woof and warp.
The tips of their eyelashes they hung with tears, while they let loose their tongues against the sun,
Saying: 'Oh! Glory of the World, one moment still! So suddenly you should not yet have come!'
Then Zāl cast his cord down from above and descended from the tower of his auspicious mate.

Missing in these short extracts in English is the 'music' of the original, which – especially at length – is sonorous, sombre and grand, sometimes even when the theme might seem to call for lighter treatment. (I refer here principally, of course, to the poetry's own inherent music, though it must never be forgotten that a great deal of Persian poetry was intended to be, and was in fact, musically accompanied.) This difficulty in conveying what we have called the 'musical' effect stands in the way of most translations from Persian poetry, though the effect in question may vary greatly from poet to poet.

The greatest *romantic* poet to write in Persian, Niẓāmī (d. 1209), defies direct translation utterly and completely: this is partly because he displays a close-packed learning and allusion, rather like *Paradise Lost*, which calls for a great weight of explanatory notes; but partly also because his special 'musical' tone is achieved by daring and sustained innovations in the use of language. This is a pity, indeed, for the treatment of his themes is highly original, at once mystical and dreamlike, yet sharply circumstantial and naturalistic. Whether he wrote of star-crossed lovers or the legendary career of Alexander the Great, he was able to appeal for centuries to nearly all the

Islamic world; and in our own day he is admired as their own laureate by the Persian-speaking peoples of the Soviet Union, so much so that Soviet scholars are undoubtedly the world's leading experts on Niẓāmī. Fortunately, a good impression of his subjects and their treatment can be grasped pictorially in almost any great museum, for his five masterpieces, known as the *Khamsah* or 'Quintet', have been widely copied as precious manuscripts and superbly illustrated by miniature-painters through the centuries. For illustration few, if any, other Islamic works remotely approach Firdawsī's epic and Niẓāmī's *Khamsah*.

From the greatest all-round Persian poet, Sa'dī (d. *ca.* 1290), we have many things, including some very fine prose. But primarily he exemplifies yet another age-old aspect of Persian literature, delight in story-telling and wit and wisdom, largely for their own sake no doubt, but ostensibly to illustrate and make palatable regular doses of moral exhortation. Again, this is not always exactly to traditional Western taste, especially since the worldly-wise Sa'dī tends to mix lofty moral counsel with practical low-cunning and meek compromise. But he is an incomparable artist, and his courageous words to the great often come as a heartening surprise. Much of Sa'dī's material is too long for easy quotation, but here is a typical pseudo-autobiographical vignette of great distinctness. It is used to convey advice of a general character with mystical overtones, i.e. you can best find your way in life by attaching yourself to a mystical adept who already knows the way, like a child clasping the hand of a parent when in a crowd. The actual advice goes on at considerably greater length than we are able to quote:

> Often am I minded, from the days of my childhood,
> How once I went out with my father on a festival;
> In fun I grew preoccupied with all the folk about,
> Losing touch with my father in the popular confusion;
> In terror and bewilderment I raised up a cry,
> When suddenly my father boxed my ears:
> 'You bold-eyed child, how many times, now,
> 'Have I told you not to lose hold of my skirt?'
> A tiny child cannot walk out alone,
> For it is difficult to take a way not seen;
> You too, poor friend, are but a child upon endeavour's way:
> Go, seize the skirts of those who know the way!

Here, again, in quite different style, is a tale in prose and verse, pointing a moral of political significance. The hero is conventionally one of the heroic Persian rulers from the 'good old days' when justice ruled the land:

> They tell how, when some game was being roasted for Nūshīrvān the Just during a hunting expedition, no salt was available. So an attendant was sent to a village to get some. Nūshīrvān said: 'Pay for the salt, lest the village be ruined and a bad precedent be established.'
>
> When asked what harm could come from such a small amount, Nūshīrvān replied: 'The first foundation of oppression in the world was little, but those who came after added to it so that it reached its present culmination.'
>
> If the king eats one apple from the garden of a subject,
> His attendants will dig up the tree by the roots.
> For every half-egg the sultan allows to be taken unjustly
> His troops will put a thousand fowls upon the spit.
>
> A tyrant of ill fortune will not endure,
> But the curse on him abides for ever.

This last tale belongs to a dual category in Persian literature. One is that of *belles-lettres*, elegantly written, entertaining prose of an 'improving' character; the other is what is known technically as the 'mirror-for-princes' style. This form is so typically Persian that even when it occurs in Arabic the models and examples are nearly always taken from pre-Islamic Iran, often necessitating some explanation for the benefit of the Arabic reader. The most famous of such works is the *Book of Political Science*, by the great minister to the Seljuks, Niẓām al-Mulk (assassinated 1092). Here is a short passage from the section on the duties of a ruler:

> It is the king's duty to enquire about the condition of his subjects and his army, both far and near, and to know how things go, both great and small. If he does not do this it is a fault, and people will attribute it to negligence and tyranny, saying, 'Either the king knows about the mischief and depredation going on in the country, or he does not know. If he knows about it and does nothing to retrieve or prevent it, it is because he is an oppressor like the others and acquiesces in oppression; and if he does not know, he is most negligent and uninformed.' Neither of these opinions is a good thing.

Niẓām al-Mulk's prose, though supple and unaffected, falls short of true elegance. This is not the case with a work, *The Book of Qābūs*, composed by a North Persian ruler of about the same period, allegedly for the guidance of his son. An astonishing range of advice is covered, personal and political, serious and light-hearted; and the young prince is even told how to make out in various ways if he should lose his throne, including (if necessary) by recourse to hard work! Here is the opening of Chapter 23, 'On Buying Slaves':

> When you wish to buy slaves, be prudent. The buying of men is a difficult science; because many a slave may ostensibly be good, but, looked at scientifically, turns out to be the opposite. Most people imagine that buying slaves is simply one of the several modes of trade, not understanding that the buying of slaves, and the science thereof, is a branch of philosophy. Anyone who buys something which he does not thoroughly know may be defrauded therein; and the most difficult type of knowledge is the knowledge of human beings. The faults and virtues of men are many; a single fault may conceal a hundred thousand virtues, while a single virtue may conceal a like number of faults.

Undoubtedly the most famous of all medieval Persian writing in *belles-lettres* is the work known as *The Four Discourses*, by a twelfth-century author who is otherwise largely a figure of uncertain and shadowy outlines. It consists primarily of four elegant essays on the art of being respectively a confidential secretary in government service, a poet, an astrologer, and a physician; each essay is illustrated with several delightful, if largely apocryphal, stories about real practitioners of these arts. It is the sort of work that infuriates the pedantically accurate scholar, concerned for dates and hard facts; but its real value lies in its lively picture of contemporary Persian life, not only as lived in courts and great houses, but also in the market-place, the slums, and the countryside. Here is the earliest-known story about 'Umar Khayyām (Omar Khayyam), allegedly a former teacher of the writer, which is intended to show 'Umar's skill as a foreteller of the future. 'Umar had prophesied that he would be buried in a place where the blossoms would fall on him twice a year – a statement that the writer had found puzzling:

> When I arrived at Nishapur, it was four years since that great man had veiled his face in the dust, and this lower world had been orphaned of him. I went to visit his grave on a Friday (for he had the claim of a master on me), taking someone with me to point out his tomb. He took me out to the Ḥīrah Cemetery; I turned to the left, and found the tomb situated at the foot of a garden-wall, over which pear- and apricot-trees thrust their heads, and on his grave there had fallen so many blossoms it was hidden beneath the petals. Then I remembered that remark which I had heard from him in the city of Balkh, and tears overcame me because throughout the wide world, and in all the regions of the habitable quarter, I had nowhere seen anyone to equal him.

Mention of 'Umar Khayyām will undoubtedly arouse curiosity as to where Fitzgerald's *Rubā'īyāt* belongs in the scheme of Persian literature. First, it should be said that Fitzgerald did not translate, but rather re-worked and adapted, much abbreviating in the process. Secondly, as we indicate in Chapter 10, 'Umar is more famous in Iran for his scientific achievements. (Even the last author affirms that, despite his skill in prediction, he was too great a *scientist* to take astrology very seriously.) But Fitzgerald did capture successfully the uniquely Persian spirit of mysticism paradoxically allied to pessimism, together with yet a third element: the very un-Islamic cult of the irrational, wine-induced or otherwise, which was felt to make bearable, if not acceptable, the emptiness of both this life and eternity. If, however, we would see this central Persian affirmation at its most characteristic and sublime, equally in concept and in expression, we must look to Ḥāfiẓ, the foremost lyric poet of Iran (d. *ca.* 1390). Just as Firdawsī, Niẓāmī and others took the unwieldy, monorhyming Arabic poetic forms and adapted them to long, multi-rhyming Persian narrative and argument, so Ḥāfiẓ took them again, following upon Sa'dī, and trimmed them down to a new form designed to make the most of brief lyric effect. Even so, his best work is too long to quote in full in this short essay. But here, remembering that in this case above all we shall miss the lyric 'music', are a few brief extracts:

> I saw the green acres of Heaven and the sickle of the new moon/ And this reminded me of what I'd sown and reaping-time...
>
> The times are bent on mischief once again:/ I'm caught again in drunkenness and the mischief of my companion's eye./ I never cease to wonder at the way the wheel turns,/ No knowing whom earth will take next...
>
> You who live dangerously, proclaim at the market-entrance:/ Oyez! Hearken, you dwellers in loose-living's lane!/ Some days since, we lost the daughter of the vine;/ She went to do what she was minded: Beware! Beware! Be on your guard!...
>
> O you who're constantly deluded with your Self,/ We'll excuse you if you have no love./ But don't go round with those who're crazed for Love,/ For you are famous for your precious intellect./ Your head holds

> not the drunkenness of Love:/ Go, you who're drunk on grape-juice!...
>
> I will not hold my hand from wanting till my desire is realised:/ Either my body attains my heart's beloved, or my heart will leave my body./ Open my grave when I am dead, and look/ How smoke arises from my shroud at the fire that's in my innards./ Show your cheek and all humanity will grow distracted and bewildered;/ Open your lips and cries will rise from men and women both...

Fortunately, this fragmentary quotation does less injustice to Ḥāfiẓ than to some Persian poets, and even less injustice to Persian poetry as a whole than might be the case in other literatures. This is because we are dealing not so much with linear, logical development as with a stream, or rather a whirlpool, of consciousness. Each double-line is usually self-contained, the centripetal force of the whole being provided by multi-level imagery and word-play rather than by closely articulated ideas. What the reader may not have noticed, in this quick review, is the *range* of peculiarly Persian mood: nearly *all* the things we have mentioned are in these few lines: not only the mystical and the pessimistic, the irrational, the preoccupation with wine in one way or another, but also earthly love and the ever-present desire to please a – hopefully – generous patron. Above all, perhaps, there is the typically Persian note of devil-may-care defiance, an urchin-gesture at ultimately all establishments, political, social and religious alike, for they are all seen as in a sense hostile, an imposition from 'outside'.

One great poet about the purity of whose mystical concern there is no doubt at all is Jalāl al-Dīn Rūmī, founder of the Whirling Dervish Order (d. 1273). His output, particularly in poetry, is vast, powerful and rough-hewn – like a huge, boldly drawn map of a whole continent, or rather of two continents, for his bifocal vision superimposes the spiritual world upon the natural, perceiving the wealth of images in both. His verse contains everything: all the age-old Middle Eastern legends and histories, crude and obscene anecdotes, details of daily life, sublime speculation, rough-tongued advice, and a fair share of humour. A typical line of his runs: 'Truth is concealed in falsehood like the taste of butter in buttermilk.' This line introduces a pithy and abstruse discourse on the real and the illusory, which ends, even more roughly than he began: 'From a drunk's ramblings you can deduce the existence of bartenders!' It is pointless to try to give a real impression of this craggy, mountainous genius in a little sketch like the present, but we may fairly conclude with another typical line or two, in which Rūmī speculates on the rich multiplicity of natural creation in conflict with the white simplicity of the divine:

> The wonder is that colour welled from that which has no colour: how, then, did colour rise to fight the colourless?/ Or is this not real warfare, but a ruse for divine purposes, like the pretended competition of the donkey dealers?

Many religious people in the West might well be shocked by this way of looking at things, as many in Islam, in Rūmī's own time and since, have certainly been.

Out of the hundreds of notable figures in medieval Persian literature, some twenty of whom are great by any standard, we have mentioned less than ten. Unfortunately, if we are to say something about modern times, we must be even more unjust than this. We have no time, for example, to analyse the vast amount of 'near-literature' produced by historians and others. Nor can space be found for the much fine Persian poetry written in India and the Ottoman Empire during the medieval period and later. Nor, again, can we even review the great volume of by no means insignificant Persian literature produced between, say, 1500 and 1850. Fortunately, what we can aver with some confidence in these cases is that virtually none of this material differs markedly in theme and style from the main classical and medieval trends that we have presented. The types we have so far described were to serve as models, wherever Persian was written, for nearly 1000 years.

Putting this another way, we may say that by the mid-nineteenth century Persian literature had become stereotyped and repetitive in both content and language. This inevitably meant that, quite apart from wide-spread illiteracy, the literature neither reflected the real life of the people nor was it understood by them. Whatever the artificialities and limitations of the medieval period, when literature was primarily a courtly production, this double cleavage between the nation and its literature had not existed then. For one thing, the medieval society had been a far more open one, with the majority of life's proceedings visible to all and well comprehended by most. By the mid-nineteenth century this was no longer so.

In the last 100 years Persian literature has moved effectively into modern times. But the process has been slow and uneven, just as the political, economic and social changes in Iran came somewhat later and more slowly than in the Ottoman Empire. The operative forces were as we have described them elsewhere: Western imperialism – acquisitive and technically well equipped, but also by its very nature highly revolutionary – touched Iranian society and at many points penetrated it painfully. On the part of a few people, mostly among the small, wealthy intelligentsia of the time, there was interest and even excitement at the new developments; but fear, insecurity and resentment gripped the vast majority. Before long, virtually nobody in Iran could have clear-cut and simple feelings either way about the volume and diversity of changes that were pressing in upon them or still impending in the remoter distance. At least, however, literature began to concern itself again with difficult realities and urgently felt ideals. It became in the first stage highly political, markedly satirical and journalistic. The literary language became simpler: some would even say its currency was debased. All in all, it was a long time – well into the present century, in fact – before Persian writing began again to ring wholly true to the test of national expression and national appreciation, as it did for so long with Firdawsī and the others we have cited.

When Persian literature began to find its feet again as literature, its writers were still preoccupied with what they regarded as the West's most significant literary creations, the drama and the novel. In the event, however, their own best work has been done not in these fields, but in those areas which – even despite enormous innovations – could be in some way related to traditional genres: poetry and the short-story. There are at the present day literally dozens of competent and interesting poets and short-story writers, and scores more who are less gifted. Their themes and styles, though often derivative, are as diverse as can be imagined: they include not only virtually everything Western, but also certain features with special Iranian relevance, e.g. the social problems of modernisation, and stylistic experiments relating to the particular nature of the Persian language. If Persia's political situation were easier, internally and externally, we should doubtless see even greater variety. On the other hand, a Communist régime might prove more constricting to literature than the Shah's present rule.

The man commonly regarded as the greatest figure in modern Persian literature, Ṣādiq Hidāyat (Sadegh Hedayat) who committed suicide 1951, does not translate well because, like Niẓāmī some 800 years earlier, his language is rich and vivid, and his material is full of allusions needing annotation. His friend Buzurg (Bozorg) 'Alavī (an exile, who is Professor of Persian in East Berlin) translates magnificently; but the present Iranian government resists popularisation of his work (which, ironically, has also begun to displease the Communists). Of his half-dozen best books, the most impressive date from the years he spent in prison under a previous régime: *Prison Paper-Scraps* and *Fifty-Three Persons*. 'Alavī often introduces the tragic and horrifying by means of the commonplace, and even the sentimental. One of the episodes from *Prison Paper-Scraps*, 'The Comet', begins in the following innocent, but slightly foreboding, Graham Greeneish manner:

> Everybody can see the comet but once in his lifetime. Some, like me, can't even see it that once. In 1912, when the comet appeared in the sky, I was five or six years old. My mother and sisters had gone up on the roof to see this remarkable star, and they were also pointing it out to me and saying: 'Did you see it? Do you see its tail?' My mind couldn't properly grasp what a star was, and I didn't know what 'comet' meant. I couldn't see it, but I said I had.

Literary affirmation in Persian has often been, and can still be, strident and grim. But there is a quieter affirmation, too, resting in the cyclical commonplaces of daily life. Here, to conclude, is an extract from a modern poem by a poet-politician, M. S̱ābitī (Sabeti), which has much of the grace of a Japanese *haiku*. It speaks of the severe Persian winter, but takes comfort in the life-giving snow:

> The snow has come, capping every woman and mountain,/ And this year its coming is very precious./ The world for whiteness is like a royal falcon's breast,/ The welkin in blackness like the wing of a swallow./ People have all fled from land and market,/ Hiding in their houses like bees in the hive.

In some ways, this poem is extremely modern and actual, but there is not a statement or a word that would not be easily understood over the last 1000 years. Few nations can equal that degree of linguistic and literary consciousness and continuity.

Turkish *ghāzī* bowman fighting in Europe. Miniature from a fifteenth-century Turkish manuscript

8

Turkish literature through the ages[1]

ELEAZAR BIRNBAUM

Turkish literature is not just that of the land now called Turkey, where Turks began to settle some nine centuries ago. It is or was current in many regions of the vast area stretching from Eastern Europe to the Great Wall of China. In pre-Christian and early Christian times, the Turkic[2]-speaking peoples lived in east-central Asia; over the centuries group after group migrated towards the west and south-west across Asia. Their oldest written monuments are some long funerary inscriptions set up in a Mongolian valley during the eighth century. These describe in vivid prose the legendary origin of the Turks, and their battles with the Chinese. The polished style suggests that the origins of Turkish literature go back much farther into the past. Early Turkish oral literature included a wide range of verse in a variety of forms: lyric, pastoral, didactic, epic and elegiac. Many specimens are included in the remarkable *Dictionary of the Languages of the Turks*, compiled about 1074, by Maḥmūd al-Kāshgharī, a Central Asian Turk who had settled in Baghdad.

In the early Middle Ages groups of Turks were converted from their ancestral shamanism to Buddhism, Manicheism, Christianity and Judaism; old Turkic translations of some of their religious works survive. But Islam had a much greater impact, and its most effective propagators amongst the nomadic Turkic tribes were wandering Turkish dervishes.

[1] The italicised Islamic terms and names in parentheses in this chapter represent the Turkish forms.

[2] The term 'Turkish' has long been used as an adjective in two senses: (a) broadly, relating to Turks anywhere in the world; and (b) more narrowly, pertaining to those of the political entity called Turkey, or its predecessor, the Ottoman Empire. To avoid ambiguity, 'Turkic' has in recent years come into increasing use in the former sense.

The rise of Islamic Turkish literature: forms and themes

Since the ninth century, the most powerful religious and cultural influence on the Turkic peoples has been Islam. With it came the study of religious and literary masterpieces in the two major Islamic tongues, Arabic and Persian. The dominant external influence on Turkish writers has been Persian literature. Until the present century traditional Turkish higher education always included the Persian classics, which became models even for original works in Turkish. It was in the Persian, rather than in the Arabic, forms that the standard Islamic literary genres were adopted. Thus in poetry *'arūż*, the quantitative system of prosody, was taken over, with its metres and poetic forms: the *ghazal* (Turkish *ġazel*), a kind of lyrical sonnet whose main themes were love and wine; the monorhyming *qaṣīdah* (*ḳaṣīde*) for panegyrics; the rhymed couplets of the *masnavī* (*mesnevī*) for epic, narrative and didactic works; the quatrain (*rubā'ī*) for epigrams. Since the Arabo-Persian metres are based primarily on the difference between long and short vowels, a distinction natural to these languages but far less to Turkish, it became accepted practice for poets to incorporate loanwords from Persian and Arabic as required, when to do so would more easily achieve a smooth musical effect. As a result, classical Turkish came to have at its disposal the entire vocabulary of three languages, and with it the possibility of expressing a vast and sophisticated range of meaning and feeling. This Turkish literature of the educated classes shared with Persian essentially the same literary conventions, traditions and terminology. The attitudes of Ṣūfī mysticism influenced all writing and completely dominated poetry, which sang mostly of love:

whether of God ('real love'), or simply erotic love of a man or woman ('metaphorical love') is usually unclear, and was intended to be so. What R. A. Nicholson wrote of the Persian masters applies equally to the Turks: 'By tantalizing the reader, by keeping him, as it were, suspended between matter and spirit, . . . [the poets] pique his ingenuity and double his pleasure. Nearly every line is a play of wit. Love, Wine and Beauty are painted in the warmest, the most alluring colours, but with such nicety of phrase, that often the same ode will entrance the sinner and evoke sublime raptures in the saint.' (*Selected Poems from the Dīvāni Shamsi Tabrīz*. London, 1898, p. xxv.)

Classical Turkish poetry is mostly very subjective, and such material or physical details as may be mentioned also have conventionally accepted metaphorical and spiritual meanings. Spontaneity and originality of the kind that are prized in Western poetry are neither sought nor valued. By such standards, the mark of true poetry is the beauty with which a central 'point' is expressed, rather than the idea itself, (and that idea may well be conventional). Since, typically, realism is avoided, the expression of subjective emotion can become an intellectual exercise in virtuosity involving, not only meaning and musical effect, but also a wide range of figures of speech. (Sometimes the results are reminiscent of the 'conceits' of Elizabethan literature.) Metaphors are primary and are used with astonishing variety. Intricate word-play is exceedingly popular, and allusions to the whole range of Islamic learning – from religious law and history to Persian legend, and from geography to astronomy – abound. A Turkish classical poet was of necessity a very educated man, who was expected to display his learning, but with a light touch. A favourite figure was ætiology – a graceful yet patently fictitious statement of cause and effect: 'tireless and restless, the bewildered sky revolves, night and day. Perhaps his aim is union with you' (Fużūlī); 'Each morning comes the breeze, to visit your tresses; yet, fearing their chains, he stays not, but away he flees.' (Şeyḥī)

According to classical theory the *beyt* (verse or couplet) is poetry's basic unit. It should contain one central 'point' or idea, and its two halves should be intimately related, not only formally but also in the meanings (primary, secondary and even tertiary) of the carefully chosen words, as well as in the allusions and association of ideas conjured up. Each couplet should be an independent artistic unity. It should not be linked grammatically or semantically with the preceding or following verses. Yet there should be echoes and parallels both in the music and the thought, connecting it – if only by a gossamer thread – with many of the other lines. Each verse is a jewel in itself; the verses together form a necklace. In the hands of a master such poetry can be a feast of wit and virtuosity, of genuine feeling and exquisite taste. Originality is acceptable, and indeed highly regarded, but only when it is exercised within the confines of tradition. Real talent is seen as the ability to express with strength yet delicacy, in a new and elegant way, the kind of feelings regarded as appropriate to poetry. There should of course be no triteness or banality, nor may the numerous canons of poetry be transgressed. Form is relatively more important than content. The fine network of primary and other meanings and allusions linking the words and images makes 'straight' translation an impossible task.

There are several distinct though related Turkish literatures, each with parallel currents of (a) classical or court, (b) popular secular, and (c) popular religious works. And besides these, there is 'modern' literature. The two principal geographical groups are the areas linguistically represented by (1) Eastern Turkish, from old Uyghur to classical Chaghatay and its successor dialects; and (2) Western (or Oghuz) Turkish, consisting of Ottoman (Anatolian) Turkish, and Āẕerī (the language of the Azerbaijan region).

Eastern Turkish literature, including Chaghatay: Luṭfī Navā'ī, Makhdūm-ḳuli.

A long allegorical poem called *The Knowledge that Brings Happiness* (*Ḳutadġu Bilig*) is the oldest extant literary work of Turkish Islam. Written in 1069, this is essentially a didactic political essay in an artistic form. During the next three centuries Muslim Turkish literature gradually adopted Persian literary norms, as both languages were cultivated side by side at the courts of culture-conscious Turkish princes in the flourishing Central Asian cities of the lands which are presently Uzbekistan and the other Soviet Central Asian republics, as well as in Afghanistan, Iran, northern India and Pakistan, and western China. In the fifteenth century, poets and painters, architects and scholars found especially generous patronage at the various courts of the Timurid sultans, who were interested in the arts not only for their own sake but also for the prestige which accrued from having capitals that were recognised as cultural centres. Although different Turkish dialects were spoken, a common literary language,. Chaghatay, developed and gained acceptance over a vast territory. In it works were written and read, enjoyed and criticised, right down to the end of the nineteenth century. The greatest of the Chaghatay authors is universally acknowledged to be 'Alī Shīr Navā'ī (1441–1501). Second to him comes his predecessor and teacher in poetry, Luṭfī (*ca.* 1367–*ca.* 1463), whose innovative groundwork paved the way for Navā'ī's achievements. At a time when the inherent problems of adapting the forms of Turkish to the technical constraints of Perso-Arabic prosody had not yet been overcome, Luṭfī showed how this might be done. What he wrote had a rare musicality; he was a highly skilled craftsman in the use of alliteration and rhyme, and developed the rhyme-refrain very effectively. His personal touch brought a new kind of naturalness to the contrived literary conventions of his time. His *ghazals* often evoke a pleasurable thrill of recognition, as the reader comes upon a familiar saying or proverb artfully embedded within a verse:

> For joy the rose 'bursts out of her garments', because
> people compare her with you!

Or a metaphor drawn from everyday life:

> My heart seeks your mouth but cannot find it:
> maybe the little one is playing hide-and-seek!

(A small mouth was regarded as beautiful). Luṭfī also showed unparalleled mastery of the *tuyuġ*, a rare and difficult form of quatrain peculiar to Turkish. He seems to be the only author to have written a great number.

The prestige of Persian letters at Turkish courts in Central Asia and Iran had for centuries inhibited the full evolution of literary Turkish, so that its function had been largely relegated to practical use, and to books intended for the non-élite, e.g. popular religious works. It was rather avoided by Turks with literary pretensions, who preferred to write for a larger audience in Persian, the polished prestige language read by all educated Persians and Turks. None but the small Turkish élite knew Chaghatay; its development as a unified major literary language must be credited to Navā'ī. As friend and minister of Sultan Ḥusayn Bayḳara of Herat, he lavished support on its writers; but much more important is the influence of his own books, numbering more than thirty, in verse and prose, in a wide variety of styles from the simple to the ornate. His poetry comprises some 48,000 verses, almost equally divided between his four *Dīvāns* (collected poems) and his five allegorical romantic epics. Though a brilliant and inventive writer, he freely acknowledged his debt to the great Persian poets.

Navā'ī was blessed with wit and humour. In a prose work containing a fearless critique of contemporary society he brands some teachers as 'executioners of innocent children'. He is not shy of using bold and even extravagantly comical metaphors in his poetry: 'These are not stars but cotton wool, which the heavens have stuffed in their ears. – So great are my sighs for you, oh my sun [i.e. beloved]!' One of his last works, *The Two Languages on Trial*, sets out to prove that Turkish is, if anything, even better fitted than Persian to be a medium for great literature; it is able to express nuances with equal elegance and even more economy and precision. Navā'ī stabilised Chaghatay as a literary medium and his works served as models until the end of the nineteenth century.

To turn to Bābur, the Turk who conquered India and founded the Moghul dynasty there in 1526 – he not only wrote competent poetry, but also fine literary criticism. Best of all is the fresh and lively prose of his memoirs, the *Bāburnāma*. Chaghatay went on being studied in Muslim Indian court circles until the British occupation. Central Asia continued to produce many authors, but as time went on, their language became less uniform. Features of the local dialects crept in with ever greater frequency.

While the educated classes enjoyed Chaghatay literature, it was unintelligible to most of the town, village and steppe population. They had their own parallel folk literature. The most popular poet is, perhaps, Makhdūm-ḳuli (1733–*ca.* 1782), an educated Türkman, who cultivated the forms of folk poetry in secular love lyrics, and also wrote didactic works and religious songs. Religious poetry had been popular for hundreds of years throughout Central Asia, in a style going back to the hymns of Aḥmad Yasavī, a mystic and saint of the twelfth century. These songs remained widely current until the Bolsheviks took over these regions, which were incorporated into the Soviet Union in 1924. Local languages were now elevated to independent literary status. The largest among these were Uzbek, Kazak, Türkman and Kirghiz. The Arabic script was abolished, in favour of Latin alphabets (1927–28), which were themselves replaced in 1940 by modified Cyrillic ones, each slightly different, so that related languages would be less mutually intelligible. Thus the break with the unifying influences of the Islamic and Chaghatay past was completed. The various modern literatures in these languages have by now become more closely related to Russian literature than to any in the Islamic world.

Western Turkish literature, including Ottoman and Āẕerī: Fużūlī, Bāḳī, Yūnus Emre.

Bigger, richer and more diverse than the Eastern Turkish literatures are those that developed in 'Western Turkish' i.e. the language of the Ottoman Empire and Turkey, and of its much smaller neighbour to the east, Āẕerī. Āẕerī was always under strong Ottoman influence; at the same time, however, several essentially Āẕerī poets were popular in the Ottoman Empire – usually in Ottomanised form. The Turkish *ghāzī* warriors who broke into eastern Asia Minor in 1071, gradually spread across the peninsula. For the first couple of centuries the Seljuk rulers, though ethnically Turks, used Persian as their official written language, while Arabic was the main language of scholarship. When the Seljuk state broke up in the latter part of the thirteenth century, the Turkish leaders of the small *ghāzī* successor states, as a rule, knew little of Persian and Arabic. Consequently Turkish became much more important in their local court circles, and, as a result, many Persian literary works were translated into it. The local poetry came under increasing influence from the Persian. Developments in western Turkish paralleled those in Chaghatay. At the regional courts the Persian metrical system was adopted and a new kind of Turkish literature grew up. For some time its practitioners were still in close touch with the language of the common people amongst whom they lived, but after the middle of the fifteenth century this changed. During the previous century and a half the small Ottoman state had steadily been expanding, until it included most of Anatolia and much of the Balkans. The capture of Istanbul in 1453 gave the Ottomans a new capital with ancient imperial traditions. Their court soon became an almost self-contained entity where a very sophisticated, if artificial, literature matured. Turkish words were often displaced by Persian and Arabic loanwords with supposedly more poetic overtones. Turkish writers strove to develop an acceptable blend of the native literary tradition with the more polished one of their Persian neighbours. Their pioneering efforts may have looked somewhat clumsy to later Ottoman generations, but considerable merit was shown by some of these early authors, such as Sheykhī (Şeyẖī, d. 1431) in his lyrics and his romantic epic *Khusraw and Shīrīn*. Still greater skill, wit and grace marks the work of Nejātī (Necātī, d. 1509), the earliest master of the *ghazal*. His way of introducing local imagery and proverbs is reminiscent of Luṭfī's work in Chaghatay, a century earlier and half a continent distant.

By the sixteenth century classical Ottoman (court) poetry had achieved maturity. Authors were no longer constantly looking over their shoulders at the Persian masters, but took pride in their own distinctive creations, which developed some fresh imagery and new themes. Only a few of the greatest can be mentioned here; perhaps the most outstanding are Fużūlī and Bāḳī. Fużūlī (d. 1556) was not in fact a typical Ottoman. He was born into an Azerbaijani family in Iraq, where he seems to have spent his entire life. The Ottomans conquered Baghdad in 1534, and so Fużūlī's later work was largely subjected to Ottoman linguistic norms, but his early output was entirely in the Āẕerī dialect. He was very well educated in all fields of Islamic learning, and left prose and verse in Persian and Arabic, as well as in his native Turkish. In all of them his deep scholarship is evident. Like most of the poets, in his verses he constantly takes up the theme of love. In his case, however, this is not just the conventional pastime, but arises from his all-consuming passion for the Divine, which pervades almost every line he wrote. A contemporary biographer described him as 'prostrate on the path of (mystical) self-annihilation', his 'heart wrecked by love'.

Fużūlī held the mystical *ṣūfī* doctrine that all beauty in the world is merely a reflection of the divine beauty, and that one who loves another, really loves the element of divine beauty within him. Fużūlī therefore occasionally addresses his verses to a human lover, but in general the direct object of his yearning is God himself. Unlike so many in quest of their beloved, what he seeks is not 'Union with the Beloved', but the quest for its own sake, for Union would bring an end to the sweet sadness of longing, and without this pain, life would not be worth living:

O Lord, make me very familiar with the calamity called love./ Let me not for even an instant be far from the calamity called love.

This verse comes from *Leylā and Mejnūn*, Fużūlī's allegorical epic. Based on a 'Romeo and Juliet' episode from Arabic literature, which had been beautifully reworked in Persian by Niẓāmī (d. 1209), the theme was again taken up by Fużūlī and re-created into a highly original and very moving tale of spiritual love. The beautiful and unattainable Leylā represents God, and Mejnūn the poet himself.

Fużūlī's greatness is particularly evident in his *ghazals*, which are distinguished by their pathos and human compassion. The rhythm is musical and the language and form deceptively simple. They are spontaneous and deeply felt, and the centuries since they were written have not dimmed their inner fire. No other Turkish poet has been so widely read, learned by heart, admired and loved throughout the Turkish world from the Balkans, and across Asia to the frontiers of China. His influence on all three major Turkish literatures – Ottoman, Āẕerī and Chaghatay – has been immense, and he still remains unequalled in poetic power. It seems impossible to render his *ghazals* into a non-Islamic language in a way which will give even an inkling of their beauty, harmony and sincerity. While Fużūlī was essentially a serious man, he had a good sense of humour, which shows through in some of his word-play and puns. In one of his verses he remarks:

The preacher describes Hell. Go to his sermon, you bigot, and see what Hell really is!

In one of his lighter *ghazals* about love and wine almost every word has two different meanings – one a lyrical expression common in love poetry and the other a scientific technical term. To make sure no one takes him too seriously his penultimate verse advises:

Better far than a thousand lessons offered by a professor in the college/ is the goblet proffered by a beauty in the tavern!

Fużūlī is the supreme master of feeling in Turkish poetry. In technique, however, he was surpassed, half a century later by Bāḳī (1526–1600), who is generally recognised as the great master of form. The ambitious young scholar's talent for poetry matured into genius; he solved (for himself at least) the remaining problems of blending into a unified whole the three linguistic elements (Persian, Arabic and Turkish) of Ottoman poetry. In his hands the technical difficulties vanished. His smooth-flowing lyrics have been aptly described as 'finely tooled with the care of a jeweller'.

Bāḳī's subjects mirror the pleasant aspects of upper middle-class Ottoman society. He writes of love, youth and nature: like all happiness, they are transitory, and he bids us enjoy them while we still can. The sophisticated multiple word-play and the musicality of his word choice, especially the way in which the sound echoes the sense, give his poetry a very distinctive cachet. Even as a young man he already knew how to achieve a majestic, almost orchestral effect. A panegyric to Sulaymān the Magnificent won him that Sultan's friendship. The attachment was mutual, and is perpetuated in a moving elegy which Bāḳī wrote eleven years later, when the aged Sultan died, while leading his army on a campaign in Hungary. Here are a few of the opening lines:

Oh man, whose foot is caught in the trap of fame and glory!
How long will you be taken up with the desires of this restless world?

Think of the day when the spring of your life will end,
And your tulip-coloured face will turn to autumn leaves!...

How long will unheeding sleep yet obscure understanding's eye?
Are you not warned by the fate that befell the king – that lion of war –

That royal master-cavalier of this fortunate realm,
For whose swift-wheeling steed the world's field was too much confined?

The Hungarian infidels bowed their heads before his flashing sword,
The men of Europe admired the temper of his sabre.

Graciously, like a rose petal he laid his face to the ground.
The Treasurer of the Ages placed him, like a jewel, into His treasure chest...

Many other poets of the classical period are deserving of mention, but lack of space obliges us to confine ourselves to just one more, a poet who is very pleasant to read, and somewhat ahead of his time as a stylist. In Turkey the first thirty years of the eighteenth century were called the Tulip Age. The upper classes spent as much time as they could relaxing in the beautiful tulip-filled gardens of their elegant new country mansions, communing with nature, and their friends, in unabashed luxury. The spirit of the times was delightfully captured in the songs of Nedīm (d. 1730) whose light touch and simplicity of style, make him a most enjoyable poet.

The classical poetry discussed in the last few pages was cultivated by the educated élite. The populace at large would have found it difficult to understand: they lacked the education and sophistication to do so. Their artistic needs were served by simpler material, both secular and religious. The minstrels were themselves usually nomads or peasants, who would wander around the country singing verses composed by themselves or other minstrels in the ancient Turkic syllabic metre, to the accompaniment of a kind of guitar. (Some are still active to this day.) The subjects chosen deal with elementary experiences and emotions: human love, yearning, sorrow, the round of country life. Their range also includes some epics and ballads. The treatment is of course fairly simple in content and in form, and the style is cliché-ridden and predictable. Most folk poets have been shadowy figures. Even the most gifted of the universally popular ones, Ḳarajaoghlan (Ḳaracaoğlan), is hard to pin down, his basic biography being submerged beneath conflicting legends, but he probably lived between the fifteenth and seventeenth centuries. His songs, still widely sung, show a true appreciation of the beauties of nature. Pieces inspired by longing for the distant village in which he was born, have, for centuries, struck a responsive chord in the hearts of those far from home. The beloved who figures in this folk poetry is very recognisably human and undoubtedly female. She is objectively, if conventionally, described – sometimes she is even referred to by name and village. This, of course, is in marked contrast with the treatment in classical poetry, where the description is so generalised that the object of the poet's passion normally remains a mystery – whether divine or human, whether man or woman is ambiguous.

The other major type of folk-poetry is religious. The simple style of the hymn was spread by immigrants from Central Asia to Anatolia. A saintly mystic named Yūnus Emre (d. 1320) developed the art to new heights of power and beauty. Thanks to his unique understanding of the souls of his own people, his hymns are still sung and loved all over Turkey. Himself a highly educated Muslim, he realized that if he was to transmit to his uneducated brethren the spiritual message of Islamic mysticism, he must adapt the techniques of the wandering minstrels of secular poetry. Thus most of his poems are in the syllabic metre; their vocabulary is almost confined to Turkish words and those loanwords from Arabic and Persian which were current in popular speech. His favourite themes are the paradoxes of despair and hope, sin and pardon, suffering and joy, life, death and the afterlife, and above all, man's longing for God and union with him.

Only one other religious poem has shared with those of Yūnus Emre the love of all classes of Turks: the *Mevlid* ('Birth'), a long and moving description of the birth and life of Islam's prophet. Composed early in the fifteenth century by a preacher, Süleymān Chelebi, in a simple form of the quantitative metre, it is still chanted with devotion on major family occasions, as well as on Muḥammad's birthday.

In assessing the art of another culture, due weight must be attached to the judgment of the bearers of that culture. The Turks have generally considered their finest work to be their poetry, and that is why we have given it pride of place in the present article. Turks of all classes, educated and illiterate, today as in the past, know quantities by heart. There is, however, also much notable Turkish prose. The styles run the gamut between simple and incredibly ornate, depending on the intended readership and purpose. At one extreme lie the rather artless folk tales and epics, often a mixture of legendary, religious and historical elements. Some have their source in pre-Islamic oral literature, while such adventures as the *Baṭṭālnāme* and various *Ghazavātnāmes* portray Islamic heroes and their battles with infidels in central Asia, Anatolia and the Balkans. Modified colloquial Turkish is the basis of their style. Somewhat more sophisticated, though still essentially simple in language, is the group of *Histories of the House of 'Os̱mān*. During the classical period good, clear and attractive prose was written by Evliyā Chelebi (Çelebi 1611–84), whose huge *Book of Travels* is entertaining and packed with information. There is also Kātib Chelebi (1609–57), a civil servant who was at the same time an unusually wide-ranging original scholar, noted for his excellent writing in history and geography, and for his essays and bibliography. İbrāhīm Pechuylu or Pechevī (Peçuylu, Peçevī, d. 1649) employed a similar style in his partly autobiographical history. But most of the major historians wrote in educated 'middle prose', neither colloquial nor high flown. Probably the most widely read history of the Ottoman Empire since the first quarter of the eighteenth century is that ascribed to Na'īmā (but actually drafted about 1655 by Shāriḥ ül-Menārzāde). It is famous for its lively, often dramatic, narrative. At the other extreme of prose writing lies the exaggerated *inshā* tradition of professed and often pretentious works of literary art and artifice, whose writers flaunted their learning by employing hosts of obscure expressions strung together in rhyming cadences of flowery, complicated sentences. However, in the hands of a master this kind of writing can be fascinating. *The Crown of Histories* by Sa'deddīn (d. 1599) is the most highly regarded chronicle of this kind. After poetry, history is the Turkish genre that is best developed. In writing their chronicles, the historians found fulfilment as educators, scholars and artists. The same may be said of biographical literature. 'Secular' prose developed early and became surprisingly plentiful in Turkish, long before the same was common in Persian and Arabic.

Tanẓīmāt literature: Western influence

The modernisation of the Ottoman Empire was formally initiated by the *Tanẓīmāt* ('Reorganisation') of 1839. Military men were sent in considerable numbers for technical training in France, and thus came into contact with French literature and Western ideas. The reforms in Turkey created the need for men with modern knowledge. So the educational system was broadened to provide an alternative to the religious colleges. Consequently a new kind of writing developed; its first phase was called 'the *Tanẓīmāt* literature' (*ca.* 1850–90). The founder was İbrāhīm Shināsī (Şināsī 1826–71). He had been sent to France by the Ottoman army to study statistics, but devoted most of his interest to French literature, absorbing its values and translating its classics into Turkish. It was Shīnāsī who initially supplied much of the reading matter for graduates of the new-style Turkish education. To obtain a wide readership for Turkey's first two private newspapers (which he founded in 1860 and 1862 respectively) he had to create a simpler prose, capable of expounding new concepts and subjects. It had to be instantly intelligible, yet not colloquial, as that would have been considered vulgar. From that time onwards, newspapers and periodicals have played a key role in popularising new ideas, methods and standards in prose and poetry, and have acted as powerful agents of literary, social and political change. Irregularities in the supply of news caused editors to search for ways to maintain reader loyalty. One means was the employment of regular columnists, who wrote on a wide variety of topics of current interest; another was the printing of novels and short stories, often specially written for serialisation, or translated from the French. Shīnāsī himself took up new subjects, not hitherto regarded as literary. He pioneered in drama, writing the first modern play, the more daring in that it treated a sensitive social theme: the position of women in Ottoman society (1859). His pupil and collaborator, Nāmıḳ Kemāl (1840–88), a far better writer, contributed greatly to the development of the new writing. To sum up: the major changes introduced by the *Tanẓīmāt* literature were a radically different style as the vehicle for new themes (e.g. social, religious and political) not previously considered as literary in character, and new genres: the novel, the short-story, drama and the western type of essay. All of these were powerfully assisted in their growth by the new journalism. Gradually the old classical literature went out of fashion.

New literary schools crystallised around several periodicals. Towards the end of the nineteenth century, the *S̲ervet-i Fünūn* group, led by Tevfīḳ Fikret in poetry and Ḥālid Żiyā Uşaklıgil in prose, fostered a French-inspired ornate literary style promoting 'art for art's sake'. Later on came symbolism, excellently interpreted in the work of Aḥmed Hāshim (1885–1933).

Modern literature

Of particular interest because of its long-term importance is the 'National Literature' (*ca.* 1910–*ca.* 1930) which followed the theories of the sociologist Żiyā Gökalp (1876–1924), stressing the centrality of 'Turkishness' in public life and letters, as against the cultural pluralism of traditional Ottoman society. During this period and the next (post-1930, called 'Republican Literature'), the young writers propagated his doctrines on social themes and his advocacy of a simple literary style. Among the best productions are short-stories and novels by 'Ömer Seyfeddīn (1884–1920), Ya'ḳūb Ḳadrī Ḳaraosmanoğlu (b. 1889) and Refīḳ Ḥālid Karay (1888–1965). All these writers took as their themes, for their predominantly upper middle-class readers, the harshness of village life and the undesirable features of town life. The short-story appears to have been the outstanding genre of this period. The typical author was a member of Istanbul's middle class, but the subject of his choice would most likely be the village or small town, even though he would generally have little intimate contact with either.

The short-story writers and novelists who began writing after the late 1940s have often been very different from those of the previous period. Some were peasant boys who had been trained as teachers in Village Institutes. They revolutionised literature, by displaying, with stark realism and from the inside, what kind of life was led by the villagers who constitute eighty per cent of Turkey's population. Mahmud Makal (b. 1933) was the first authentic peasant voice. His book of partly autobiographical stories, *Our Village*, had a tremendous impact on the literary scene. Today the most popular writers include many of plebeian origin, not only from villages but increasingly from small towns. Some, like Yashar (Yaşar) Kemal, whose *Memed My Hawk* portrays the adventures of a Turkish Robin Hood, are acquainted with traditional folk-story-telling techniques. Poor characterisation, lack of depth and polish, as well as excessive sentimentality are sometimes concealed by the swift pace of action in recent novels. Not surprisingly many of these authors are unacquainted with any foreign language, and have never been exposed to great literature.

The vocabulary of written Turkish has changed more in the past half century than during any previous period. From the middle of the nineteenth century, the movement for the 'Turkification' of the language steadily gained strength. Theorists, from Shīnāsī onwards, deplored the way authors tended to avoid purely Turkish words in favour of borrowings from Persian and Arabic. Later writers, under his influence, urged that only loanwords that had entered popular speech should continue in written use. Still later, the presence of even these was felt to be undesirable in principle. One basic aim of the Turkish Language Society (founded by Atatürk in 1932) was to replace such 'Ottoman' words by native Turkish ones. Where none existed, the resources of other Turkic languages were called in to fill the gap, or neologisms were created, some scarcely intelligible. The purist movement is still alive today, although in an attenuated form. Frequently a whole series of Ottoman words expressing various shades of meaning has been replaced by a single 'pure Turkish' equivalent. The result has been more impoverishing than enriching to the language and literature.

Very little has been said about drama because it has been of minor importance. There are some mildly dramatic traditions: the old Karagöz shadow play (reminiscent of Punch and Judy); and the *orta oyunu* – acted sketches replete with slapstick and folk humour. In addition there is the *meddāḥ*'s performance, where a story-teller imitates all the various stock characters. Real drama appeared on the scene in the second half of the nineteenth century, as a western art form. Plays by Molière, Shakespeare and other foreigners have been popular in educated circles for more than a century. Most of the Turkish plays written before the Second World War are not particularly good. Those of the past twenty-five years show somewhat more promise. As for the cinema, its enormous output is aimed at the urban lower classes, and as art is very primitive.

Literary criticism of a kind was implicit in the Ottoman *'Biographies of Poets'* genre, but the modern form is not yet very well developed. Two important critics were professors at Istanbul University. Mehmed Fu'ad Köprülü (1890–1966), a brilliant scholar, was the first Turk to put the historical study of all the Turkish literatures on a sound basis. Ahmed Hamdi Tanpınar (1901–62), an essayist with the heart and eye of a poet, was also noted for the musicality of his own verse.

The poetry of the Republican period is marked by several overlapping currents. Except in the work of one remarkable poet, Yahya Kemal Beyatlı (1884–1958), who expressed in harmonious verse his nostalgia for all that was best in the Ottoman past, the quantitative metres and subjects of the classical literature were finally abandoned after an existence of more than 800 years. With the rise of nationalism, the old Turkish syllabic stress metre, which had continued in use all the while for popular secular and religious verse, became the only vehicle for the writing of poetry by an educated élite, who simultaneously cultivated 'folk' themes and the modern topics fashionable in contemporary European writing. Soon afterwards free verse was introduced by Nazım Hikmet (1902–63), an innovative poet of rare talent. It was left to Orhan Veli (1914–50) to make a complete break with all previous Turkish poetry, by deliberately ignoring metre and rhyme, and refusing to limit his choice of subjects, some of them totally 'unpoetic'. And yet his work is not haphazard: it sometimes shows artistry, power, feeling, and humour, especially satire. Most of his followers were inferior. With Cemal Süreya, in the late fifties, begins the still more unconventional school of 'Meaningless Poetry', which even Turks find obscure. Free verse in the hands of a poet can be effective, but its use by a multitude of undisciplined imitators has resulted in a flood of mediocrity. There has recently been evidence of a return to rather more traditional styles.

Fazıl Hüsnü Dağlarca (b. 1914) is widely considered to be Turkey's greatest living poet. He has participated in many of these changes in poetic mood, technique and taste. A versatile, original, sometimes sensitive and powerful talent, he is also very prolific – perhaps too much so. Many of his later writings involve social and political criticism, and seem to be artistically inferior to his earlier output.

Turkish literature, from its pre-Islamic origins in Central Asia, and its classical Islamic sophistication to the present blending of traditional folk elements with modern western currents, is a fascinating study. Before it lies a challenging future.

Wall tile from Granada

9

Islamic art: variations on themes of arabesque

R. SANDLER

The arabesque is an ornamental design that is closely associated with the art of the Islamic world. But the word arabesque is also used to refer to works of art that have about them an element of fantasy, a graceful flourish, a preference for the ornate, and flowing, curving lines. It is in this sense of the word, as well as the first, that Islamic art will be treated in this chapter. For there is an unreal quality about Islamic art that suggests a source of inspiration apart from the actual world. Buildings, whether they serve a serious religious intention, or a lighter mundane purpose, are decorated with such intricate designs and wonderful materials that they are rendered fantastic and other-worldly. Solid walls are disguised behind elaborate plaster and tile decoration, and the prosaic function of vaults and arches, covered with elaborate floral ornaments, is rendered secondary. Domes are filled with brilliantly-coloured radiating designs of infinite patterns, giving the effect of bursting fire-works, rather than stone or brick structures. Walls, domes and ceilings are often covered with arabesque designs which give the impression of intricate lacework. Architectural features such as the surrounding wall and the inner courtyard, as well as the decorative effects mentioned above, convert an Islamic structure into a self-sufficient paradise. The Islamic painting, too, conveys a world untouched by reality, inhabited by delicately-drawn figures which play a role in the ornamental whole.

It was the Arabs who adopted certain ornamental leaf designs of the ancient world and developed them into a new type of ornament called the arabesque. At first, classical motifs and forms were used to decorate Islamic objects. But naturalistic forms of decoration were gradually eliminated; patterns became more abstract and a new style of decoration incorporating the arabesque was evolved. The marked sense of rhythm which pervades Arabic poetry and music was expressed visually in a design of decorative leaves and branches which could be intertwined in different and fanciful ways, and divided to form an endless number of new variations. The arabesque suited very well the Islamic artistic desire to fill an entire surface with ornamentation. Spaces ranging from the curve of a huge dome to the cover of a small metal box were covered with continuous repeat patterns.

The arabesque is a major element of Islamic art at all times, and occurs in objects made throughout the Islamic world. Persian, Turkish and Indian artists used this ornamental form as well as the Arabs who invented it. It was used for every type of decoration: for architectural decoration, for carved wooden and stone surfaces, for painted surfaces, in the decoration of pottery, glass, metal work, bookbinding, in book illuminations, and in the patterns of Islamic rugs. The leaves and branches of the arabesque are found in combination with various types of geometric decoration, plant and animal forms, human figures and patterns of flowers. Arabesque designs mingle with figures and animals to decorate pottery produced in twelfth-century Iran, and in fourteenth- and fifteenth-century Spain. We find a design of floral elements and abstract linear motifs filling the surface of an early ninth-century ceramic plate produced in Iraq, as well as being used for architectural decoration, stone carving and a crystal beaker produced in Egypt during the Fatimid period. The Arabic script, also a basic form of Islamic ornament, is often combined with the arabesque; in some cases, the arabesque forms a background for the calligraphy, while in others, the letters themselves end in ara-

Turkish dish (Iznik), sixteenth century. This is typical Iznik ware in its use of a sprayed design of realistic flowers which would be coloured in red, blue and green

Decorative carving near the Mihrab of the Cordova Mosque. Note the characteristic arabesques

Mosque lamp. Syrian or Egyptian, probably twelfth century

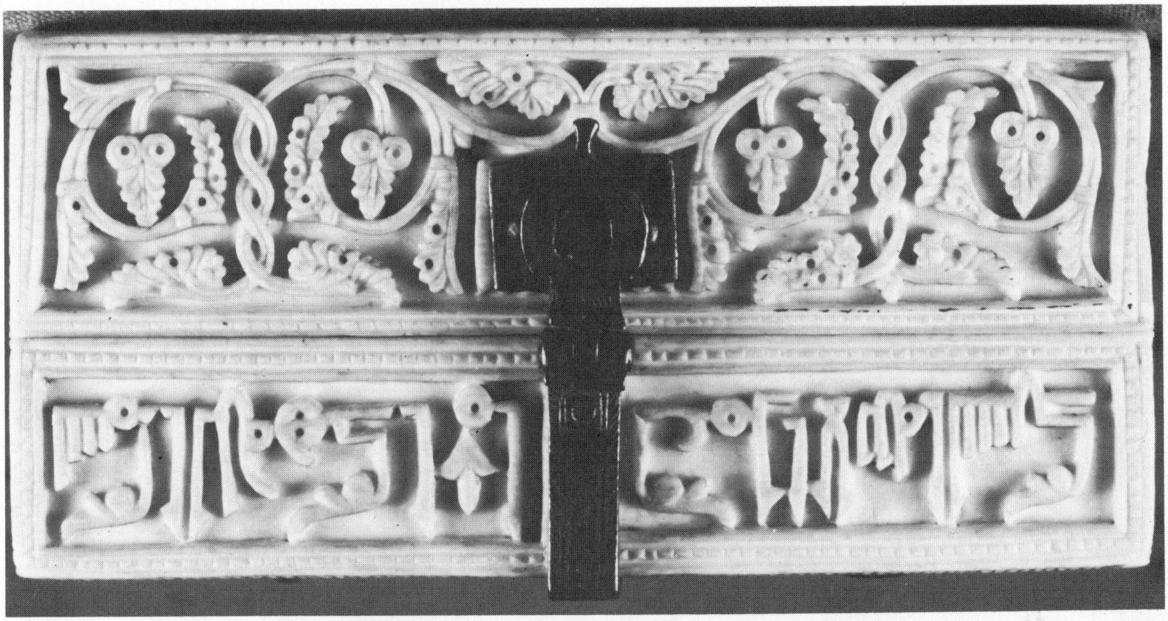

Ivory casket. Cordova, 962. This is a typical Mahgribi adaptation of the Kufic script and combination of letters and leaves

Earthenware dish, Samarqand, ninth century. The decoration around the rim is a Turkic adaptation of the Kufic script

besques, or letters and arabesques may be interwoven.

While a great proportion of Islamic buildings have been lost due to, among other factors, earthquakes and poor building materials and techniques, some of the buildings constructed centuries ago are still standing today to give us some idea of what Islamic architecture looked like at the highest peak of its development. Architectural decoration became progressively more ornate, particularly in the eastern part of the Islamic world. The entire exteriors of buildings were faced with decorative tiles and glazed bricks displaying geometric designs, arabesques, scroll patterns and floral designs, all in brilliant colours. Lustre-painted tiles were used for interior wall decoration transforming the walls into blazing sheets of gold.

The structure of the Shaykh Luṭf Allāh Mosque (built in the Persian city of Iṣfahān between 1602 and 1608 by the Ṣafavid Shāh 'Abbās, and named after his father-in-law, who was one of the foremost preachers of the day) is a simplified version of the common plan of the Persian mosque (which is in turn, a modification of the Arab mosque plan). The entrance portal of the mosque leads directly into the domed interior (more commonly, the entrance portal leads into a court surrounded by walls which are broken in the centres by towering portals, and the largest of these portals leads to the domed sanctuary). In contrast to the simple structure of the mosque, the decoration, both exterior and interior is exceedingly complex. The ground of the tile-work on the outside of the dome is a unique unglazed buff yellow, rather than the usual glittering blue. The dome is decorated with glazed white, turquoise and deep blue arabesques which entirely cover the soft yellow surface of the dome. The combination of unglazed and glazed decoration gives a quivering glitter effect to the surface of the dome when the sunlight strikes it. The decoration of the interior of the dome seems to lead the eye upwards towards its centre, as the rings of ornamental bands filled with arabesque patterns become smaller and smaller. In Ṣafavid times, the mosque faced the great royal polo ground, as if to emphasize the Islamic connection between the secular and the religious. To-day, the polo ground has been turned into a garden, and the mosque is artfully reflected in the pool in the middle of the garden.

The Ottomans preferred the flower as an ornamental device, and the interiors of the mosques and palaces in Istanbul are like flower-gardens with their multi-coloured floral tiles. The huge complex of the Topkapı Palace of the Ottoman Sultans still stands to-day, overlooking the Bosphorus. One notices here the Ottoman decorative preference for naturalistic flowers in the tile-work: we find the tulips, roses, carnations and hyacinths also found on Ottoman pottery.

Like the Topkapı Palace, the Alhambra Palace in Granada, completed during the middle and last half of the fourteenth century, stands on a hill above, and removed from, the city. In contrast to the undecorated exterior of the palace, the interior is decorated in an extremely lavish manner. The walls are covered with a combination of tile and stucco work, which is truly astonishing in its intricacy. Use has been made of highly ornamental patterns of Arabic inscriptions, in combination with abstract linear elements and arabesques, but despite the complexity the inscriptions still remain readable. Geometric shapes dominate the tile-work. The colours are strong, with shades of green, orange and blue predominating, and the fact that the shapes are generally large makes the colours appear even stronger. Every conceivable surface area is decorated; even the roof of the Royal Baths in the harem is dotted with star-shaped windows which were once covered with red glass. Each of the many separate units of the palace is arranged around an outdoor court, giving the feeling of immeasurable peace and tranquillity. The only sounds, except for those which rise up from the city, come from the numerous fountains and water basins in the courts. Water courses which begin outdoors, continue on into the interiors, extinguishing the difference between outdoor space and indoor space.

As in Islamic architecture where decoration assumes more importance than the structures themselves, so in painting, great attention is paid to ornamentation and the pattern of composition. The Islamic painter did not create pictures out of ordinary life, but sought to convey in his painting an idyllic world, or one illumined by a religious, mystical or ethical ideal. In this, he was, no doubt, influenced by the Islamic perception of the world. Islam understood the world to be only part of a totality, one half of which was inhabited by man, and the other half by God. The world had little value in its own right: it was merely the stage for man's enactment of God's

Iṣfahān, Shaykh Luṭf Allāh Mosque. The overall decoration is both subtly symmetrical and ornate. The sparing use of the arabesque design on the dome is particularly effective

Granada, The court of the lions, Alhambra. The continuation of water courses into the interior is typical of the Moorish use of water to span long distances

Ivory box, late medieval Spanish-Moorish. The figures are very similar to those found in contemporary European Christian churches. The eagle on the left was used as a symbol of power by European kings and knights

Embossed silver casket, Moorish, 976. The rim of the lid is decorated by Arabic writing

will and for God's creativity, rather than a panorama of self-starting variables. Furthermore, both the form and the methods of Islamic painting militated against the portrayal of an individual concept of reality. Islamic pictures are nearly always illustrations of literary, historical and religious texts, and it is not until recent times that we find individual artists departing from traditional subjects and methods to examine social and psychological truths in their work.

The Muslim painter was just one of the many who contributed to the Islamic art of the book. The first to work on a manuscript was the calligrapher, who copied the text and transformed the letters into decorative elements in their own right. Next came the illuminators who gilded and painted the title pages and margins of the book. Often, the Islamic miniature is surrounded by margins of delicately-drawn leaves and flowers of gold, which are as pleasingly decorative as the paintings themselves. Spaces were left for the illustrations and finally it was turned over to the painter. The calligrapher shared enormous prestige with the painter, and the name of the calligrapher often appears along with that of the artist of a particular manuscript.

The artists were supported by royal workshops, for at all stages in Islamic history, Islamic rulers drew the literary and artistic élite of the empire to their capitals, often vying with one another for the particularly gifted. Schools of painting were formed, centred in a particular city, and artistic traditions were handed down from one generation to the next. The atmosphere in which the artists worked tended to dilute artistic energy and spirit. The sense of unreality transmitted to the pictures resulted, no doubt, as much from the inbred isolation of the artists, as from the range of their subject matter. Every so often, a painting did appear which was recognisably greater than most. The greatness often lay in the individual painter's creativity within the bounds of his subject matter and techniques, or the breadth of his view of the totality of the painting, and sometimes, but here very rarely, in the sympathetic and humanistic portrayal of his characters.

In spite of a common misapprehension that Islam prohibits the representation of human figures, figural motifs occur in Islamic painting from the very beginning, and there is no prohibition against them in the Qur'ān. But during the eighth century, those who took the commandment against graven images to the extreme became opposed to the imitation of human and animal forms, and these types of forms are not found in religious buildings or as part of the decoration of the Qur'ān. One feels that this attitude inhibited the Islamic use of figures, even when it did not prohibit their use; for while human figures are used to elaborate stories, they are rarely more than yet another decorative element, and are used in much the same way as geometric and plant motifs are used, that is, in the service of a decorative whole.

As they had no pictorial tradition of their own, the early Islamic artists used the models provided by the cultures of the conquered territories, particularly those of Byzantium and Iran. Gradually, they fashioned an art of their own which was neither Byzantine, nor Persian, but a new combination of all the cultural traditions which contributed to Islamic civilisation.

The earliest surviving Islamic miniature paintings are drawings of medical herbs and the ways in which they are prepared for medical application. These drawings serve as explanations for an early thirteenth-century Arabic translation of a Greek medical text, produced at the 'Abbasid court in Baghdad. The herbs are drawn in a simple manner, against an undecorated backdrop. In one of the miniatures, the stance, the dress and the facial characteristics of the two doctors preparing a medicine are clearly copied from Byzantine models.

Only a limited range of books was illustrated during this early period of Islamic painting: medical treatises, books about animals, a few volumes of lyrical poetry. One popular Arabic classic describing the imaginary adventures of its bohemian hero (the *Maqāmāt* of al-Ḥarīrī) was illustrated many times and in many different areas of the Islamic world. Three separate copies of this text indicate the debt of Islamic painting to other cultures, as well as the evolution of a new style. An early copy of the text shows figures with Byzantine-type haloes, and it is clear that contemporary and earlier Christian paintings served as models for the illustrations. In another copy, the figures do not have haloes, but they are elongated in the manner of classical painting and are draped in the classical style. The faces of the figures are replicas of Hellenistic models, the colours are subdued and the background is flat and undecorated. In yet another rendition, the combination of eastern and western models is very noticeable. The figures are

Page from a Persian chronicle, Mughāl school, about 1595. The border depicts an earthquake in the city of Rayy. The text at this point deals with the Caliph Mutawakkil, killed by the Turks in 861 in Baghdad, and his successors

Painting from an early thirteenth-century Syrian copy of al-Ḥarīrī's *Maqāmāh*. The figures are noticeably affected by Byzantine art and their heads are bare, contrary to Islamic custom

Painting from a copy of al-Ḥarīrī's *Maqāmāh*, made in Baghdad in 1237. Unlike the figures in the slightly earlier Syrian copy these figures are wearing turbans short and stocky rather than tall and languid, and they are wearing tunics and trousers similar to the costumes found in subsequent Islamic pictures; their turbans mark these pictures as belonging definitely to the Islamic world. The faces of the figures are a cross between Byzantine and Mongol. The colours are varied, gay and brilliant rather than subdued. The background is dotted with shrubbery and simply-drawn flowers reminiscent of the earlier 'Abbasid herb drawings. The shapes of the figures are outlined in a decorative manner so as to call attention to the composition rather than to the individual figure. As time went on, the eastern and western manners of painting were blended more subtly to form a new and distinct style of painting in Persia.

The first paintings to survive in large quantities are those which belong to the Mongol period, and histories of painting in the Muslim East usually begin with these. However, a school of book-painting existed before this period, but because of the scarcity of examples, very little is known about this school. A painting from the only surviving illustrated manuscript of the pre-Mongol period indicates clearly the direction which Persian painting was to take. This miniature is extremely intricate in its total effect. The background is decorated with large palm-shaped, continuous scroll patterns. Instead of dominating the picture, the figures are made to blend into the decorative whole by being grouped in a pattern which imitates the background design. The decorative scrolls convey a sense of rhythmic movement, while the figures on their horses remain static, as though caught in mid-action.

The complexity of artistic tradition in Mongol Iran is shown in a late thirteenth-century painting of Adam and Eve in which old styles are continued and new ones added. The semi-nude figures of Adam and Eve are somewhat unique in Islamic painting. Central Asia provided the models for the figures which are drawn in a solid manner. The flat background is punctuated with grass and flowers which are rather primitive and blunt, in the style of the early 'Abbasid herb drawings. The colours are bright, as in the third rendition of the Arabic adventure story mentioned above. A painting from the same period and the same area of northwestern Iran shows the definite Far Eastern influence on the development of the Mongol style. The treatment of the subject matter, a multi-coloured phoenix, the finely-drawn trees and flowers, and the water, are Chinese in inspiration. A three-dimensional effect is given to the picture through the addition of a number of planes of action.

By the early part of the fourteenth century, many manuscripts of the *Shāhnāmah*, the long poem recounting the adventures of the kings of Persia, had been copied and illustrated with miniatures. A multitude of paintings show the ancient Persian kings hunting, being crowned, fighting their enemies. While some of the paintings are extremely successful in conveying something of the powerful narrative and the deep emotions, others seem to reduce the action of the poem rather than to develop it. Perhaps much depended on the artist who appears to have exercised some degree of choice as to how to approach his subject and which aspect of the story to dwell upon. Three different paintings of the same tale from the *Shāhnāmah* illustrate this point. In the first painting, the king visits the humble home of a peasant and his wife. Although the setting as depicted in the poem is the simple home of the man and his wife, and the king is travelling incognito, the latter appears seated on an elaborate throne, surrounded with richly embroidered pillows. In a second picture of the same tale, painted in a different city, the king sits on a simplified throne. While both painters seem to have been following an ancient model for the king, the first artist chose to develop the kingly aspect to the utmost degree. In the third painting of the same tale, the king does not appear on a throne but rests against his saddlebag, in the room with the man and woman. The fact that the king is supposed to be overhearing the conversation between the two is shown by the position of the couple who have their backs turned to the king. Obviously, this aspect of the story has been ignored in the first two paintings, in favour of portraying the king in all his kingly glory, regardless of the actual details of the tale.

A number of minor schools of painting arose in different localities after the end of the Mongol dynasty. Some of the paintings produced at this time show the difficulty of portraying action without the use of artistic judgment whereby certain figures are assigned key importance, while others are made less important. The figures are all of equal size, and the same amount of detail is applied to each one. As a consequence, the eye is positively overwhelmed.

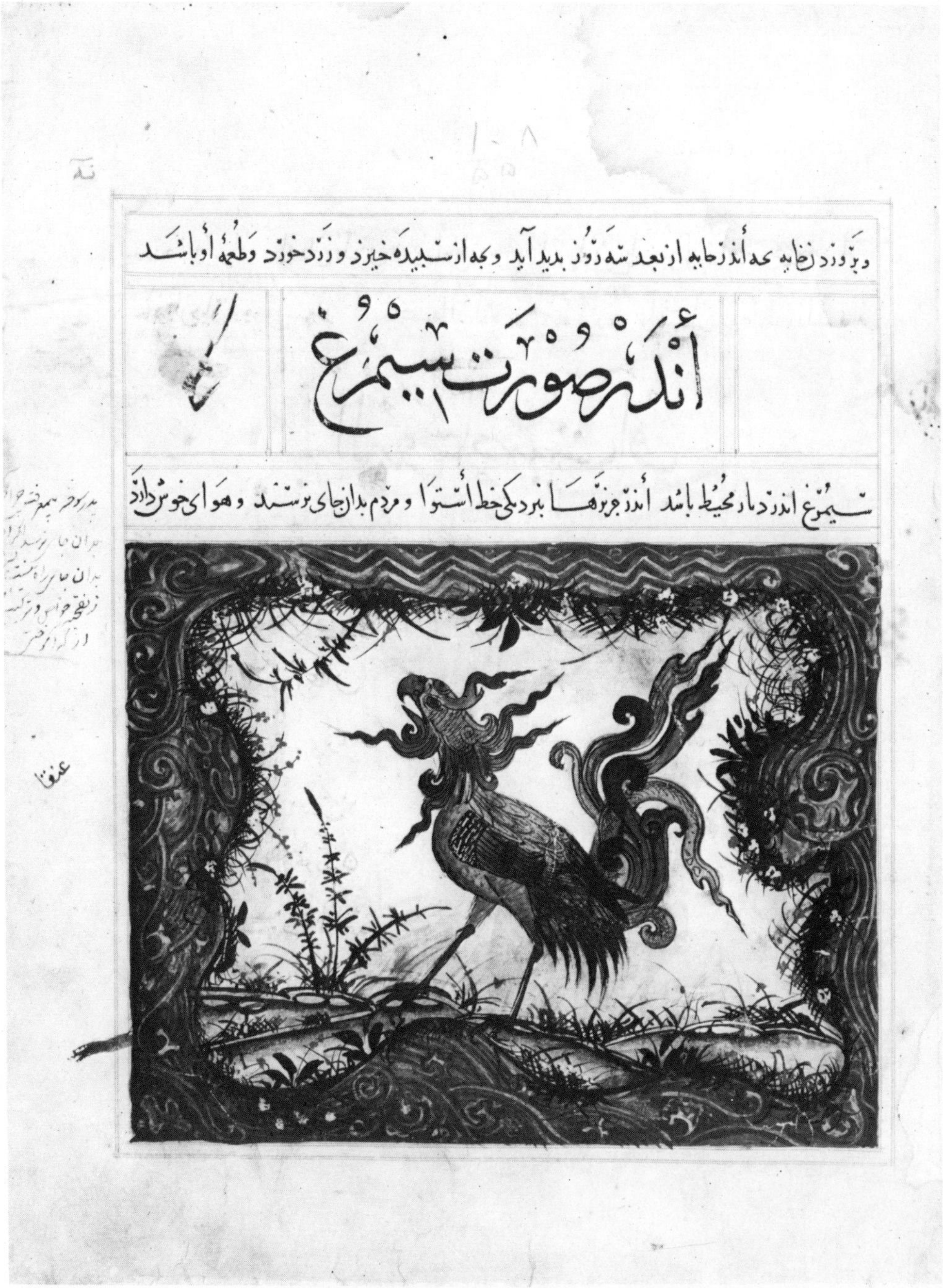

Painting from a late thirteenth-century Persian copy and translation of an Arabic work entitled 'The Uses to Which Animals Can Be Put'. The title caption reads 'Concerning the Form of the *Sīmurgh*'. The *sīmurgh* is a sort of phoenix of Persian legend. Above the caption details are given of the *sīmurgh's* birth and habitat and it is compared with the Arabic fictitious bird called the '*anqā*

Painting from the late thirteenth-century Persian manuscript mentioned on p. 103. The stylistic features are discussed on p. 102.

The figures and animals tend to be drawn on a large scale and strung across the width of the picture, filling the entire space. The total effect is one of overcrowding, as if an ill-conceived stage design had squeezed together too many actors on to a small stage. This shortcoming was eventually mastered by the introduction of a high horizon which lengthened the picture and provided more room for the figures to move about.

The new high horizon was at first used in a simple way, with the figures occupying large spaces on different planes of action. But the new horizon provided the means for making the pictures more and more complex and detailed. The paintings became intricately-worked decorative patterns, developing a tendency that was present in Islamic painting from the very beginning. The landscape scenes, now drawn in a very delicate manner, gave way to more complicated scenes which often involved ten or more groupings of people, all following their own activities. A single painting could move from an outdoor scene indoors to a palace, with different rooms of the palace being shown. Lacking perspective, outside and inside areas were separated by such devices as palace walls. All the details of highly decorated walls and floors, as well as the details of the costumes, were present in the more ornate of these paintings.

The *Shāhnāmah* continued to be illustrated, while other books familiar in the 'Abbasid and Mongol periods became less popular. New works appeared: histories of new rulers, and enlarged and continued renditions of older histories. From the mid-fifteenth century, another work of Persian literature rivalled the *Shāhnāmah* as a popular subject for illustrations. This was the *Khamsah*, a collection of five poems by the poet Niẓāmī. Usually, only one or two popular scenes from a work were selected for illustration, and in only a very few rich volumes were most of the scenes from the story illustrated.

One of Niẓāmī's poems most frequently illustrated by Persian painters is the love story of Laylā and Majnūn, the children of Arab chieftains. A miniature from an early sixteenth-century copy of this poem shows Laylā and Majnūn in the schoolroom where the boy Qays falls so deeply in love with Laylā that he is called by his schoolmates, Majnūn or 'the possessed'. Laylā and Majnūn sit in a classroom richly decorated with tiles showing geometrical mosaic patterns, arabesques and floral scrolls. The variety of colours is startling: shades of red and blue, white, yellow, gold, black, orange, brown, green and beige. Bookstands, pencil boxes and ink pots are scattered about the floor. Pupils read or doze; in the foreground, one boy pulls another boy's ear. To the left of the classroom scene, two boys are playing in a courtyard indicated by a change of wall and floor decoration. At the head of the class sits the old bearded teacher who holds a rod in his hand. A boy standing on the roof is the only person portrayed in a fairly naturalistic way; he displays annoyance at the racket below him. The faces of the other children are unusually serene, and they sit or kneel in stiff, stylised positions. One has the impression of a magnificently-patterned embroidery – extremely pleasing in its decorative detail, but flat and incapable of involving the onlooker.

From the end of the twelfth century, Egypt and Syria were closely tied together once more and some of the miniatures so favoured by the Mamlūk rulers in Cairo were painted in Syria. The figures in the miniature paintings of the Mamlūk school are, generally speaking, like dolls or puppets. The paintings are predominantly decorative rather than interpretive. The repertory of subjects is the same as for the rest of the Islamic world. A miniature from the popular adventure story by al-Ḥarīrī mentioned above shows a king being entertained. There is nothing at all realistic about this work. The figures are arranged in a decorative circle around the king, and we are looking at an ornamental setting rather than a picture of a king being entertained. The figures are non-Muslim, modelled after Byzantine types.

In the middle of the fifteenth century, the Ottoman conqueror of Constantinople established a court school of painting in this former Byzantine capital. The Ottoman Turkish Sultans imported painters from Persia, and a good deal of work done in Turkey was an imitation of the Persian style. But a distinctly Turkish style of painting gradually evolved that was realistic and fresh in comparison to the pictures we have been discussing. The Turkish miniatures are simple and much less sophisticated than Persian miniatures. Turkish paintings tend to illustrate the history of the day, the lives of the Sultans and ordinary city life, and this served to give them a quality of actuality wholly missing in the more idyllic Persian paintings.

Painting from an Egyptian copy of al-Ḥarīrī's *Maqāmāt*, dated 1334. The painting combines eastern and western Islamic influences

The unique realism of the Turkish paintings is paralleled in one other group of Muslim paintings: those produced in Mughal India. While the early paintings reflect the Persian tradition, a decidedly non-Persian style developed in India. Like the Ottoman painters, the Muslim painters in India illustrated historical events – battle scenes, court life and hunting scenes; intimate scenes of the emperor and his harem or family, and actual portraits of the emperors record the real lives of the Muslim nobility. A painting showing soldiers and oxen pushing a cannon up a steep hill depicts an actual historical incident during the emperor Akbar's campaign in Rajastan. Notwithstanding the mass of detail, hundreds of figures, trees, part of the emperor's encampments, and the emperor himself standing at the top of the hill with his attendants, the painting imparts something of the crush, confusion and hardship of a military campaign. The strong, deep colours, very different in texture from the colours found in Persian paintings, are inherited from the Hindu tradition.

While a great proportion of Islamic paintings subtly convey the idea of a dream-world, a painting of a dream of the Indian emperor Jahāngīr, expresses quite deliberately the emperor's desire for peaceful relations with the Shah of Persia. Jahāngīr, slightly taller and more imposing than the Shah of Persia, embraces the Shah who responds somewhat submissively. The emperor stands on a lion, while the Shah stands on a lamb, indicating Jahāngīr's wishful

Mughal painting depicting siege operations during the emperor Akbar's campaign in Rajastan, c. 1600

thinking about their relative strength. The wishful dream is understandable; what is surprising is the attempt to portray the unattainable, when the bulk of Islamic paintings confidently portray paradise attained.

The old historical romance declined in popularity in Persia, and during the late sixteenth and seventeenth centuries the taste of the age turned away from battles, to studies of single figures and pastoral scenes. Pictures were collected and mounted in albums for noble and wealthy patrons. Miniatures from literary texts were separated from their original manuscripts and inserted into the leaves of an album, but more often painters produced separate portraits or prepared panels of calligraphy for the albums. Although literary manuscripts continued to be illustrated during the seventeenth century, the emphasis was on the preparation of album leaves, and this continued well into the nineteenth century.

Although Persian painting was influenced by European painting before the seventeenth century, this influence was intensified by the direct contact between European and Persian painters in the middle of that century. The results of this influence were disastrous for Persian painting. A picture entitled 'Convivial Party', attempts to substitute perspective for the traditional high horizon, with highly unsatisfactory results. The figures are larger than the figures in older Persian miniatures, but even less life-like. The people eating and drinking together are stiff and unrelaxed, perhaps echoing the reaction of the Persian painter himself to the new European subject matter and techniques.

As is the case with other spheres of life in the Islamic world, the values which produced Islamic art have gradually died away, and the art of this world has been overwhelmed by Western ideas and techniques. Modern buildings in the Middle East are Western-inspired, although free use is still made of indigenous decoration. New office and administrative buildings are often constructed with the aid of Western advisers. Middle Eastern architects design buildings which reflect Western taste, and new residential districts are largely Western in appearance.

However, along with decay there has been growth. Islamic artists are learning how to look at the world around them for inspiration, and how to use the new Western techniques in the service of their art. Subject matter is now attuned to the problems of each of the Middle Eastern countries, as well as to worldwide artistic developments. Artists examine the life of the people and nature, and deal with social injustice and the suffering of the poor. Where once artists worked in the rarefied atmosphere of the court, and for the tastes of the court, modern artists use their art to express political views (and have often been forced to leave their countries because of this). The battle between the old and the new is complicated by the fact that the old is indigenous and the new is alien. And there is the problem of public taste which seems to have been non-existent, or at least, conventional, for centuries.

While the Islamic heritage is discernable in some of the more traditional artists, many of the modern painters have opened up their work to a surprising degree. One particular work is faintly reminiscent of the calligraphic rendering of words, although the shapes are much larger and blunter, really not at all like the delicate calligraphy of old. A poster made up of computer printing has been produced in Iran, and the subject of women, and relationships between people, are explored in new and unromantic ways in paintings produced in Iraq and Kuwait. The use of original techniques is very noticeable in scenes of labourers in the Lebanon and a bullock-cart in Pakistan, half abstract, half life-like. Certainly, Islamic art is not any longer the art of the arabesque, but what it will be is not yet apparent.

Workers' Monument in Liberation Square, Baghdad. The figures are in various poses of heroic action. The sign in Arabic on the right reads 'The People's Garden'.

A contemporary painting of a street scene by a pupil in a school in Jiddah, Saudi Arabia. The openness of life in the street contrasts sharply with the covered-up facade of the houses

Astrolabe, Cairo, 1236, brass with silver and copper inlay

10

The Middle East as a world centre of science and medicine

G. M. WICKENS

The average man in the West takes science and medicine for granted, not only as activities likely on the whole to benefit him, but as the necessary accompaniments of civilised life. Indeed, for many people civilisation itself would be defined primarily in terms of achievements in science and medicine. If this point of view is not to be absurdly naive, it must be qualified by a realisation that it is not universally valid by any means. There have been great civilisations, like the Inca, for example, which lacked any real science and practised only a somewhat rudimentary medicine. On the other hand, there have been societies which, despite the highest skills in science and medicine, have hardly deserved the title 'civilised' – like the Nazi regime of 1933–45. Even in our own contemporary Western society, the correlation is no longer always very obvious; and some people argue plausibly that the arts of civilisation currently flourish best where science and medicine are not conspicuously to the fore.

Be that as it may, it always remains necessary to explain why and how a given society comes to concern itself with science, and what sort of science it concerns itself with. (Medicine often develops as a natural and consequential human application of science; the primeval fears of humanity sustain an abiding interest in an activity that constantly produces surer and more numerous cures for all the many ills of body and mind.)

One must begin with some definition of science and medicine that will illuminate the case for Islam, making clear what we may and may not expect in the period when the Middle East was a great centre of science and medicine. Modern science in its strictest sense (and this includes medicine) is observational, experimental and relative. It deals primarily in observed processes and relationships (neither in simple 'facts' nor in elaborate 'theories' of the old-fashioned sort); it demands lengthily repeated, measured reproduction of the observed phenomena (one instance, or even several instances, in uncontrolled circumstances being of no use whatsoever); and it constructs limited and infinitely modifiable hypotheses on the basis of these observations and experiments (again, these are no longer stated as grandiose and immutable 'laws' such as were the very hallmark of science up to about 1900).

Modern science, furthermore, has no purpose in itself beyond the investigation of an immediate problem, and the relating of that problem to certain (but not necessarily many) others. Accidentally or (in applied science) deliberately, it offers man increasing knowledge and control of himself and his environment. But it no longer looks to find ultimate 'causes' or answers to any of the great questions of the religious devotees, thinkers, poets or artists. Thus, modern science disregards authority as such, whether it be the authority of earlier scientific findings or that of religious experience; and its concern with pure, if fallible observation, measurement and hypothesis places it outside the very dimensions of philosophy, theology, literature or art. Paradoxically, this means that the average man, and even the specialist himself, while awed by science, has long found himself even less 'at home' with it than was his remote ancestor with Nature in the raw. The happy honeymoon from about 1700 to 1900, when science was accepted in the West as an exciting new component of general culture, is now irrevocably past. General culture now has to make radical accommodations with science to ensure its own meaningful survival.

One must realise that science, in the full sense that we have been describing, is a purely modern, Western creation: whatever apparent foreshadowings of it are found in other times and places, they are either fragmentary or else accidental and unconscious. Neither Islamic nor any other traditional science ever went to such objective, sceptical, relative, and existentialist lengths as these.

Islamic science and medicine, like all pre-modern types, *were* generally respectful of authority, and operated within a framework of religious, philosophical and human reference. There was, it is true, considerable observation and experiment, but this was usually confined to details or to practical matters (agricultural, medical, metallurgical, etc.), on which the less technologically-minded Ancients had made no received pronouncement. If the Ancients were known to have spoken, whether from observation and experiment or merely out of reflection or wishful thinking, little further investigation was usually undertaken. Moreover, even where there was fresh observation and experiment, there would always come into play, far too early and too definitively, an elaborate process of theorising, categorisation and pattern-making. Neatness, design, symmetry, numerical harmony, circularity – these were sought at all costs, and out of all proportion to the observable realities. Like its counterpart in the medieval West, this was a great advance on mythical or superstitious accounting for real phenomena; it was even, in some cases, an advance on the scientific work of the Ancient Greeks. But it is difficult to see how any of these postures – Ancient Greek, medieval European, or Islamic – could ever of themselves have developed into modern science as we know it. All three were caught in one or more blind alleys, and the cataclysm that was to provide a way out would take place only in the West. Nevertheless, modern science could not have got started without a footing in these earlier researches.

Islamic science and medicine began, somewhere around the years 650–700, in a complex tradition deriving from the Greeks, the Persians, the Indians and even the Chinese. By about 600 the originality and vigour of Greek science and medicine, as exemplified by Aristotle, Ptolemy, Archimedes, Hippocrates and Galen, had long since disappeared throughout virtually the whole of the post-Hellenic Middle East. Some tradition still survived, now mediated as much in Syriac as in the original Greek; but even the occasional flicker of *new* life in such places as Alexandria, was too often smothered by the occult and mystical beliefs and practices endemic in Egypt. Moreover, during the fifth and sixth centuries, religious persecution in Eastern Christendom and a growing obscurantism towards scientific endeavour had driven many Syriac-using scholars of the Nestorian heresy from the Byzantine Empire to Persia; here, among others, a renowned school of science and medicine was built-up in Jundishāpūr. This basically Greek school was enriched by influences native to Persia, and by continued contacts with other dissident Byzantine scholars in India and China. It still flourished at the time of the Islamic invasions of Persia, around 640.

The rulers of the first great Islamic empire, the Umayyads, had no interest in science as such. Medicine was more personal, and they brought physicians (mostly Christians and Jews) from Jundishāpūr to look after their health in Damascus – and also, incidentally, to look after other affairs, for these were men of wide competence. With the change in capital to Baghdad, when the 'Abbasid line assumed power in 750, not only did a more intellectual climate develop, but Persian influences in particular became pre-eminent at all levels. Diverse works on science and medicine were now translated into Arabic (from Greek, Syriac, Middle Persian, etc.) as part of a great campaign to exploit earlier creativity, thought and experiment in all ages. The preoccupation of rulers with their health was still a powerful driving force, and mathematics and astronomy were important to such vital pursuits as agriculture, irrigation and land-survey; but a genuine intellectual curiosity for its own sake was active between 800 and 850, and the impetus of this age carried the Islamic civilisation forward for some three or four centuries to come.

The most famous of the translators of this period was Ḥunayn ibn Isḥāq (809-77), himself a physician with a strong attachment to Galen. More than this, together with his son and his nephew, he produced perhaps the greatest corpus of *general* translation by any one group in the whole history of the Islamic translation movement. (His influence more than any other led to Galen's domination of medicine in the Middle Ages and later, both in Islam and in Christian Europe. This does not, of course, explain why such deference should have been paid to a Greek physician *at all* over so long a period – that being a general reflection of society and intellectual climate.) To sum up, then, we have by the mid-ninth century a large, though incomplete, body of material in Syriac and Arabic that fairly adequately represents the intellectual heritage of the great ages of the past. It would be added to and corrected in some points over the next fifty years, but the substantial bulk was already available. At best, it provided a stimulating take-off point for new endeavours; at worst, it would be constantly digested and commented on by scholars for nearly 1000 years to come. Much of this material would eventually reach Western Europe, particularly through translations from Arabic into Hebrew and/or Latin in Spain. In some cases the translations were bad, with misleading new errors compounded upon old; and some works were themselves spurious, at least in their ascription to a particular great name such as Aristotle; at the same time, Western Europe might of itself never have obtained the Greek originals at all, as in fact in some instances it never has.

By about 850, this material was Islamic only in the following senses: that it had been chosen to suit new and growing needs of the Islamic civilisation, though the actual selection was often made by non-Muslims; that it was largely available in the primary cultural language of the Islamdom of the time – Arabic, which had by now almost wholly ousted Syriac as Syriac had earlier ousted Greek; and that there were an increasing number of Muslims, both translators and direct students, who were thoroughly familiar with it. But, even by 850, apart from the active side of the Jundishāpūr tradition as carried on in Baghdad, this scientific-medical material was still largely inert and bookish. However, a time would shortly come when all this material was both activated and truly Islamicised.

Even by this period, one branch of science was apparently very active – the primitive chemistry we still call by the Arabic form 'alchemy'. Alchemy, like astrology, conjures visions of superstitious dabblings in the 'black arts'; but this is a mere folk-memory, for alchemy, like astrology, has a respectable – if mistaken – basis in scientific theory. The theory in this case is that all matter is composed of one or more of the four anciently accepted elements: earth, air, fire, and water; that all metals are essentially identical; and that accordingly all that is needed to convert base metals like iron into noble metals like gold is an agent (called an 'elixir': another Arabic form) to re-arrange the elements. (Modern atomic science says something similar, but the reasons and processes involved are immeasurably more complicated than was then realised. The cost is also staggering.)

The most famous name in this early alchemical research is that of Jābir (before 800?), though much (if not most) of what is attributed to him seems to belong to a later period. Characteristically for an alchemist, his name is linked with occult practices, esoteric religious doctrines, and revolutionary social and political ideas – to say nothing of an interest in the mystical properties of numbers. He did much incidental work with metals and salts, and this was useful in developing foundry techniques and glazing processes for tiles and other ceramics. Once again, what impeded real advances here – and what would do so, in both East and West, for centuries to come – were less the wilder fantasies than the faulty, if elegant, theories that were considered immutable: e.g. that the elements were four in number, and were the precise ones handed down by the Ancients, that metals were seven, and so on.

Also active at this fairly early period, in all sorts of scientific ways, was the great philosopher al-Kindī. He was particularly interested in sound (an offshoot of his concern with music), in meteorology, specific weight, tides and optics. Most of his actual writing is now apparently lost, but in its day it enjoyed enormous prestige in both East and West. Again, just after 850 there appears a cooperative treatise on mechanics, dealing particularly with the movement and pressure of water. At about the same time several works were written on animals, plants and stones, though their scientific value is often sacrificed to literary conventions. Much new *practical* work was also being done in pharmacy, as the growing Islamic civilisation opened the market to both new drugs and remedies and the strange new skills that went with them. Finally, sugar-cane and musk, attractive novelties though they must have seemed at the time, became insignificant beside the first successful Islamic paper-manufacture at Baghdad, just before 800. (It would be several centuries before this Chinese craft was practised in Europe.)

We come now to the period, *ca.* A.D. 900 to *ca.* 1100, when Middle Eastern science and medicine became a flourishing and integrated function of Islamic society as a whole; a function, moreover, largely performed by Muslims themselves, though Christians and Jews always remained particularly important here as compared with most other areas of social and intellectual activity. Above all, in this period these activities yielded really original results, in contrast with the earlier two centuries of passive pupillage to an ancient culture itself already more or less static. Unfortunately, the freshness and vigour would not last beyond 1100; thereafter Islamic science and medicine would themselves lapse into the conservative repetitiveness from which only the violent irruption of Western culture would eventually 'rescue' them.

Two other points should be made here. First, that an abnormally high proportion of the great Muslim scientists and physicians continued to come from a Persian background, though their scientific work was usually recorded in Arabic (which played a comparable part to Latin in medieval Europe). Secondly, that while these activities were *in fact* an essential part of Islamic society, they were never formally recognised in theory; what were called 'The Islamic Sciences' were studies concerned with the elucidation of God's word and purpose: textual analysis, Arabic linguistics and literature, history (particularly of the life, actions and sayings of the Prophet and his Companions), and the Law. Virtually all other intellectual activity was lumped together as 'The Foreign Sciences'. Unfortunately for the Middle East the formal, official attitude again became dominant as society itself lost its resilience and drive. In the West, while education *officially* connoted, from about 1550 to about 1850, little more than a particularly dry study of Greek and Latin texts, society in fact met its own dynamic needs by allowing and encouraging all sorts of other investigations outside the formal educational framework.

The sciences that flourished most strikingly during the period 900–1100 can be classified under three general heads: medicine, mathematics and astronomy. Many other things were done, but it was in these three branches that by far the most significant contributions were made to mankind's scientific heritage. If these contributions were practically all in matters of particulars, without any general breakthrough, there are good and obvious reasons for this, given the respect shown in Middle Eastern society at that time to 'authority'; and given, too, the preoccupation with premature and elaborate theorising, and with religious, philosophical and human frames of reference. It is not that the modern Western way is essentially better, for quite clearly it leaves vast masses of people most unhappy. Scientific achievements of the Western kind demand a high price in terms of attitudes and procedures; and *no* society, at that time or for centuries thereafter, could remotely contemplate paying such a price.

Given these limitations, then, let us try to see why these three sciences – medicine, mathematics and astronomy – were able to advance so far beyond other branches. First, medicine. Despite all the ancient jokes about the casual attitudes of doctors to life and death, many physicians at this time had to take an independent and original line in observation, diagnosis and treatment. The realities of disease in the medieval Middle East were too obtrusive for it to be otherwise – to say nothing of the obvious inadequacy of many of the findings of the Ancients, and the ever-threatening penalties for failure. If independence and originality are, so to speak, in the air, some individuals will be outstanding for such qualities; and so it was in medieval Islam. Given its excellent start and the conditions it now encountered, medicine, then, could hardly fail to prosper – at least up to a saturation point of originality adequate to a society that would itself soon become static once more.

The case of mathematics is almost the reverse. No scientific activity could be better suited to the conditions generally prevailing; for mathematics is *par excellence* the great field of pure theory, of elegant and economical demonstration in the abstract, of the rational recognition of beauty in the ordering of things. It is only in our own age that other aspects of mathematics have emerged under the pressure of application by the true, experimental sciences: such aspects as the theory of number, randomness and probability, non-Euclidean geometry, and topology. In medieval Islam these pressures were not operative, and mathematics accordingly developed very effectively to meet the needs of the social and intellectual climate prevailing.

The case of astronomy parallels that of mathematics, for it is the true science nearest to classical mathematics – at least when it is practised with the simplest of instruments for observation and measurement. Before the age of the telescope, let alone of radio-telescopy and space-exploration, astronomers made all sorts of discoveries beyond the general astronomical lore inherited from the Ancients of many nations. But certain discoveries they could not make with the instruments then available; above all, they missed those discoveries that would upset the

Moghul emperor engaged in astronomical observation, with astrolabe, zodiac tables and hourglass. An early seventeenth-century border design from Shah Jahāngīr's Album

whole pattern of their astronomical and other thinking, e.g. that *none* of the heavenly motions at all was perfectly circular, or that the planets were not merely five in number (seven, with sun and moon), and so on. As with mathematics, this is *not* a situation in which social and intellectual attitudes inhibit all advancement (which was partly the case for alchemy); rather is considerable advancement possible, within the limits set, precisely because of the largely theoretical nature of the fields in question and the lack of technological or true-scientific pressure or support. In observation and calculation (whether for agricultural or astrological purposes), practically everything that could be done was done, at times with remarkable accuracy.

Before we discuss a few of the great names and their contributions, it may be well to deal briefly with any misplaced feelings of superiority, on the part of modern Western man, in such matters as astrology and flat-earthism. Astrology (like alchemy) was based on a reasonable – if partly mistaken – scientific theory, namely that the heavenly bodies influenced the earth and its inhabitants. By the time we are speaking of (and this was largely true also for Western Europe somewhat later), most educated Muslims were at least sceptical about the scope of such influences; they might well accept the seasons and the tides as controlled in this way, but many doubted that their daily lives were similarly affected in minute detail. Moreover, official Islam (like official Christianity) generally condemned astrological prediction as blasphemous impertinence. Nevertheless, many people – and particularly the great and powerful – were as addicted to astrology then as now; and some astronomers earned their keep by preparing astrological tables and horoscopes. As to flat-earthism: Eratosthenes of Alexandria calculated the earth's circumference with considerable accuracy some two centuries before the Christian Era. His findings were sometimes overlooked, even when similar calculations were made later by Islamic scholars; but practically no educated person in medieval Islam (or, later, in medieval Christendom) really believed the earth was flat. Al-Bīrūnī (d. 1048) and others even suggested the possibility of the centrality of the sun in a solar system, with the earth both revolving around it and turning on its own axis; but, for various reasons, this did not then seem the most likely hypothesis.

Middle Eastern medicine at its peak was strong in observation and diagnosis, and in treatment by drugs; it was weakest in surgery. Two reasons, among others, may be suggested for the latter. First, though anatomical knowledge was more accurate than in the contemporaneous West, it was still handicapped by similar socio-religious objections to the use of cadavers for research. (As an exception, eyes seem to have been freely available, and Islamic ophthalmology was outstanding.) Secondly, while many surgical techniques had been known from ancient times (e.g. trepanning, amputation, Caesarean section, minor internal operations, etc.), at the same time anaesthetics, sterilisation and shock-neutralisation were all so primitive that recovery was rare. In one respect, the Middle East in the period 900–1100 had far outdistanced the West: in the provision of many great public hospitals, in the Jundishāpūr tradition, with proper budgets, permanent staffs, and the freely donated services of many distinguished physicians.

Let us look briefly now at two out of all the several hundreds of names still on record. Typically, they are both Persians, known to the West respectively as Rhazes (d. 923? or 932?) and Avicenna (d. 1037). Rhazes began professional life as an alchemist; but even there his work was markedly rational and unmystical, emphasising laboratory organisation and technique. Like Jābir, mentioned earlier, his alchemical researches have passed into the permanent chemical lore of the wider world. When he eventually abandoned alchemy (and several other scientific activities) for medicine, he took these same qualities into his new work. He 'humanised' medicine by considering the patient's problems and attitudes; and he did much to remove its ancient priestly pretensions to mystery and infallibility. He had a better knowledge of anatomy than many of his colleagues. Perhaps the best known of his 100 or more medical writings are those on smallpox and measles, and on kidney- and other 'stones'. But his medical encyclopaedia (*The Comprehensive Work*, in 20 volumes) covers the whole range of medical knowledge, contrasting what the Ancients said with his own clinical experiences and opinions. Much of his work was translated into Latin and later into other Western languages, and he was quoted and commented upon in Europe until well into the nineteenth century.

Avicenna's talents were manifold, with medicine often subordinated to philosophy and state-affairs. He was also well versed in general science, writing on such topics as geology and meteorology; in alchemy he firmly opposed research on the transmutation of metals. His medical skill was comprehensive rather than specialised, but he did important original work in ophthalmology and also on infection. He too wrote a medical survey, called *The Canon of Medicine*. Despite its bulk and its very complex classification, it gained pre-eminent acceptance. Translated early into Latin, it practically dominated European medicine until well into the seventeenth century.

Despite the long-lived influence of Middle Eastern medicine on Western medical practice, few Arabic medical terms have entered European languages. In the cases of mathematics and astronomy, however, Western languages are full of Arabic words (as they are also from alchemy), but the influence of these sciences themselves is much less. In many cases (e.g. with the formula for the addition of angles; and with work on fractions and on a type of logarithm), some Middle Eastern discoveries seem to have remained unknown in the West and were made afresh by Descartes, Leibniz, Napier and others.

Islamic mathematics rests on two broad foundations: Greek geometry, and Indian arithmetic and algebra. But the Middle East mathematicians made striking contributions of their own in all three fields, and also in trigonometry. Their most effective advance in arithmetic was, of course, the organisation of the decimal system called by us 'Arabic numerals', about which more will be said in Chapter 11. But the glory of Islamic mathematics really lies in other fields. The very word 'algebra', of which these people now made an exact science, refers in Arabic to an operation with equations; and it was here that particularly remarkable things were achieved, e.g. by Omar ('Umar) Khayyām (known to us primarily as a Persian poet), who advanced from the quadratic to the cubic stage. What limited their full development of algebra was the lack of systems of coordinates and mathematical notations. On the other hand, the Islamic mathematicians laid the groundwork for analytical geometry, and they virtually created plane and spherical trigonometry. Baṭṭānī (d. 929) placed

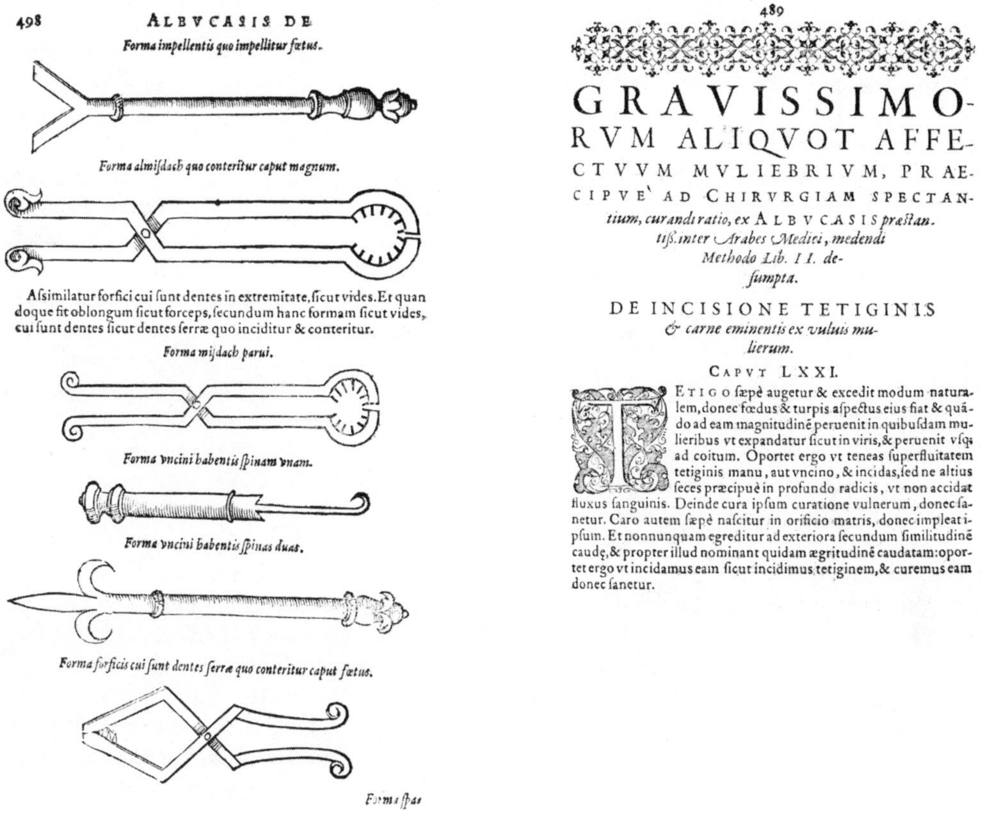

498 ALBVCASIS DE

Forma impellentis quo impellitur fœtus.

Forma almiſdach quo conteritur caput magnum.

Aſsimilatur forfici cui ſunt dentes in extremitate, ſicut vides. Et quandoque fit oblongum ſicut forceps, ſecundum hanc formam ſicut vides, cui ſunt dentes ſicut dentes ſerræ quo inciditur & conteritur.

Forma miſdach parui.

Forma vncini habentis ſpinam vnam.

Forma vncini habentis ſpinas duas.

Forma forficis cui ſunt dentes ſerræ quo conteritur caput fœtus.

F:rma ſpas

489

GRAVISSIMORVM ALIQVOT AFFECTVVM MVLIEBRIVM, PRAECIPVE AD CHIRVRGIAM SPECTANtium, curandi ratio, ex ALBVCASIS præſtantiſs. inter Arabes Medici, medendi Methodo Lib. II. deſumpta.

DE INCISIONE TETIGINIS & carne eminentis ex vuluis mulierum.

CAPVT LXXI.

TETIGO ſæpè augetur & excedit modum naturalem, donec fœdus & turpis aſpectus eius fiat & quádo ad eam magnitudinẽ peruenit in quibuſdam mulieribus vt expandatur ſicut in viris, & peruenit vſq; ad coitum. Oportet ergo vt teneas ſuperfluitatem tetiginis manu, aut vncino, & incidas, ſed ne altius ſeces præcipuè in profundo radicis, vt non accidat fluxus ſanguinis. Deinde cura ipſum curatione vulnerum, donec ſanetur. Caro autem ſæpè naſcitur in orificio matris, donec impleat ipſum. Et nonnunquam egreditur ad exteriora ſecundum ſimilitudinẽ caudę, & propter illud nominant quidam ægritudinẽ caudatam: oportet ergo vt incidamus eam ſicut incidimus tetiginem, & curemus eam donec ſanetur.

Illustrations and a chapter opening from a Latin translation of a treatise by Albucasis on diseases of women

trigonometrical ratios on an elegant new basis by substituting the sine for the old clumsy use of the chord; he also popularised the tangent and the cotangent, which interested him in connection with the shadows on a sundial. Despite the abstract nature of these researches, and their lack of integration into the other sciences and into society at large, time and again, there arise these unlikely departure points taken from ordinary life: legal disputes over land surveys, musical scoring (particularly important for fractions), time-and-distance relationships and so on.

Astronomy, as originally known to the Islamic Middle East, was a mass of lore inherited from the Ancients – particularly from Egypt and Babylonia – and mediated through the genius of the Alexandrian Greek Ptolemy (d. *ca.* A.D. 150). Ptolemy propounded a system of revolving, transparent, 'star-studded' spheres, set one inside the other like a Chinese puzzle, with the earth at the centre. It more or less accounted, with the addition of a few epicycles here and there, for all phenomena observable at the time, and it was never seriously challenged in the Middle East – or in the West until the seventeenth century. What Islamic astronomy did, primarily, was vastly to refine all the observations and calculations involved, renaming many of the stars and constellations in the process (several of these, such as Aldebaran, Altair and Betelgeuse, are with us still). To do this, they improved both the main instruments used, the armillary sphere and the astrolabe, and built them much bigger to minimise error. So good were their star-maps and astronomical tables that they were used in both Europe and the Far East for centuries to come. Again, two outstanding names deserve special mention: Baṭṭānī and 'Umar Khayyām, both already cited in connection with mathematics.

Baṭṭānī worked on such matters as the timing of new moons, the length of the solar and the sidereal year, the prediction of eclipses, and the phenomenon of parallax. The latter is of fundamental concern for astronomers; it also brings us to the verge of relativity and the space-age. But here again, it was as with his discoveries about the path of the earth and other bodies: they might have led to a really fundamental challenge to Ptolemy; but the habit of authority was too strong, and the system was patched up by adding a few more epicycles. 'Umar Khayyām's great accomplishment was to participate in revising the old Persian solar calendar: the result was a calendar still not superseded, even by the main calendar now used in the West.

Why the Middle East never invented the all-essential telescope and microscope remains a mystery, for at least one man (known to the West as Alhazen, d. 1038) did ingenious work in focusing and magnification, and with a primitive form of camera. But it was not to be. Moreover, as we have indicated, the practically essential lines dividing medicine, astronomy, mathematics and philosophy were often blurred, with the same man working on all four, and philosophy (or theology) too easily taking precedence. Problems like those of infinity or atomicity lent themselves to intellectual speculation; and rigorous observation and analysis seemed superfluous. This was perhaps truest in Spain, with such otherwise great names as those known to the West as Averroes (d. 1198) and Avenzoar (d. 1162). In general, in the sciences, Spain was renowned for astronomical tables and botanical studies, though much else was cultivated, even if without great originality. For the West, of course, her overwhelming contribution was her part in the *transmission* of much of this learning and research.

About the period of decline, or rather stagnation (roughly 1100–1800), in the scientific life of the Middle East, little need be said here. Much, if not all, of this mass of knowledge was handed down in academic digests and commentaries; and also in popular works of literature and entertainment. What eventually happened had already been foreshadowed in a science with very practical implications, that of geography. Starting again from mainly Greek bases, the Islamic Middle East was soon producing its own accurate accounts of people and places both far and near, with precise measurements and locations. Already, by about 820, the meridian degree had been computed with only 1 per cent error, thus giving a very fair estimate of the globe's dimensions. Yet, while for centuries to come *practical* Middle Eastern travellers and traders journeyed enormous distances by both sea and land, *formal* Islamic geography rapidly congealed into a mass of received facts, sometimes erroneous and increasingly outdated, and spiced with fantasy and conjecture. Islamic scholars of the ninth and tenth centuries in general knew more about the West than did their descendants of three and four centuries later, and the gap between fact and fancy, real and ideal, was only to widen – with a partial exception in the case of the Ottoman Empire at its height.

When such a wide gap lasts for too long a time, both individuals and societies are due for trouble. Small wonder, then, that this civilisation was to undergo extreme shock and trauma when the outside world finally obtruded in a form it could neither assimilate nor ignore.

Page from an Arabic copy dated 1222 of the *Materia Medica* by Dioscorides (Greek physician, c. A.D. 40). The top picture shows a consultation and the lower a physician declaiming on the virtues of a medicinal herb

11

What the West borrowed from the Middle East

G. M. WICKENS

In the broadest sense, the West's borrowings from the Middle East form practically the whole basic fabric of civilisation; and they date from the earliest times, long before history began to be recorded some 5000 years ago. Without such fundamental borrowings from the Middle East, we should lack the following sorts of things among others (unless, of course, we had been quick and inventive enough to devise them all for ourselves): agriculture; the domestication of animals, for food, clothing and transportation; spinning and weaving; building; drainage and irrigation; roadmaking and the wheel; metal-working, and standard tools and weapons of all kinds; sailing-ships; astronomical observation and the calendar; writing and the keeping of records; laws and civic life; coinage; abstract thought and mathematics; most of our religious ideas and symbols. Whether all these things were actually invented from scratch in the Middle East (and it seems probable that most were, while the rest were intensively developed there), it was from the Middle East that they came to the West over the ages, particularly between 1000 B.C. and A.D. 500. There is virtually no evidence for any of these *basic* things and processes and ideas being actually *invented* in the West. Of course, without the initial help of the Middle East, the West might conceivably have gone through some (even many) stages of independent development, like Ancient China or the civilisations of Northern India. Or it might perhaps have remained totally independent and developed its own, somewhat lopsided, civilisation, like those of the Central and South American Indians. Equally probably, it could easily have remained near where the South African Bushmen or the Australian aborigines were until recent years: very well adjusted to survival in their surroundings, courteous and dignified, interesting to anthropologists and psychologists – but hardly 'civilised' in any meaningful, high-culture sense of the term.

The borrowings to be discussed in this article, however, are not these early basics, but the later, less familiar, less essential things taken at random from Middle Eastern culture between about A.D. 800 and 1800. The sort of thing in question might be suggested by a provocative sub-title originally envisaged for this article: Sherbet and Tulips, Tens and Tabby-Cats. For things or names like these (usually both) we are indebted to the Middle East in all sorts of fascinating and mysterious ways, of which we shall be able to indicate only a few. But first some words of caution. Any attempt to trace borrowings of this kind is always difficult, requiring as it does a knowledge of many languages, and also a sound acquaintance with economic and cultural history over wide areas. One special reason for our difficulties is that these borrowings lie essentially in the domain of trade (imported foods, cloths, implements, weapons, ornaments, and luxuries of all kinds); and trade – especially in pre-modern times – has always been a secretive, economical and practical business. Merchants usually have seen no reason to waste time and money, or to help governments or competitors (or inquisitive historians), by writing long accounts of the source and special value of their imported wares. Occasionally, we are lucky enough to get a Marco Polo-type travel-journal; sometimes a merchant's private files survive by accident; but most of the time we are obliged to make deductions from passing references in the records and literature of the times, or from the names that have come into the language along with the new things themselves. This last is by far our most common source of information, and a very perilous one it is to employ.

Here are some of the curious pitfalls of this method on which we are obliged to place so much reliance. First, there are an incredible number of purely chance resemblances. For example, the Celtic *skean* is practically identical with an Arabic word for '*knife*'; but whatever borrowings took place in the dawn of history, Celts and Arabs did not exchange sharp blades at any time, and neither needed the other to supply them with a name for so basic an instrument of human survival. Secondly, these words have to be traced from English, through French and Italian or Spanish, to Turkish or perhaps Urdu, and on to Arabic or Persian, according as the object in question travelled through one or more of these various areas of Middle Eastern and, later, Western culture. In this process of travel, all sorts of things may happen to the name and even to the object. 'Magazine', for example, particularly in the sense of a storehouse for goods or munitions, comes from the Arabic, but by no means directly. The Arabic plural *makhāzin* was adopted as a singular by the Italian traders of the late Middle Ages (e.g. Genoa or Venice), either direct from an Arabic-speaking country like Egypt or, more likely, from Turkey or Persia, where Arabic plurals were often used as singulars. Then, as an Italian word *magazzino*, it passed into Old French as *magazin* (modern *magasin* = 'shop') and thence to English. Nowadays, of course, it is most familiar to us in the sense of a 'storehouse' of interesting articles and pictures, a miscellaneous weekly or monthly periodical. Finally, in this abbreviated catalogue of problems that arise in tracing borrowings of things by their names, we must be sure which way the borrowing is going. If you met the modern Persian word for a smart big-city store, *maghāzah*, you might assume either that it was taken direct from the Arabic above, or that it itself had given rise to the modern French word *magasin* in the same sense. Neither would be true: *maghāzah* was borrowed *back* from the French in modern times, when smart stores on Western lines began to appear in Iran. This is where cultural and economic history can sometimes be usefully employed as a check on linguistic data. Incidentally, even this proven back-borrowing may have been not direct but through Russian, for nineteenth-century Russia sometimes served as a cultural staging-post between France and Iran.

In a study of this untidy process of intercultural loan, almost anywhere will serve for a beginning, so we may return to Sherbet and Tulips, Tens and Tabby-Cats, and see some actual examples of these curious workings. In North America, of course, and in the world closely influenced by it, a sherbet is a sort of flavoured water-ice. (In Britain until recently it was a sort of cheap fizzy, sweet powder, once much loved by poorer children.) The word, though neither of these precise things themselves, comes to us through Turkish and Persian from Arabic, where it simply means 'drink'. (In Middle Eastern usage, it early came to refer in particular to a sweet watery drink.) From the same Arabic root also comes our word 'syrup', the original form being this time not *sharbat* but *sharāb*; again, there was once in English a word 'shrub', in much the same sense as 'syrup', so that it looks as though both 'shrub' and 'syrup' came into English from the same source, but by different linguistic routes. The Arabo-Persian word *sharāb* itself now commonly denotes 'wine'. If you compare this with 'sherbet' and 'syrup (alias "shrub")', you will see another problem in tracing borrowings: the fact that the original word and/or the borrowings often shift their meaning, their object of reference, with the passage of time. (Perhaps the most notorious example of such a shift is the word 'alcohol', which in the original borrowing from Arabic first denoted 'antimony powder'.) Anyway, here is a good example of our indebtedness to the Middle East in the area of food and drink. Other items of this kind are: Shish-kebab, pilaf (or pilau), Turkish delight and halva. Three of these, it will be noted, are still sufficiently new and foreign to preserve an un-English look and a somewhat fluid spelling, as well as to be used still only in reference to a clearly exotic item. One day, they may become more Anglicised and given wider or different application.

With 'tulips' we are on very safe ground, for their introduction into Europe from Turkey, ultimately from Persia, is fantastically well attested in literature. Indeed, in the sixteenth and seventeenth centuries Europe went through a literal tulip-mania, both for the flower itself and for its characteristic shape in clothing, art, ceramics, and so on. There were even financial scandals attending tulip-promotion schemes, particularly in Holland. Once again, the word itself passed through Italian and French: the original Persian word *dulband* meant essentially a 'turban' or 'turban-shape', quite different words normally being used for the tulip itself.

The 'invention' of Tens (the third item in our list) has already been alluded to in Chapter 10. Again, the system itself may have been initially invented in India (as Middle Easterners themselves generally believed), but it was from the Middle East that the West derived it, as is suggested by our common term 'Arabic numerals' and its predecessor 'algorisms' (a corruption from the name of the mathematician al-Khwārizmī, d. about 844). The essence of the system is to use an individual sign for each digit from 1 to 9 and a special sign for a nil-number. After 9 the same signs are used again, but placed in a second or third column to the left of the original, when they gain a power that is ten- or one hundred-times as great, and so on. Exact tens or hundreds are kept properly spaced with zeros. Similar fractional *reductions* are made by placing to the *right* of the original unit-column, with a special separator between the unit and the decimal fraction (in the West this takes the form of a dot or a comma). This essentially simple system was nearly as great a revolution as the art of writing. It enabled the performance of rapid and complex calculations of all kinds that were quite impossible with the old letter-for-number system; and unlike the latter it could be extended indefinitely into multiples of enormous size. Modern computers have found its limitations, but its simplicity assures it of a long life to come as the basis for our day-to-day calculations. Yet despite its enormous convenience and its potential for far-reaching research, the system advanced only very slowly in the medieval West; and the clumsy old Roman numerals have survived in many areas until to-day (clock-faces, monumental date-inscriptions, book-prefaces, sub-paragraph numberings, and so on). Naturally, this is one case where the importation did not bring new names, for people do not borrow familiar words like everyday names for numbers. However, the unfamiliarly large or small is another matter: just as the modern Middle East has borrowed 'million' and so on from the West, so the medieval West borrowed 'cipher' and 'zero' (both from the Arabic *ṣifr*) to designate the new nil-number.

In the case of Tabby-Cats, there is no evidence that the animals themselves were borrowed (at least in historical times), but the reference to striped markings certainly was. Textiles were perhaps the commonest medieval Middle Eastern art-form with practical application, and most cities specialised in one or another variety. 'Attābīyah was a quarter of medieval Baghdad famous for its striped silk, which was accordingly known as *'attābī* (and then *tābī*) material. The term came into English, with the material, through Spanish and French. An enormous number of cloth-names are of Middle Eastern origin: 'fustian', from Fusṭāṭ (a name for Old Cairo); 'taffeta' from the Persian *tāftah*, meaning 'twisted' or 'woven with a twist'; 'muslin', from Mosul, in Iraq; 'damask', from Damascus; and so on. The names are sometimes easily recognised, but often the passage through several languages has disguised them from all but the expert linguist. Sometimes the same town gives us different forms for different products: apart from damask, for example, Damascus was famous for its magnificent swords and daggers, which underwent a special decorative process known as 'damascening'. These blades, and copies of them, were accordingly universally known as 'damascenes'. Another Damascus borrowing is 'damson'.

Sometimes a case of borrowing that looks essentially simple will prove to have many unsuspected complications. Take the Islamic word *dīwān* (it is uncertain whether it is Arabic or Persian in origin, but it is found in one form or another in all Islamic languages). Originally, it seems to have meant: (a) a flat bench of some kind; (b) a collection of documents (which might be anything from state-records to poems). At a fairly early stage of Islamic history, a third meaning became common: either because civil servants sat on a bench (cf. our reference to judges as 'the Bench'), or because of their preoccupation with files of papers, the word *dīwān* came to connote also something like a government department. The third meaning passed through Spanish to French as *douane*, with particular reference by now to a 'customs-office'. The second meaning did not apparently travel westwards, presumably because the West already had its own system for filing reports and poems! But the first meaning became very widespread indeed as 'divan', a sort of Oriental couch without arms or back. Until modern times, practically all similar words in common use were Middle Eastern in origin: 'Ottoman' speaks for itself, but few people might suspect the same of 'sofa' or 'mattress'. (Interestingly enough, many of these terms have disappeared from general use nowadays, especially in America, in favour of such 'upper-class', English-sounding names as 'chesterfield' and 'davenport', which tell us less about origins than about the supposed taste of the buyer.) As 'ottoman' would suggest, most of these

Middle Eastern furniture-borrowings took place through Turkey, during the initial large-scale commercial contacts, in the sixteenth and seventeenth centuries. At that relatively late period, the words themselves travelled more quickly and the various languages were better known, so that distortion and disguise are much less of a problem in identification than in the case of the medieval loans.

So far we have said something about trade, food, clothes, furnishings, implements, and general luxuries. We have also touched, with arithmetic, on the great scientific borrowings more fully treated in Chapter 10; and, with *dīwān*, we have referred briefly to borrowings in administrative organisation, particularly on the civil side. A more extensive area of borrowing than this concerns things military. Three examples must suffice here. The English word 'admiral' comes from the French *amiral* (the 'd' was inserted at some stage under the impression that the name had something to do with the 'admiration' due to this exalted rank). The French *amiral* derives, probably through Spanish, from the Arabic *amīr al-*, 'commander of the . . .', whatever the armed force in question might be. In other words, the Arabic term itself does not necessarily refer to a naval commander but to a high-ranking officer generally. Here was an innovation of enormous strategic importance, for supreme commanders, apart from kings, were not a normal feature of Western campaigning for many centuries, reliance being placed instead on the old anarchic system of Germanic–Frankish loyalty to the band-chieftain or boat-captain. Another borrowing of fundamental importance in the same way is the English word 'arsenal'. The word comes, *via* Italian *arsenale*, from the Arabic expression *dār as-ṣinā'ah*, 'craft-house, workshop'. The non-expert might well be sceptical here: were there no workshops in the West, and could the word 'arsenal' really come from a word looking so different? The answers are fairly straightforward. In the first place, while Western craftsmen in the early Middle Ages were certainly capable of making weapons and building vessels, they lacked (and often suffered for lacking) really large-scale centralised organisation of these activities until it was introduced from the Middle East. The linguistic jump is not so great as it seems: when terms are borrowed in this way, one of the commonest casualties is the initial, imperfectly heard consonant: hence the disappearing 'd' ('orange' is another good example of this, this word having begun with an 'n' in the original Middle Eastern forms). As to the inserted 'l' in 'arsenal', this was probably an attempt to cope with the heavy Arabic guttural while still giving the word a satisfactory Italian sound to finish with. Finally, in this short military list, we may cite the important feature of medieval fortification, a 'barbican', i.e. a tower guarding a gate or a bridge. It is fairly certainly from an Arabo-Persian compound meaning 'gatehouse' or 'house on the rampart'. (Many Middle Eastern military terms – e.g. *sepoy/spahi* for the very word 'soldier' itself – go back to Persian, for the conquered Iranian Empire was a great model of civil and military organisation.) While the name 'barbican' survives for a station on the London Underground, close to the old London Wall, the object itself disappeared with the widespread use of modern artillery.

By now perhaps, despite the quick superficiality of this sketch, the classes of borrowings from Middle East to West have become fairly clear, though the actual process of borrowing was of course random and untidy and long drawn out. In general, quite apart from all the *basic* borrowings we mentioned at the outset, the *secondary* borrowings also cover, though not evenly, the whole spectrum of civilised life. So far, in this survey, there are large ranges of this spectrum that we have had to leave aside; and we shall find little room for them in the rest of this article, if we are to bring out other particularly interesting features. For example, several chapters apiece could easily be devoted to the enormous debt the West owes the Middle East in the matter of musical instruments and notation; or, again, in the particularly Middle Eastern crafts of carpet-weaving, ceramics and glass-making. People in the West still recognise and cherish a fine Persian or Turkish carpet. But the other crafts are no longer sought after and imported; and the influences that all these crafts have exerted in the West are so far back in time, and have become so much a part of our own practices by now, that it has become difficult to single out striking features for comment in terms that will seem to have a modern relevance. Let us now, therefore, look at the borrowings again in general and from various other points of view.

There are some borrowings that advertise themselves loud and clear. A few examples at random: Arabian horses, gum Arabic, Turkish tobacco, Morocco leather, Iraqi dates. These are usually commodities which the borrower already enjoys in a general way, but of which he now acquires a finer or more specialised type. Incidentally, these names are often among the least reliable indicators. Turkish tobacco, for example, or Turkish towels or Turkish baths, are certainly all Middle Eastern importations to the West, but their connection with Turkey is largely incidental. (There were some comic renamings of many of these 'Turkish' items during the First World War, when the Allies wished to disown all obligations to their current enemies.) If Turkey, however, has been over-credited for loans in which it was only a middleman, there is at least one example of a grave injustice going the other way. The popular food *yoghurt* is Turkish through and through in both name and fact (though other Middle Eastern countries make a similar preparation); but all the promotional literature in the West insists on its origin in Bulgaria or some other part of the Balkans. Perhaps the most misleading place-name in a supposed borrowing is that of 'Jerusalem artichoke': 'Jerusalem' here is merely some non-Italian's attempt to cope with the Italian word *girasole*, 'sunflower'. The plant was in fact almost certainly unknown until it was discovered in North America, whence it has been widely exported.

Next let us consider those borrowings which are not accompanied by names at all, or where the names are incidental or fragmentary. We have seen the case of the decimal system, with 'zero' or 'cipher'. Another example is chess, where the one really vivid clue, in English, to its being brought from Persia (and perhaps ultimately India) lies in the expression 'checkmate', i.e. *Shāh māt* = 'the king is at a loss'. A deep-rooted misconception about this phrase is found in almost all works of reference: the expression does *not* mean 'the king is dead', which would be equally poor Arabic or Persian and an unthinkable piece of treason in a game of royal associations. Some other Western languages, particularly German, have preserved more of the original Persian chess terms and kept them reasonably intact: *shāh māt* = *Schachmatt*; *rukh* = *Roche* (cf. our 'rook'); and so on. We shall return later to the problem presented by the discrepant preservation of Middle Eastern names in various Western languages. Meanwhile, let us point out that these borrowings without names, or with few names, may be highly important (as, for example, with windmills or paper-making) or fairly 'trivial', like chess. Either way, they have become so far absorbed into the cultural life of the borrower that any foreign names have been either rubbed away entirely, or translated, or stick out here and there like an odd thorn in clothing worn in rough country.

A third type of borrowing is the sort where the name neither is blatantly advertised or obvious, nor has it become lost or badly distorted or washed out in translation. We started out with some of this class: sherbet, magazine, tulip, tabby, and so on. Here the name is foreign and can be shown to be so, but it has been so effectively 'Englished' that no speaker normally thinks of it as borrowed in any way. At the same time, the object it refers to has been either de-exoticised by repeated use over the centuries or converted into something nearer the generally familiar. These words cover all aspects of life. Apart from those we have just reminded ourselves of once more, we have taken particular note of the 'military' words (like 'admiral' and 'arsenal') and many terms relating to cloth and furnishings. A few others in this 'familiarised' type of borrowing are: coffee (originally an Arabic poetic term for 'wine'!); tariff (originally a 'statement'); jar; lemon; rice; tare (in weighing: originally 'something to be discounted'); lilac; apricot; cotton; satin; talc; sultana. In actual origin, not all such are strictly Islamic (for example, 'apricot' comes through Arabic from Greek, and 'satin' through Arabic from a Chinese port-name); but the transmission and development of all of these, and of hundreds more, was very definitely in the Middle Eastern Islamic period. Once again, it must be stressed that the Islamic world at its height was extremely cosmopolitan and energetic, a great importer and exporter, besides being a re-worker, of foreign wares and ideas of all kinds. Even after its great period was over, an enormous proportion of this 'merchandise' still circulated *within* the Islamic world, ready for appropriation by the shrewd and acquisitive West.

Some borrowings carry an ironical overtone, which would have given serious scandal at the time if all the facts had been known. Medieval Europe, for example, greatly esteemed two monopoly products of the royal workshops in the Middle East – gold coins and brocaded silks, the latter often interwoven with threads of precious metal. Now such objects not only had very 'Islamic' motifs, but they were inscribed with ornate Arabic lettering containing such things as quotations from the Qur'ān. (Needless to say, such writing could not usually be read in the West or even recognised as writing at all.) The coins no doubt would have been valued for their high gold-content and workmanship, no matter what was written on them; and in any case, they were usually crudely overstamped with a Western marking. But the silks were a different matter, for they were often all unwittingly used – either in the original or carefully copied – for Church vestments and hangings. Some few of these can still be seen in museums and ecclesiastical storerooms.

We referred earlier to the fact that although actual borrowings must have been spread pretty evenly throughout Western and Central Europe, the linguistic evidence for them varies in amount and intactness from country to country. We have, of course, been concerned here chiefly with English evidences, but the problem would look rather different if viewed from the standpoint of French or Italian or German. Two lands to be particularly careful about in this connection are Spain and Portugal; for while the Iberian peninsula, during its occupation, received a more marked impression than other places from Islamic culture, the languages alone would suggest that the effect went even deeper than it did. Practically every Spanish word beginning with *al-* and its variations is of Arabic origin, and there are many others besides. But it would clearly be absurd to suggest that Spain had to borrow from the Middle East the actual concepts themselves for 'passage', 'bedroom', 'cupboard', 'builder', 'damage', 'mayor', and so on. What happened here is much the same as in Britain during the Viking settlements: whatever the Vikings may have brought that was novel in the way of things or life-style, their linguistic influence went far beyond such bounds. The resident Anglo-Saxons, for example, certainly had legs and a name to refer to them by, but by an intelligible linguistic displacement the word we now use, in this and many other common instances, is Norse. What Spain did receive from the Middle East and the Arab world in particular (apart from a legendary high-culture), and what she in turn transmitted to most of Europe, was all manner of agricultural and fruit-growing processes, together with a vast number of new plants, fruits and vegetables that we all now take for granted. The Arabs of Spain were in fact among the world's most remarkable gardeners and cultivators.

One type of borrowing not so far touched upon is the temporary or artificial. The Imperialist period of modern Middle Eastern history produced many of these. The two centuries of British rule in India, for example, introduced into Britain (and ultimately other countries) many things from that subcontinent's varied cultures, including above all the Islamic. Such things and terms as 'gymkhanas' and 'jodhpurs' have become part of the Western world's way of life, at least among the better-off, and the increased popularity of curry has been fairly general. But an enormous number of others have disappeared in the 20-odd years since the Anglo-Indian era came to an end. Particularly quick to vanish were the several Urdu words and expressions that found their way into British army slang and thence to the population at large. Words like *dekko* ('look'), *bolo* ('shout'), *jildi* ('quick') and *rooti* ('bread') were widely used in Britain as late as 1945, but most mean nothing at all now to a younger generation. Even the many technical terms from Anglo-Indian life that were used by Kipling and other writers and taken for granted by Western historians of India (*sepoy, subadar, durbar*, rainy season, up-country, the hills, and so on) must now be explained in glossaries or avoided altogether.

Even less worthy of mention as genuine borrowings are the artificial Orientalisms for which wealthy or would-be prestigious classes have had passing crazes: the Prince Regent's fascinating but grotesque little Taj Mahal in Brighton, for example; or the innumerable 'Islamic' coffee-tables and metal trays that adorn many Western homes aspiring to a degree of refinement. Nor can one include as borrowings, though they are of course understood or verifiable in English, such concepts and terms as harem, odalisque, Vizier, Mulla, hookah, and so on. These are merely exotica for which the West has developed a comfortable, and often misleading, 'tolerance' of its own.

A true borrowing, in the sense we have used it in this chapter, fills an immediate need and continues to fill it for a long time: in doing so, it affects the borrower's way of life and usually his language in some permanent form. In this sense the borrowing must be desired, assimilable, not overwhelming or disruptive. What went in the opposite direction, from about 1800 on, did not fulfil these requirements in most cases. This is why we cannot include a companion, 'mirror' chapter with so simple a title as the present one.

Cordova, Mosque. Sixteenth-century cathedral within the former Umayyad mosque founded in the eighth century by ʿ Abd al-Raḥmān I on the site of a Roman temple and a Visigothic church

12

Christendom vs. Islam: interaction and co-existence

R. M. SAVORY

The existence of Islam has always made the West profoundly uneasy. Islam was the only major world religion to be revealed *after* the rise of Christianity, and consequently it was, from the moment of the revelation of Islam in the seventh century A.D., viewed by Christendom as a direct threat and challenge to itself. The threat of Islam to Christianity was increased by the fact that Muslims regarded Islam as having superseded Christianity. In Muslim eyes, Christianity was an earlier, and imperfect, form of Islam. Muḥammad was the last, the 'Seal' of the Prophets. Consequently, the problem of how to deal with Islam was perhaps the most important problem facing medieval Christendom.

The problem posed itself on two levels: the political and military, and the theological. On the political and military level, Christendom had two possible responses open to it: military counter-action (crusades); and more or less peaceful co-existence. On the theological level, Islam could be regarded as a Christian heresy, as a schism within the ranks of Christians, or as a new religion.

By the end of the seventh century A.D., the Mediterranean had become a Muslim lake, with Muslims controlling the whole southern shore of the Mediterranean from Anatolia to the Straits of Gibraltar. In 711, the Arabs seized Gibraltar and, within the next few years, overran the Iberian peninsula and crossed the Pyrenees. The defeat of the Arabs by Charles Martel at the battle of Poitiers in 732, though only a minor reverse for the Arabs, in fact marked the extreme limit of Muslim penetration into Europe for some six centuries. Despite the impressive Muslim conquests, however, the West saw Muslims as only one of a large number of enemies (Norsemen, Slavs, Magyars) threatening it at that time. Initially, therefore, the political and military reaction of the West was limited and *ad hoc*.

On the theological and religious level, the reaction of the West was strong, sustained and, almost without exception, hostile. Hostility was based on fear, and fear had its roots in ignorance. Christendom feared Islam, and therefore misrepresented it. Christians were ignorant of Islam, at least in part, because Christendom, prompted by *odium theologicum*, had no desire to understand or tolerate Islam. During the nearly five centuries between the revelation of Islam and the launching of the First Crusade, most Christians took an apocalyptic view of Islam. They identified Islam and its Prophet, Muḥammad (commonly represented as an impostor), with the Beast of the Book of Revelation, or with the Anti-Christ. They were content to represent Islam as a religion of violence, as a form of idolatry, as a religion which pandered to man's sexual appetites in this world and the next. They remained almost totally ignorant of Islam's real beliefs and doctrines.

For its part, Islamdom – to use a convenient term coined by G. M. Wickens – was equally ignorant of the Western world, but for quite different reasons. Christianity was forced to be aware of Islam, if only because Islam claimed to have superseded it, but, although aware of it, it did not try to understand it, because Islam was something to be suppressed and, if possible, destroyed. Islam, on the other hand, was ignorant of the West because it was indifferent to it. In the Muslim view, since the revelation of God to His Prophet, Muḥammad, supplemented and made perfect all previous revelations, it followed that Islamic civilisation was superior to Christian civilisation. The Islamic world, stretching from Spain across North Africa to the Middle East, was the centre of the civilised world. Since the West was stagnating during the Dark Ages, while Islam was at its peak, Muslims saw no reason to modify this view. I risk labouring this point because it is one which it is very difficult for us, reared on school textbooks which see world history almost exclusively in terms of European history, to grasp. Yet Muslim historians and geographers rarely bothered to distinguish between different countries or races in Europe, but lumped all Europeans together under one blanket term, 'Franks' – otherwise characterised as 'the northern barbarians'. The latter term was used by a Muslim *qāḍī* in Toledo, writing in 1068. Using a concern for science as a criterion for assessing the degree of civilisation attained by the nations of the world, he arrived at the following classification: the civilised nations were the Indians, Persians, Chaldees, Greeks, Romans (including Byzantines), Egyptians, Arabs and Jews. The Chinese and the Turks got honourable mention as 'the noblest of the unlearned nations'. Everybody else was classified as either 'northern barbarians' (the Franks), or 'southern barbarians' (Negroes). This cultural arrogance, though justified to a degree in the eleventh century, was to have disastrous results for Islam when maintained after the Renaissance.

After the battle of Poitiers, Islamdom and Christendom settled down to three and a half centuries of co-existence; at best, this co-existence was on a cold-war basis and, from time to time, hostilities were renewed. During the ninth century, the Arabs gradually conquered Sicily, and brought the islands of Corsica and Sardinia under Muslim rule. The region in which there was the greatest degree of contact and interaction between the two civilisations was Spain. There, a rich and flourishing culture developed – in many ways a unique culture, to which Arabs and Berbers, Christians and Jews each made their distinctive contribution. The fusion of Arab and Byzantine architectural styles produced such original masterpieces as the Great Mosque at Cordoba, the Alcazar at Seville, and the Alhambra at Granada. A prosperous trade grew up between Spain and North Africa, Constantinople and the eastern Mediterranean.

This fascinating experiment in co-existence was not permitted to endure. Christendom had not reconciled itself to a permanent Muslim presence in Europe, especially as this presence could not be ignored, for Islam, far from withering away, had produced great philosophers and scientists. In particular, the Muslim presence could not be ignored on the level of religion. Not only had Muslims resisted conversion to Christianity, but many Christians and Jews had become converts to Islam, and had learnt Arabic. The Archbishop of Seville was forced to have the Bible translated into Arabic – not for missionary purposes, but for use in his own community. A contemporary Christian writer expressed his disgust at the situation in the following terms:

> Where is the layman who now reads the Latin commentaries on the Holy Scriptures, or who studies the Gospels, prophets or apostles? Alas! all talented young Christians read and study with enthusiasm the Arab books; they gather immense libraries at great expense; they despise the Christian literature as unworthy of attention. They have forgotten their language. For every one who can write a letter in Latin to a friend, there are a thousand who can express themselves in Arabic with elegance.

In the eyes of the Christian church, such a situation could clearly not be allowed to continue, and, soon after A.D. 1000, Christendom abandoned the idea of co-existence with Islam and resorted to military counter-action. The 'Reconquista', or reconquest by the Christians of Muslim Spain, took nearly four centuries. In 1492, the combined forces of Castile and Aragon stormed the last Muslim stronghold, Granada, All non-Catholics were eventually expelled from Spain, and the nearly seven and a half centuries of Muslim presence there were thus terminated. In 1061, Christian arms won Sicily from the Arabs; some of the latter fled to North Africa, but those who remained attempted to civilise their rude Norman masters. One of these, Roger II (reigned 1130–54), employed Arab architects and geographers, and was the patron of Arab poets. The Normans minted coins which bore inscriptions in Arabic, and used the Muslim calendar. In fact, Roger II adapted himself so well to Muslim culture that he was dubbed 'the Pagan' by his fellow-Christians. Two factors in particular had helped Western Christendom to go over to the offensive against Islam at this time: the first was the adoption of Christianity about A.D. 1000 by the Vikings and the Magyars, an event which freed Christendom from the constant pressure of these barbarians; the second was the collapse of the Umayyad Caliphate in Spain in 1031 and the resulting half-century of anarchy in Muslim Spain.

The 'Reconquista' thus brought to an end the first phase of Christian–Muslim interaction, the roughly three centuries of uneasy co-existence in western

Surrender of Granada, the last Muslim stronghold in Spain, to the forces of Ferdinand and Isabella (1492)

Europe. Within a few years, Christendom carried its counter-attack into the heartlands of Islam in the Middle East, when Pope Urban II declared a holy war against Islam, and the First Crusade was launched in 1095. Most people, if asked to define the period of the Crusades, would probably designate the two centuries between the capture of Jerusalem by the Crusaders in 1099, and the final expulsion of the Crusaders from the Holy Land in 1291. These two centuries, however, cover only the period of the eight major Crusades. The crusading spirit was far from dead, and in 1396, 100,000 men, the largest Christian army to take the field against the 'infidel' since the First Crusade, marched down the Danube to be defeated by the Ottoman Turks at the battle of Nicopolis. Not until 1453, when the Turks entered Constantinople, did the crusading zeal of the West begin to flag, and Christian hopes of recovering the Holy Land begin to fade. The balance of power in the continuing struggle between Islamdom and Christendom had shifted once again and, as the disciplined armies of the Ottoman Turks, the most formidable Muslim fighting-machine in history, pushed further and further west to the gates of Vienna, Western Christendom was forced once more on the defensive.

Most people, if asked why the First Crusade was launched in 1095, would reply, 'Because Jerusalem was captured by the Muslims in 1070, and it was necessary to restore the Holy Land to Christian hands', or something to that effect. The inference is that, prior to 1070, Jerusalem and the Holy Land were in Christian hands, and that the First Crusade was therefore a logical reaction to the capture of Jerusalem by the Seljuk Turks in 1070. Nothing could be further from the truth. When the Crusaders invaded Palestine, they were invading territory which had been an integral part of the Islamic World for 450 years. All that happened, when the Seljuk Turks captured Jerusalem in 1070, was that power was transferred from one Muslim dynasty to another, but this statement is an over-simplification.

The Fatimid Caliphs, who surrendered the territory to the Seljuks, were Shi'ites of the Ismā'īlī, or 'Sevener' persuasion. The Fatimids, after initially disputing with the Byzantines control of Syria, had enjoyed generally peaceful relations with their powerful Christian neighbours. The advent from Central Asia of the Seljuk Turks, who, as Lane-Poole put it, had 'embraced Islam with all the fervour of their uncouth souls', heralded a return to Islamic orthodoxy in Syria and Palestine, and ultimately in Egypt itself. The religious fervour of these new converts to Islam meant that a harder line was taken in regard to the Christian minorities under Seljuk rule and, in particular, meant that difficulties were placed in the way of Christian pilgrims wishing to visit the Holy Land. Although the pilgrimage of Christians to the Holy Land had been resumed in A.D. 670, only thirty years after the capture of Jerusalem by the Muslims, it was not until the ninth century, when Charlemagne established his protectorate over the Christian East, that the flow of pilgrims assumed significant proportions. During the tenth century, the pilgrimage to the Holy Land became fashionable, and was undertaken by many nobles and high dignitaries of the church. The normal pilgrimage route, by sea from Italy, was supplemented, after the conversion of King Stephen of Hungary to Christianity about the year 1000, by an overland route via Constantinople. In the eleventh century, the pilgrimage became even more popular, especially in Normandy, France and Germany. In 1064, for instance, only a few years before the capture of Jerusalem by the Seljuks, some 7000 pilgrims from Germany visited the Holy Land. After 1070, such pilgrims were liable to be molested, and were subjected to harassment of various kinds, and needed an armed guard in order to be able to travel in safety.

The capture of Jerusalem from the Fatimids by the Seljuk Turks in 1070 was an event which had far-reaching repercussions in the Christian world – especially the eastern Christian world. The second Seljuk achievement was of even greater consequence to the Christian world. This was the Seljuk defeat of the Byzantine army at the battle of Manzikert in 1071. This battle, one of the decisive battles of world history, 'struck a fatal blow at Christian imperial power in Anatolia'. The Seljuk victory shattered the Byzantine line of fortifications, a thing which the Arabs had never been able to achieve, and thus opened the way for the Turkicisation of the whole of Asia Minor. Ultimately, it made possible the establishment of the Ottoman Empire, which for more than six centuries maintained its imperial power in the Middle East and eastern Europe, and it was thus indirectly responsible for the creation of modern Turkey.

These, then, were immediate causes of the launching of the First Crusade. The call for help uttered by the Byzantine Emperor, Alexius I, was a double one: 'help me recapture Jerusalem, so that pilgrims may once more proceed without interference; and help me throw back the tide of Turkish invasion in Asia Minor'. The response from the rulers of Europe was a poor one. In fact, not a single crowned head accompanied the crusading host, variously estimated at between 100,000 and 600,000 men, which assembled at Constantinople in 1096–7. For this reason the First Crusade is sometimes termed the 'Barons' Crusade'. Several of the crowned heads were, so to speak, *hors de combat* by virtue of being under sentence of excommunication at that time; these were Philip I of France, William Rufus of England, and the Holy Roman Emperor himself, Henry IV. Spain was fully absorbed with the 'Reconquista', and the majority of the troops for the First Crusade were French, or Normans from southern Italy.

There was a variety of reasons for the eagerness of the Crusaders to go to the Holy Land – most of them economic. By the eleventh century, the population of France had increased beyond the capacity of its natural resources. Palestine was represented as a land flowing with milk and honey, and, after the establishment of the Latin Kingdom of Jerusalem in 1099, settlers flocked to 'Outremer', as the fabulous land beyond the sea was called. The Latin Kingdom, too, offered an outlet for the younger sons of the nobility, who, under the feudal system then in force in Europe, had little opportunity for advancement. In other words, it acted as a colony which temporarily alleviated certain serious economic and social problems associated with feudalism.

It also solved a social and military problem which had become increasingly acute in the eleventh cen-

The famous Crusader castle 'Crac des Chevaliers' in Syria. After resisting numerous sieges the castle was finally stormed by the Mamlūk Sulṭān Baybars in 1271

tury, namely, how to absorb or divert the bellicose passions of the barons. The Popes had tried desperately to harness their warlike energies to the concept of 'just' and 'holy' warfare, by such devices as consecrating the arms of the knight to the defence of justice and protection against oppression. Consequently, the call for assistance from the Byzantine Emperor was heaven-sent, as far as the Pope was concerned. At the Council of Clermont, in 1095, Pope Urban II, with great political skill, succeeded in diverting the barons from their fratricidal quarrels, and uniting them in a common struggle against the infidel, a struggle which he endowed with the sanctity of a Holy War.

The great Italian commercial cities were eager to support the Crusades because of the prospects of unlimited profit and commercial expansion. Venice, Genoa and Pisa established on the Syrian coast great emporia from which they supplied the Latin Kingdom with food and munitions. The spiritual impulse was thus supplemented by the profit motive.

Thus the motives for the First Crusade were, to say the least, mixed. Through an irony of history, before the Crusaders reached Jerusalem, the Seljuks, whose capture of the city and restriction of the pilgrim traffic had been the principal reason for the Crusaders going to the Holy Land, had surrendered the city to an army sent from Egypt, and Jerusalem was restored to Fatimid control. Since Fatimid control of the Holy Places had apparently been satisfactory to Western Christendom before, logically no reason now remained for assaulting Jerusalem. The crusading barons may have been unaware of the changed situation; or it may have been too subtle a point for them to grasp. Whatever the reason, they proceeded to lay siege to Jerusalem and to carry the city by storm in July 1099. The butchery of the civilian population which followed cast an early stain on Christian arms.

The conquest of Jerusalem led to the establishment of the Latin Kingdom, a strip of territory about 500 miles long and at places less than 50 miles wide. Its chief cities, apart from Jerusalem, were Antioch, Edessa and Tripoli. The great Muslim cities of the hinterland, such as Damascus and Aleppo, were never captured by the Crusaders. For fifty years the Franks were in the ascendancy, and the Latin Kingdom was strengthened by the creation of some of the most famous of the medieval orders of chivalry: the Knights Templar; the Knights Hospitaller (or Knights of the Hospital of St John of Jerusalem), and the Teutonic Order.

In October 1187, the great Muslim leader, Saladin, reoccupied Jerusalem and recaptured many of the Crusader strongholds on the coast. Tyre, Tripoli and Antioch held out, and enabled the Franks to retain their foothold in the Holy Land for another century. Acre was recaptured by Richard the Lionheart on the Third Crusade, and this was followed by a treaty with Saladin which allowed Christian pilgrims safe-conduct to visit Jerusalem.

During the thirteenth century, there was a degeneration of the crusading ideal. Crusades were now launched against schismatics, heretics, and, in general, against any elements which had antagonised the Pope. For example, the Fourth Crusade was directed against fellow-Christians at Constantinople, and fatally weakened the divided Eastern Christendom. Even those Crusades which were directed against the Muslim enemy no longer necessarily had the Holy Land as their goal. The Fifth and Seventh Crusades were directed against Egypt, and the Eighth against Tunis, where Louis IX of France met his death. The Sixth Crusade, which was more in the nature of a diplomatic mission than a military expedition, was led by Frederick II. The Muslims so admired Frederick's knowledge of Arabic and Islamic culture that in 1229 they voluntarily handed back to the Crusaders the city of Jerusalem, together with Bethlehem, Nazareth and the other Holy Places – surely one of the most extraordinary incidents in the long history of the relations between Christendom and Islam! Frederick entered Jerusalem and placed the crown on his head with his own hands (he had been excommunicated, and so no one could do it for him); then he rushed back to defend his kingdom against a Papal army. Fifteen years later the Muslims recovered Jerusalem and, in 1291, the Mamlūk rulers of Egypt and Syria stormed Acre and put an end to the Latin Kingdom.

In terms of cultural interaction, the results of the Crusades are meagre. During the forty years or so between the death of Baldwin II in 1131, and the death of Amalric in 1174, a period during which the Crusader and Muslim forces were roughly in equilibrium, the Crusaders learned to live on friendly terms with the local Muslim population, but they learned little from them, and developed little of their own which could influence the West. No new poetry or art arose in the Holy Land. The great romances about the wars between Christendom and Islam, which were sung by the minstrels of the period – the *chansons de geste*, the *Song of Roland*, and the legend of the Cid – were composed by the minstrels of the West. Many words of Arabic or Persian origin entered Western languages, but it is extremely difficult to be sure whether the borrowing occurred in Palestine, or in one of the other two principal points of contact between the two civilisations – Spain and Sicily. Even borrowings in the military sphere, in military architecture, tactics, and the like, have been disputed. For instance, some assert that the Crusaders brought back to Europe the notion of the concentric castle with the central keep. Others maintain that it was developed in the West by the Normans and taken to Palestine. Similarly, it is hard to know whether siege-weapons and tactics developed during the predominantly siege warfare in Palestine were of Arab or Greek provenance. As far as the Muslims in Palestine were concerned, they showed no inclination to interest themselves in the affairs of the crusading nations, even to the point of trying to distinguish between the different national contingents. All Europeans living north of Spain and Italy, from the Pyrenees to the lands of the Slavs, were still called by the same blanket term – Franks.

The results of the Crusades are to be seen rather in the stimulation of trade and commerce between Europe and the Middle East, and in the impetus given to various social and political changes in Europe. The city states of Venice, Genoa and Pisa achieved unparalleled prosperity through their trade with the Middle East – trade which was by no means confined to the Latin Kingdom of Jerusalem. Popes thundered against trade with the infidel and issued threats of excommunication, but without effect. On the other side, the Muslim leader, Saladin, justified *his* trade with the infidel by explaining to the Caliph that the Italians brought to Egypt arms and war material. 'This', he said, 'constitutes an advantage for Islam, and an injury for Christianity.'

A by-product of this greatly increased trade between East and West was the development of banking and credit, to serve the needs of pilgrims and knights travelling to the Middle East. Once again, the Italians were in the lead in the establishment of banking firms, but an interesting feature is that some of the medieval orders of chivalry were deeply in-

The Battle of Lepanto, 7 October 1571, in which a fleet consisting mainly of Venetian and Spanish ships, under the command of Don John of Austria, destroyed an Ottoman fleet. This was the last major naval battle fought with oar-propelled vessels

volved in the banking business. As the military religious orders became secularised, various mendicant orders of friars were founded to counteract this tendency – for instance, the Franciscans and Dominicans.

The Crusades also gave impetus to social and political change in Europe. For example, they affected the Papacy. Despite the prominent part played by lay princes in most of the Crusades, the Crusades were essentially preached, organised and directed by the Popes. Although initially the Popes gained great prestige from this, the use of crusading zeal against Christian heretics in Western Europe, or against the personal enemies of the Pope, tended to discredit the Papacy. In addition, the creation of the military religious orders tended to blur the distinction between lay and clerical, between temporal and spiritual, and thus to undermine the authority of the clergy. Secondly, participation in the Crusades meant the impoverishment of many feudal lords, and the consequent increase in the power of the king. In the economic field, the most obvious outcome of the Crusades was the introduction in the West of a system of tax on personal property and income. Hitherto, taxation on land had been the norm, and so one may say that a modern taxation system in the West dates from the time of the Crusades.

An ironical but undeniable result of the Crusades was the deterioration of the position of the Christian minorities in the Holy Land. Formerly these minorities had been accorded rights and privileges under Muslim rule, but, after the establishment of the Latin Kingdom, they found themselves treated as 'loathsome schismatics'. In an effort to obtain relief from persecution by their fellow-Christians, many abandoned their Nestorian or Monophysite beliefs, and adopted either Roman Catholicism, or – the supreme irony – Islam.

To sum up, the Crusades were a total failure as a military counter-attack against Islam. As Sir Steven Runciman has succinctly put it: 'the Crusades were launched to save Eastern Christendom from the Moslems. When they ended the whole of Eastern Christendom was under Moslem rule.'

The fifteenth century ushered in the third phase in the long history of interaction between Christendom and Islamdom, a phase which may be characterised as the 'exotic' period. The end of the religious wars in Europe had meant a slight decline in *odium theologicum*. Already in the fourteenth century Wycliffe had declared that even Muslims might obtain salvation (hitherto thought to be the exclusive privilege of Christians), and had asserted that both Christians and Muslims were prone to the same vices. In the fifteenth century, Thomas Gascoigne put forward the novel idea that Muslims did not want to be converted to Christianity, since they found the disputes between the Christian sects abhorrent, and were not impressed by the ethical or moral standards of the Christians with whom they had come into contact (principally Venetians and Genoese). In the same century, the Qur'ān was for the first time subjected to serious exegesis. With the advent of the Reformation, the Pope for many Protestants took the place of Muḥammad as the Anti-Christ, and much of the polemic formerly directed at the Prophet of Islam was now aimed at the Vicar of Christ.

The military strength of the Ottoman empire obliged the West to resign itself to another period of co-existence with the Islamic world. The three great Islamic empires of the sixteenth and seventeenth centuries, the Ottoman, the Ṣafavid and the Mughal, were treated as part of the known world, and diplomatic relations between these empires and European princes were conducted on the basis of equality.

The West, ceasing for the moment to see the Islamic world as the abode of unimaginable evils and vices, put in its place the concept of the 'exotic East', the home of the rare and the bizarre, of fabulous riches and voluptuous delights. In 1704 there appeared Galland's translation of the *Arabian Nights*, and more and more Islamic literature in translation became available in Europe. There was increased study of the Arabic language, and chairs of Arabic were established at Oxford and Cambridge Universities. More people, especially merchants, travelled to the Middle East, but their accounts of life there were not always reliable, and many merely fed the needs of a public avid for *exotica*.

This improvement in the relations between Christendom and Islamdom was not to last. The advent of the nineteenth century marked the rise of imperialism in the West. As the West lost its fear of the Ottoman Empire, now in decline, it also lost much of its temporary respect for Muslims and for Islamic civilisation. The Western imperialist powers attempted to conceal their economic and political objectives under a veneer of altruism. As they saw it, there were people in Asia in need of good government and, in the West, there were people who not only knew how to govern but were eager to confer the benefits of good government on others. England therefore shouldered 'the white man's burden', and France devoted itself to its 'mission civilisatrice'. The technological superiority of the West over the East which was the product of the Industrial Revolution brought with it an unshakable belief in the superiority of Western civilisation over Islamic civilisation. If the West was going to confer on the East some of the benefits of this superior civilisation, such as good government, it was logical that it should demonstrate to Muslims the superiority of another aspect of Western civilisation, the Christian religion. So with the government officials went the missionaries, and the nineteenth century saw a fusing of the colonialist/imperialist attitude toward Muslim countries with the Christian attitude toward the Islamic faith. The two levels of possible reaction by the West to the problem of Islam, the political-military and the religious, were thus once more united, and united as they had not been since medieval times.

It is not surprising, therefore, to find a great similarity between the medieval view that it was safe to speak ill of Muḥammad because his malignity exceeded whatever ill could be spoken of him, and the tone of nineteenth-century missionary tracts which exhorted the Muslims of India to abandon the false religion which they had been taught. There were even echoes of the old crusading spirit. When the French occupied Algeria in 1830, they declared that they had in mind 'the greatest benefit to Christendom'. Similarly, Canning's solution to the 'problem' of the Ottoman empire was to bring it into modern Europe under Christian tutelage. When the French invaded Tunis in 1881, they considered their action a sacred duty 'which a superior civilisation owes to populations which are less advanced'.

The Islamic reaction to this double onslaught by the armies and administrators of Western powers and by Christian missionaries, was both religious and nationalist. Colonial peoples did not accept the West's belief in its superior moral culture or its superior religion, but believed rather that the West owed its dominance to the accident of prior industrialisation. It is possible to argue, of course, that the Industrial Revolution was the product, at least in part, of those dynamic tensions which existed in Christendom (not the least of them being the creative tension between 'church' and 'state'), but were lacking in Islam. At all events, rising nationalism in the Islamic world meant that, by the end of the nineteenth and the beginning of the twentieth centuries, the imperial powers were faced with the simple alternative of relinquishing their colonies or holding on to them by force.

For fourteen centuries, Christendom and Islamdom have confronted each other as 'two incompatible and largely hostile systems of thought, morals and beliefs'. Since the Second World War, the balance of power between these two systems has shifted once again. The loss of nerve on the part of Western civilisation, the questioning of its very moral foundations, the movement away from Christianity both by those who blame it for the West's cult of materialism, and by those who have lost all religious faith, have meant that we have entered what W. M. Watt has called the period of 'inter-religion', 'in which adherents of the various great religions are mingling with one another on an unprecedented scale'. On their side, Muslims, who only a generation ago were avidly grasping whatever aspect of Western technology they could, in the belief that therein lay the secret of Western dominance over them, share the disillusionment of many in the West with the results of technology, and are seeking other, possible Islamic, solutions. The period of the 'one world' has brought the major religions into contact with one another as never before, but, by the same token, it has brought them once more into rivalry. Each of these two great civilisations, Christendom and Islam, has always been convinced of its own superiority and self-sufficiency, and the fact that at the moment neither side holds the advantage may mean nothing more than that each sees itself threatened by a universal relapse into godlessness and barbarism.

Kurdish nomads in Iran. The Kurds have resisted many attempts to settle them as agriculturalists and still travel, despite increasing difficulties, in the mountainous areas on the borders of Iran, Iraq, Syria and Turkey. The women are unveiled, as is the custom for nomadic women in the Islamic world

13

The changing concept of the individual

R. SANDLER

The Islamic world has been largely by-passed in the modern Western search for the spiritual springs of life in favour of the seemingly more fertile ground of the farther Orient. One possible explanation for this may lie in the very different solutions which each of the three cultures has formulated, over the centuries, to deal with the problems of existence. While Western culture has progressively encouraged outward individual action, and the Orient has emphasised the interior life of the individual, Islamic culture has laid stress on the communal, social aspects of life above all else: life lived in concert with others. Rather than perceiving man as significant in his own right, traditional Islamic culture viewed him as part of a total scheme of society. The individual was encouraged to perform, to the best of his ability, the duties assigned to him by his religion or by custom, rather than to forge a subjective world for himself, based on his individual perceptions and needs.

The conceptual framework within which the individual in traditional society worked was defined for him by the religious guides, the Qur'ān and the Islamic law. Since Islam posits an intimate connection between religious ideals and society, the believing Muslim is expected to make a reality of the principles of his faith in his own life. Furthermore, he should want to extend the area where religion dominates, beyond his personal sphere, to include the political and social life he shares with other Muslims. This scheme bore heavily upon traditional attitudes regarding the function of society and the individual. In the traditional literature, the ideal society is one that enables people to carry out their religious and social responsibilities, and encourages individual action that is in keeping with the divinely-guided principles of Islam. The ideal individual is one who fulfils his religious and social obligations. Both society and the individual were judged in the light of these ideals.

An illustration of traditional expectations of the individual is found in a history of the early Muslim rule in India which describes a certain Sayyidī Maulā, a mystic living in Delhi during the latter half of the thirteenth century. While he was apparently popular with a large segment of the population, he aroused the jealousy and suspicion of many of his fellow Muslims because of his unconventional life-style; he gave lavish parties and, in general, acted in a manner considered unseemly for a mystic by assuming the demeanour of the aristocrats with whom he associated. Whereas the religious notables generally took great care to observe the congregational prayer, Sayyidī Maulā failed to participate in this practice, thereby incurring the disapproval of the orthodox community.

While the individual is held accountable for his actions in the religious, legal and moral sense, the traditional literature taken as a whole, expresses the attitude that the individual is not responsible for the larger events in his life. Some, inspired by religion, might suggest praying or attention to religious duties to make the world a better place in which to live, and more practical suggestions were also put forth in 'Guides' for rulers. But what happened on earth was largely viewed as part of a firm divine plan which man must accept. The starting point for the attitude towards the scope and area of individual activity is the Qur'ān which conveys a mistrust of action deriving exclusively from individual initiative. A modern-day Muslim businessman, living and working in North Africa, echoes the sentiments of the Qur'ān and the traditional culture in his views of man's role in society. While he regards Islam as a religion of action, he does seem to place limitations on the range of man's activities by equating individual action with individual discipline. According to him, the job of the individual is to work hard to carry out the responsibilities demanded of him by his religion. Man can do anything he wants to do, provided that God has given His consent to man's wishes. It is man's pride that makes him think that he knows more than he actually does, and it is man's pride that makes him think that he accomplishes more than he actually does. Only God knows all and is responsible for everything.[1]

The popular literature in particular conveys the idea that the individual is at the mercy of agents other than himself. The fairy tales, especially, abound in spirits of all kinds: good spirits bring good fortune and bad spirits bring bad fortune. These spirits are most often responsible for the action of the stories: things happen to the characters rather than the characters initiating the events of the stories. Just as the Qur'ān views the world as the stage for the performance of man's role as God's partner in His master-plan, so the popular literature conveys the idea of a world which is the arena for the interaction of man and fate. The world is not of man's making, and all that he can do is manipulate the factors given him: he cannot make a new world for himself. Many traditional stories (for example, some of those found in *The Thousand and One Nights*) emphasise the use of the individual's wits and wiles to triumph over the obstacles that fate has thrown in his path.

In more recent times, the behaviour of certain individuals betrays a sensitivity to the machinations of fate that is not present, to the same degree, in modern society: answers provided by science, and social and economic opportunities have altered the individual's perception of the world as being largely outside of his control. A French military observer of the desert Bedouin in nineteenth-century North Africa[2] has remarked upon the differing concepts of honour among Europeans and the Bedouin. While the European will fight to the last man, the Bedouin will unhesitatingly leave the scene of battle when they perceive that 'fate' has betrayed them and turned the tide of battle in favour of the enemy, or when they no longer see any point in overcoming the enemy. Only a readily discernable practical goal, rather than the defence of some illusive concept of honour, will make the Bedouin continue a losing battle. (The concept of man as functioning within a framework established *for* him – as opposed to *by* him – seems to spare the Muslim from the moral dilemmas which trouble individuals in the Western world, where individual responsibility is emphasised. The idea that the individual can change his situation and indeed, should change it, causes guilt when things are not as he thinks they should be. The Islamic framework which places boundaries on the range of human action, brings less emotional and psychological hardship to the individual, but less change as well.)

The spirits, good, evil and neutral, found in the popular literature are allowed to run rampant, fulfilling human desires and lending a helping hand to individuals in trouble, as well as making trouble for them (this is true also, in some measure, for the spirits found in the popular literature of medieval and later Europe). The purpose of the folk-tales (which have usually originated in a pre-Islamic milieu) is simply to tell a story, or to entertain an audience, or to express human emotions and desires. But at the level of 'high-culture', that is, the officially-sanctioned culture composed within the framework of socially acceptable attitudes, the awareness of another dimension tends to manifest itself in a sense of a moral structure that not only imparts order and meaning to a world that would be chaotic and meaningless without it, but makes social demands on the individual. To illustrate this point: in the miniature paintings which accompany the text of the Persian epic entitled *The Book of Kings* exhibited for some months at the Metropolitan Museum of Art in New York in 1972, the absence of spirits in the court scenes is very noticeable. In several of the other paintings throughout the text, small faces peer out from behind mountains and trees, secretly listening in on conversations or covertly watching events. At times, there are hardly discernible faces sketched in among the rocks of the mountains which form the backdrop for the actual events taking place, and man-size spirits interact with human characters. The painters of these pictures appear to be acutely aware of a world apart from the world of normal action. The absence of spirits in the scenes depicting the royal court conveys in a subtle and indirect manner

[1] These are the views of Hadj Brahim, the object of a study by John Waterbury in *North for the Trade, The Life and Times of a Berber Merchant*, Berkeley, University of California Press, 1972.

[2] Daumas, General E. *The Ways of the Desert*, 9th rev. ed., Austin, University of Texas Press, 1971.

The Night Journey of Muḥammad to Jerusalem and thence to Heaven. He is escorted by Gabriel and other angels. From the *Khamsah* by Niẓāmī, in a Persian manuscript dated 1542

the Muslim attitude to the ruler as the source of order, the guarantor of a proper moral atmosphere and the happiness of his subjects. As one individual whose actions affected society to an even greater extent than most individuals, the ruler was a popular target of traditional Islamic moralists.

Because of this over-riding concern with society, the traditional culture frowned upon individually motivated emotions which would lead to 'bad actions', cause turmoil and disturb the smooth functioning of society. The medieval Persian writer Sa'dī, discussing 'Love and Youth' in his *Gulistan*, regards the emotion of passionate love as a personal phenomenon which had grave consequences for society. For him, love destroys the individual's concern for the requisites of his social role, his sense of the proprieties, and of the rights and duties which would determine and shape the relationship of individuals under 'normal' conditions. Love overcomes the rational faculties by which man knows right from wrong and good from bad. He discusses love and youth in the same chapter because both of these states cause the individual to act without regard for the consequences of his actions. The youth, admired by all, can afford to be temperamental and unsociable, but with age, he becomes more willing to interact with others in a sociable manner; he becomes less selfish, more mellow and kinder. A teacher who loves his pupil is unable to fulfil his function properly and to assess that pupil rigorously. Love causes a religious man to act in a manner unbecoming a pious person. Love erases the proper distance between a master and a servant and the master is unable to keep the servant in line.

Love is the antithesis of the contentment, self-control, patience and forbearance urged by the traditional culture. Like anger, it leads to regrettable actions, with important consequences for society. Individual desires, individual joys, are sacrificed for the good of the greater whole. This is not to say that Muslims do not experience love, or joy, but only that the traditional culture encouraged certain modes of behaviour, and discouraged others. The folk-songs and folk-stories of the Islamic world are ample evidence that below the surface of allowable actions and sentiments, a spectrum of individual sentiments did exist. The folk-songs and stories convey the unhampered feelings and thoughts of people for whom the Islamic moral overlay is perhaps not so binding in practice. These stories and songs describe human love in all its vagaries, in simple and commonplace language, indicative of their relation to the lives of the people.

Present day Islamic society is in a period of transition which is reflected in changed attitudes towards society and the place of the individual in society. While the traditional literary culture tended to convey the ideals of the society, the emphasis has shifted, in recent times, from society to the individual. Observers using the framework of the scholarly disciplines document modifications in all spheres of life, and indigenous writers also describe, and reflect upon a changing society. Individuals no longer act entirely within the traditional framework; correspondingly, modern literature conveys the thoughts and the feelings of individuals in a variety of life situations, and with a broadening spectrum of experiences. This literature depicts a society in transition, and at the same time reflects a society in transition.

The phenomenon of change is taking place at all levels of society and touches the most isolated villages as well as the large cities. No individual or community can remain isolated from the outside world for long. The modern Pakistani writer Zulfikar Ghose has described an individual's response to change with sympathy for, and understanding of, the fragility of the traditional in its confrontation with new and unfamiliar ways of acting and thinking (modern Islamic governments, on the other hand, often feel exasperation at life and thoughts so tenaciously held to). He depicts[3] the acute bewilderment of a Pakistani peasant in his first encounter with the complexities of the English court-system, and the grasping business tactics of his fellow countrymen, textile manufacturers who wish to buy the peasant's land in order to expand their business premises. The peasant, who sees no alternatives to his way of life, refuses to sell his land, and the businessmen refuse to be thwarted. The peasant is portrayed as a simple man, accustomed to the simplicity and starkness of rural life, where the rhythm of life is determined by nature. Here, the individual is an integral part of his natural surroundings and of his society: the relationship between man and his land, and between man and his fellow men is highly ritualised, and the duties and obligations of individuals to each other are clearly defined and adhered to (this, of

[3] In a novel entitled *The Murder of Aziz Khan*, New York, John Day, 1969.

course applies to agricultural communities outside the Islamic world). Hence the peasant is totally unprepared for dealing successfully with situations and people completely unfamiliar to him. The author indicates the differences in the values, motivations and objectives of the peasant and the businessmen. He suggests that the peasant's concept of himself and his world, his experience and his education (all the products of the traditional society) have not equipped him to deal with the modern world. Whereas the businessmen launch several schemes to attain their end, and are ultimately successful, the peasant attempts to control the outcome to his advantage by methods which seem, in comparison, highly unsuitable: he prays and fasts, and finally accepts the unfortunate results of his encounter as God's wish, and attributes what has happened to his lack of piety.

The situation is somewhat different for a group of dissident young village men as portrayed by a Sudanese writer exploring the dynamics of change in a modern Sudanese village.[4] The young men, for the most part under twenty, some of whom are students, and a few of whom have travelled abroad, openly defy the village *imām*, the symbol not only of the Islamic religion, but of the Islamic way of life. Perhaps more important, they regard him as superfluous. The young men form one of three main groups in the village based on age and power; they are the only villagers who have been exposed to influences outside the village culture. The men who are out of the main stream of events by virtue of their age, treat the *imām* and what he stands for with respect. The group of men who are married with family responsibilities and who have a hand in every aspect of village life, assume the financial responsibility of supporting the *imām* and the upkeep of the mosque, but it is intimated that their support is merely formal, and they never attend the mosque prayers. However, since the presence of the *imām*, like the sun, is taken for granted and revered as part of the natural order of things, he is never actually challenged by this group. The *imām* and religion perform the necessary function of ordering and legitimising the life of the village: both are an integral part of the social life of the village and a necessary element of the important ceremonies of life – marriage, birth and death. The generational conflict, always present in the village to some extent, has been given a new dimension and new ammunition with the addition of a new world view. Whereas previous quarrels with conformity took place within the traditional cultural context (for example, orthodox conformity versus mystical nonconformity), the contemporary young men have been armed with an alternative world view that is at variance with all the priorities of the traditional culture. They have been exposed to new schemes for assessing the ills of the world (such as 'dialectical materialism') and presented with alternative patterns of behaviour which appear to encourage unrestricted freedom of action and the enjoyment of life, regardless of the repercussions for society and for the individual. Unfortunately, neither the economy of the village, nor the life and outlook of most of the inhabitants can accommodate these young men, and they remain isolated from the routine life of the village.

The preceding story illustrates the disruption of the psychological unity of the village in modern times. Formerly, the inhabitants of villages all over the Islamic world shared a common heritage, a common way of life, a common spirituality, common symbols of that spirituality, a common past, and a common present: and they shared a common interpretation of life. Each individual was attached to another individual socially, economically and psychologically. An anthropological study undertaken during the 1960s[5] describes the beginnings of social and economic individualisation in a village on the island of Baḥrayn where a Western-owned oil refinery trained and employed the male villagers. The village, acting as a whole, forbade its young men from participating in those aspects of Western culture that were especially repugnant to it: alcohol, card-playing, dancing, unrestricted contact between the sexes. In spite of their vigilance, however, the villagers were affected in ways that they could not foresee. Since the men were paid for their work in cash, each man now had his individual supply of money and could step outside the village system to buy whatever he wished to buy. Furthermore, the delicate balance that characterised the relationship between the men and the women was disrupted when the pattern of the men's lives changed, while the lives of the women remained the same.

At the village level, change in the traditional way of life and thought is just in its beginning stages.

[4] Sāliḥ, al-Tayyib. *The Wedding of Zein*, and other stories, By Tayeb Sāliḥ trans. from Arabic by Denys Johnson-Davies. London, Heinemann, 1968

[5] Hansen, Henny Harald. *Investigations in a Shi'a Village in Bahrain*, Copenhagen, National Museum of Denmark, 1967.

Gradually, a social unit, a community of life-styles and ways of thinking will become a mosaic composed of individuals with individual histories, experiences and attitudes (an American observer of the Egyptian scene has described the strong and affectionate ties that continue to bind the villagers who have gone to work in Cairo to their village families and community,[6] while a modern Sudanese writer has predicted the change that will come to the village when the children of the village go to the town for their education and 'the number of young men with souls foreign to our own increases . . .').[7] In the larger cities, the process of individualisation has been accelerated by a more prolonged exposure to new ideas. This phenomenon finds expression in a short story which describes a young man who spends his spare time away from his job in a Cairo foundry reading a magazine entitled 'The World'.[8] An article on 'Palace Music in the Eighteenth Century' particularly absorbs him. He is entranced by the strange foreign names, and pays no attention to his older illiterate workmate who tells him that reading a magazine will get him nowhere. These two people share the same work but they are relegated to two separate worlds by their different values and interests.

Again, in the city of Cairo, two people with different life-styles are brought together, for a brief period, by a shared experience. One of the characters in a modern Arabic short story[9] is a familiar figure in the large Islamic cities, the village dweller who comes to work and live in the city (whereas the West has by now moved on to a discussion of other problems, the situation of the villager who comes to the city, often leaving his family behind, is the central point of a great number of Islamic fictional works). He acts as the Cairo middleman for the produce which his brother grows in the country. He finds a small, modern house in one of the city's suburbs. His European-style clothes are the outward symbol of the fact that he has completed secondary school and reads the magazines, newspapers and books available in the city (his brother, who has not progressed past the village school, continues to wear the traditional *galabiyah*). His recently acquired wife is for him the epitome of life in the city: he describes her as being 'white as milk' and 'plump as a duck'. But despite his schooling, and his habit of reading (of which he is very proud), he resorts to the world of his childhood in times of despair. After years of childless waiting, he allows his wife and mother-in-law to resort to the traditional charms, rituals and services of wise old women to bring about the wanted pregnancy. He has the greatest respect for the doctor who delivers his first child, for his gentleness, experience, kindness, and his calm and cheerful manner which inspires confidence . . . a new deity with the ability to control life and death. But although he and the doctor meet on common ground as they both await the birth of the child, they inhabit two different worlds of experience. The doctor is soundly based in the city, while the man is still tied to his village. While the city provides him with the amenities of life, his very being reacts to his village on his frequent returns there, in a way that it never reacts to the city.

In the same way that individuals are emerging from their traditional social and conceptual framework, the new nations are entering phases of economic and social development that demand a new relationship between the various groups which comprise these nations. In this changed atmosphere, an Iranian woman has felt the need to redefine her area of responsibility to include her countrymen in the villages and tribal areas, as well as her family and immediate social group. The woman, trained in the United States, goes to work among the poor villagers in her country.[10] She tells of her struggle to inculcate a feeling of political and economic responsibility in the villagers: in one village, she helps to set up a rug factory which utilises the particular skills of the villagers for a financial return. But her encounter is also a lesson in mutual acceptance. She is greeted by the villagers with as much suspicion as they would show to a foreigner. Much of the woman's energy is spent trying to find a common bond between herself and people whose standard of living, attitudes and values are very different from her own. She is shocked when the parents of a young village girl who is seriously deformed by an accident, refuse to take her back from the hospital in Tehran because she will be an intolerable burden to them. She comes to the realisation, through her intense and prolonged con-

6 Gornick, Vivian. In Search of Ali Mahmoud. *An American Woman in Egypt,* New York, E. P. Dutton, 1973.

7 Sāliḥ, al-Tayyib, 'The Doum Tree of Wad Hamid' in *Modern Arabic Short Stories,* trans. by Denys Johnson-Davies, London, New York, Oxford University Press, 1967; reprinted in the collection of stories mentioned in note 4.

8 In *Modern Arabic Short Stories.*

9 Ibid.

10 Najmeh Najafi has written about her experience in two books: *Reveille for a Persian Village,* London, Gollancz, 1959 and *A Wall and Three Willows,* New York, Harper and Row, 1967.

Arab nomads, Jordan. The men are muffled against the desert winds and sand

tact with the villagers, that there is less room for even the most basic of the finer emotions in situations of extreme poverty. She eventually manages to form solid friendships with some of the villagers, through her continued contact with them, and a shared interest in the rug factory which she has helped them to establish. While the woman's relationship with the villagers has undergone a change, her wealthy family continues to interact with the villagers along traditional lines by bringing food as a paternalistic gift for the villagers on the occasion of the Persian New Year.

The contrast in the thinking of people of widely different experience is apparent in the Iranian woman's awareness of the effects of poverty and disease on the attitudes and values of the villagers, and in her plans to make the villagers economically solvent. This sensibility and the growing awareness of the villagers themselves of their economic and political potential, contrast sharply with the attitude of a poor and ignorant village woman, described in a short story by a modern Arab writer.[11] The woman desperately hopes for a miracle to cure her blind daughter who has been relegated to a lonely position outside the life of the village because of her handicap. In the case of the Iranian woman, the traditional attitude of acceptance has been replaced by a critical attitude toward society, and an appreciation of the effects of differing educational, economic and social opportunities on the lives of individuals.

The author of a novel about a journalist living in Cairo[12] also exhibits a critical attitude toward society, but he writes from the viewpoint of the

[11] In *Modern Arabic Short Stories.*

[12] Ghānim, Fatḥī. *The Man Who Lost His Shadow,* trans. by Desmond Stewart, London, Chapman and Hall, 1966.

underdog; his tone is much harsher and his work is meant to have a political impact. One of the characters in the novel is a young peasant girl who is brought by her mother to Cairo to work for a wealthy family. As the girl grows older, she realises the limitations of the relationship between her wealthy patrons and herself. With no alternatives, she is dependent on the good regard of her patrons and any gifts which they choose to give to her.

Other Arab intellectuals, in articles and autobiographies and through literary protagonists, speak of the frustrated wishes and repressed desires of the person born into the lower-class milieu. These writers point out that the difference in education and experience make for different individual destinies, and contribute to the conflicting attitudes of the upper classes and individuals born into less-privileged circumstances. They point out the vulnerability of the peasant, and the urban dwellers who live on the fringe of society – the beggars and other misfits.

In the modern world, many find the traditional codes of behaviour stifling, and are opting for a less formal framework for their behaviour. At a dinner party I attended in Tehran in the summer of 1971, each of the guests, all young members of the Iranian government circle, politely refused to be seated until each of the other guests was seated, in compliance with the traditional code of politeness. After a few moments of complete inaction, the guests laughed and sat down without further ado. In contemporary literature, individuals no longer stand solely as examples of right or wrong in the social and moral sense and they explore more personal ways of acting and thinking. The traditional codes of behaviour are examined critically in an Arabic short story about a villager who lives in fear that he will have to defend the honour of his beautiful sister, as traditional custom would demand of him.[13] Another story follows the separate thoughts and expectations of a young couple who are left on their own for an afternoon.[14] The girl allows herself to be seduced by the boy, but assumes that he will marry her. The boy, on the other hand, has doubts about marrying her and feels unwilling to 'pay the price' for his action. (The habit of accosting women, practised at various levels of intensity by young males across the Middle East, is yet another indication of a free-floating social system, particularly unsettling for a society which previously regulated relations between the sexes to a very high degree.)

Traditional concepts of the female and her role in society are being questioned as changing economic and social opportunities begin to challenge the traditional function of women. Like every member of traditional Islamic society, the woman was viewed in relation to other members of that society. She obtained her status and her legal and social rights as someone's wife, sister, mother or daughter. The woman's behaviour, in particular, had grave social consequences, for she was regarded as the keeper of the moral order, and at the same time, the potential source of moral chaos. Traditional Islamic thinking assigned different duties and responsibilities to men and women on the basis of their different capabilities. Women, thought to be delicate in their mental as well as physical makeup, personified the instinctual side of human nature, while men represented the spiritual and intellectual side. And in society, women took on the stance of modesty as a perfect fit for the male's stance of aggression and dominance. Islam is not alone in dividing the totality of human nature thus distinctly between men and women; but social and economic circumstances ensured the persistence of these attitudes, and of the roles which actualised them until now.

Changing attitudes towards women and their traditional role is apparent in much of the contemporary writing about and by women. However, the pace of change is different in each of the Islamic countries. Although the Iranian woman who went to work among the villagers (mentioned above) did manage to step outside the traditional area of female responsibility, she was the object of a great deal of criticism from her family and her husband's family because of this. Even her sympathetic husband who had also been educated in the United States, and shared her interest in her work, reacted with hostility to her 'divided' life. In turn, the woman felt guilty and uncertain about what she was doing, for the woman who goes out of the home to work is still rare enough in Iranian society to be vulnerable to the criticism of her friends and family.

The pace of change differs at the various levels of society as well. As the following story illustrates, the material basis for actual change is often not present. The heroine of a story set in Egypt[15] decides to return to the village of her dead husband and marry

[13] In *Modern Arabic Short Stories*.

[14] Ibid.

a relative of his. She regards marriage as a prison and village life as terribly confining, but she prefers the dignity and security of marriage in the village to living with relatives in the city who do not want to look after her.

Other heroines express a desire to attain an individuality of feeling, thought and action, and at the same time, show ambivalence towards the process of achieving an individual existence. The unhappy woman in a story by a Lebanese authoress[16] expresses an inability to find meaning in her family relationships, while still feeling the need for them. Her former social role has lost its contours for her, and yet she has no new role to replace it. While she pays lip service to the idea of freedom, she herself does not feel free. She compares individuals in society to grapes which have become dislodged from the bunch, and she expresses scepticism about the ability of any laws or belief-system to reassemble these individual grapes into bunches. In making important decisions about her life, such as whom she will marry, she likens herself to a puppet at the beck and call of some invisible tyrant, whose motives are unknown to her. She searches for the person under the 'mask' of her social self, a mask that displays the responses required of her, while hiding the responses of the individual underneath it.

Yet another story describes the interior discontent of a woman caught in much the same stalemate as the one above.[17] This woman feels an inner defiance toward her husband, and a sense of shame for her vulnerability in her marriage. But she has not yet reached a point of independence that would enable her to express her feeling towards a husband whose attitude towards her and their traditional marriage has undergone no corresponding change.

In comparison with the traditional literary culture, the range of ideas and sentiments expressed by modern Islamic writers has been considerably widened; this expanded range goes hand in hand with changes occurring at all levels of society. Individuals today view the world from differing perspectives which depend on such factors as age, experience, education, individual sensitivity (whereas expressions of discontent in the traditional culture were variations, most often subtly-expressed variations of the common traditional themes). Much of the work of the contemporary Arab writer, Najīb Maḥfūẓ, discusses the individual's need to come to a personal adjustment with his world. He urges not only a personal response to the world, but one which takes into account the individual's past as well as his present. Many who speak for the needs of other levels of activity (e.g. the Iranian woman working among the villagers of Iran) echo Maḥfūẓ's plea to preserve the elements of the traditional culture which give meaning to life as well as solidity to the nation. The writings of Maḥfūẓ and others touched upon in this chapter, describe individuals in the painful process of finding a new identity for themselves. A recent painting illustrates quite tellingly, the stressful situation in which many individuals in the contemporary Islamic world find themselves. The picture (by a Turkish artist) is entitled quite simply, 'Birds and Girl.'[18] A woman with a veil encircling her face and shoulders is placed within the frame of a window. She is hampered from movement beyond the window, and yet her eyes (so often described in purely conventional terms of beauty in traditional literature) look longingly at two birds perched on the windowsill in front of her. This painting conveys quickly and tellingly, the dilemma of the individual in the Islamic world today, caught between the traditional and the new.

[15] See *Arabic Writing Today, The Short Story,* ed. by Mahmoud Manzalaoui. Cairo, American Research Center in Egypt, 1968.

[16] In *Arabic Writing Today, The Short Story.*

[17] In *Modern Arabic Short Stories.*

[18] See cover of Middle East Studies Association *Bulletin,* New York, Vol. 7, No. 1, February 1973.

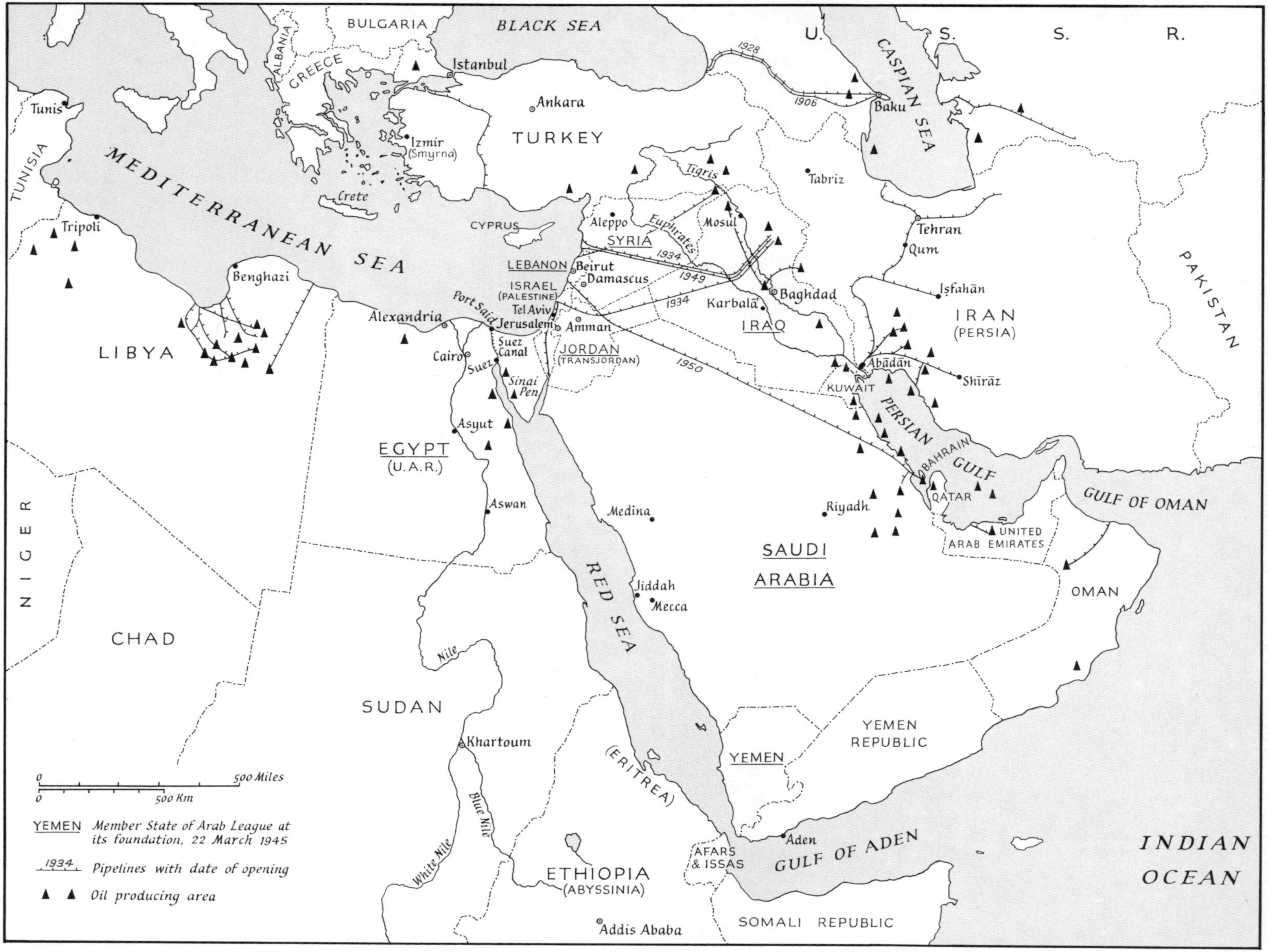

The Middle East today

14

The modern Arab world

L. M. KENNY

The Arabic-speaking world covers a vast stretch of territory, extending from the Atlantic-washed shores of Morocco in the west to the Zagros Mountains on Iraq's border with Iran in the east, and from the foothills of the Taurus Mountains and the Mediterranean Sea in the north to the Indian Ocean and the savannahs that border the Sahara Desert in the south. This is the area in which Arabic became the language of both government and people in the centuries following the Muslim conquest. The ties that bind the countries lying within these limits together are those of language, culture and religion, and an illustrious history to which all of their inhabitants look back with veneration and nostalgia.

In addition to their common heritage, the Arabs are linked by certain common political goals and economic interests, although regional and national interests tend to dominate the wider ones and to prevent the League of Arab States from becoming a cohesive and effective political organisation. There are also cultural and historical differences between the various parts of the Arab world, especially between North Africa and the eastern Arab states, and these are accentuated by geographical factors – narrow coastal plains and river valley oases separated by vast stretches of desert.

In the final analysis, the most important formative factor creating the Arab consciousness is the Arabic language, which is the bearer of their culture, the vehicle of their history and the sacred tongue of the religion of the majority. It is true that the local dialects vary greatly, but the written language – that of literature and the media – is substantially the same, possessing the power to grip its readers and to charm its listeners from Baghdad to Marrakesh.

At the present there are twenty independent Arab states, including the United Arab Emirates. How did they come into existence and take the shape they have today? Previous chapters have described the rise of the Arab/Islamic Empire and its centres of civilisation: Baghdad, Aleppo, Damascus, Cairo, Tunis and Fez, as well as the holy cities of Mecca and Medina, and how these cities became the capitals of the various successor states. Then in the sixteenth century practically the whole of the Arabic-speaking area, except central and southern Arabia, guarded by their desert fastnesses, and Morocco, protected simply by its location in the far west, fell under the sway of the great new Muslim empire that had arisen in the north in the fourteenth and fifteenth centuries, that of the Ottoman Turks.

The Ottoman and Mamlūk Empires had become neighbours by the beginning of the sixteenth century, but the conquest of the latter by the former, though probably inevitable in the long-run, was the by-product of another historic struggle, that between the Ottomans and the recently-established Ṣafavid state in Persia. Thus, after the Ottoman Sultan Selīm I, had defeated the Shah's forces at Chaldiran in 1514, he moved to secure his southern flank by crushing the power of the Mamlūks at Marj Dābik in Syria in 1516, and their remaining forces outside Cairo the following year. The Ottomans inherited suzerainty over the holy cities of Mecca and Medina from the Mamlūks and proceeded to extend their control over both littorals of the Red Sea.

The architects of Ottoman rule in North Africa were the Barbarossa brothers (a nickname meaning 'Red-Beard'), who began their careers as corsairs against Christian shipping in the western Mediterranean. Their opportunity was provided by the encroachment of the Spaniards on the North African coast at the beginning of the sixteenth century and the call of the Arab Muslim principalities there for military assistance against the Christian intruders. The younger Barbarossa brother, Khayr al-Dīn (Kheireddine), was taken into Sultan Selīm's service after the latter's conquest of Egypt, and given a band of Janissary troops. By 1574 Ottoman rule extended over the whole of North Africa, except Morocco.

If North Africa was a frontier area in the west, so was Iraq in the east, the first aim of the Ottomans being to deny it to the Persians. Egypt, Syria[1] and the Ḥijāz, however, were a different matter. The Ḥijāz, with its holy cities of Mecca and Medina, was the symbol of the Sultan's authority and sway as the most powerful Muslim ruler and the defender of Islam. Syria occupied a strategic position because it guarded the approaches to the Anatolian plateau and, furthermore, Damascus was the staging-place for the annual pilgrimage to the Ḥijāz from Syria. Most of the area between Damascus and Mecca was controlled by the bedouin, those desert nomads to whom protection money had to be paid and with whom skirmishes often had to be fought. In addition, through Syria went the great trade routes from the Persian Gulf, Arabia and Egypt, over which the commerce of the East, and of the Arab provinces themselves, passed on its way to Istanbul. The importance of Egypt as a granary for the Empire scarcely needs to be stressed, although its irrigation system had greatly deteriorated from what it had been in earlier periods. Moreover, Cairo, with its great mosque-university, al-Azhar, and related schools, was the most illustrious centre of Islamic learning then in existence. From Cairo also another great annual pilgrimage left for the Ḥijāz.

Ottoman rule brought a measure of peace and stability to the Muslim world under its control, and for four centuries it was its chief bastion against the growing power of a resurgent Europe. In time, however, it became the stability of stagnation and decay. Corruption at the centre was aggravated in the provinces by the quick succession of governors, who sought to enrich themselves at the expense of the people during their brief tenure of a year or two. In the seventeenth and eighteenth centuries new tribes of bedouin erupted from the Arabian peninsula into the Syrian Desert. With the decline in security the depredations of the bedouin increased, to escape which the settled areas had to pay protection money. Tribes located in the Egyptian Delta exacted tolls even from the Nile River boat traffic. Large areas of the countryside were depopulated and the power and influence of the towns and cities *vis-à-vis* the rural areas increased as the latter were forced to seek the protection of the former, which contributed later on to the rise of large urban land-owning families. The shrinkage in total population may be illustrated by the fact that Egypt's had fallen from an estimated ten millions in Roman times to not more than two and one-half millions in the eighteenth century, although she was now barely self-sufficient in food.

Due to the prevailing disorder and the decay of the authority of the central government, local grandees and ruling families emerged in the Arab provinces, as they did in the more central regions of the Empire. It is asserted by H. A. R. Gibb and H. Bowen in their two volume work, *Islamic Society and the West*, that during the whole of the eighteenth century not a single Ottoman governor came to office in the Arab provinces on any other basis than naked force. In order to defend their entrenched positions against the central government and other rivals, they had to build up armies of slaves or mercenaries and to equip them, all of which had to be paid for by the people in the form of increased taxation and extraordinary exactions.

In Egypt the Mamlūks had not only survived the Ottoman conquest, but, by the eighteenth century, had come to wield the real power, while the Ottoman Pasha had become a mere figurehead. The office of *shaykh al-balad* (the mayor of Cairo) became the most powerful in the country, and the officer appointed as Commander of the Pilgrimage now filled the role of commander-in-chief of the army. In 1760 both of these offices were united in the Mamlūk leader, 'Alī Bey. He made himself completely independent of the Porte, refused to pay tribute and sent his army to seize the Ḥijāz and Syria. Ousted from Egypt in 1772 by his own victorious general, he sought the aid of the Russian navy to help him regain power, but perished in the attempt.

A Russian fleet had entered the Mediterranean during Catherine II's war with the Ottomans, 1768–74, piloted there by an Englishman, John Elphinstone. This was a portentous event, for although the fleet did not remain there, its incursion a quarter of a century before Napoleon's invasion of Egypt

[1] Geographic Syria, until the end of Ottoman suzerainty in 1918, refers roughly to the area embraced by the present states of Syria, Lebanon, Jordan and Israel.

Al-Azhar Mosque, Cairo. One of the foremost centres of Islamic learning since its founding by the Fatimids in 970

presaged the extension of European power into the Eastern Mediterranean basin. This same quarter of a century saw a growing rivalry between Britain and France for commercial and political supremacy in the area.

Syria and Lebanon witnessed the rise of many prominent native leaders similar to ʻAlī Bey of Egypt, although few of them dared to make themselves completely independent of the Porte as he had done.

Iraq, like Egypt, was governed by a military Mamlūk oligarchy for most of the eighteenth century, until it was ousted by a reviving Ottoman power in 1831. Iraq was not an easy province to govern. It was rent by factional rivalries, tribal loyalties and the Sunnī–Shīʻī cleavage (northern Iraq and Kurdistan – the present Kirkuk region – were largely Sunnī orthodox, while central and southern Iraq were mainly Shīʻī and rejected the Ottoman Sultan's pretensions to being the true defender of Islam). The last twenty years of the eighteenth century brought Iraq the relatively firm and enlightened rule of Sulaymān Pasha the Great. He had been helped to power by the British, who by this time had become the dominant power in the Persian Gulf and India. In 1797 and 1798 he launched two inconclusive expeditions against the Wahhābīs, the military/Islamic-revivalist movement in Arabia. The Wahhābīs retaliated in 1801 by pillaging the Shīʻī sacred city of Karbalāʼ in southern Iraq, with indiscriminate slaughter.

The rise of Wahhabism in Arabia in the eighteenth century probably posed the most serious internal threat to the Ottoman system in the long history of the Empire. The threat was not only at the political and military levels, but also constituted a challenge to the moral and religious claims of the Ottomans as the defenders of Sunnī Islam. The movement was founded by Muḥammad ibn 'Abd al-Wahhāb (1703–92), a fearless preacher of a purified Islam, who attacked such prevailing superstitions as the reverencing of sacred trees and the tombs of saints. It was launched in 1745 upon the consummation of an agreement between Ibn 'Abd al-Wahhāb and the prince of Dar'īyah (a small town in east-central Arabia), Sa'ūd, the founder of the Sa'ūdī dynasty that still rules Arabia. Under the spiritual tutelage of Ibn 'Abd al-Wahhāb and the military prowess of the Sa'ūdīs, the movement expanded its domination until, early in the nineteenth century, they had gained control of the holy cities of the Ḥijāz. They were even able to bring Damascus under attack in 1810, although this was the high-water mark of their power. The forces of an Ottoman vassal, Muḥammad 'Alī of Egypt, were called in to subdue the Wahhābīs, and they captured the Sa'ūdī capital of Dar'īyah in 1818.

Wahhabism was a revivalist, but not a modernist movement. If one must choose a date for the beginning of the modern period of Arab history, the most likely one is 1798, the year of Napoleon Bonaparte's invasion of Egypt. His primary purpose undeniably was to disrupt British communications with India and her commerce in and through the area. He did, however, bring a band of outstanding scholars with him, and introduced European learning and the Arabic printing-press to Egypt (although it was removed again by the evacuating force in 1801). Napoleon himself returned to France after only a year's stay in Egypt – evidence of the fact that for him Europe at that time was still the crucial theatre of operations. The Egyptians, for their part, were not greatly impressed by the 'liberty, equality and fraternity' proclaimed by the army of occupation, or by their professed regard for Islam. Moreover, the French stay was too brief and relations too frequently marred by revolt on the one side and repression on the other to permit any direct, deep and lasting impression. It was a crucial turning-point, however, in that it irretrievably shattered the power of the Mamlūks and demonstrated the superiority of European military organisation and fire-power, a lesson that was not lost upon Egypt's next outstanding master, Muḥammad 'Alī (1769–1849), the 'founder of Modern Egypt'. The French expedition also signalled the fact that European power politics had entered the Middle East to stay – a not unmixed blessing.

It was Muḥammad 'Alī who seriously opened up Egypt to 'Frankish' ways and influence. He was later criticised by Egypt's outstanding reformist leader of the nineteenth century, Muḥammad 'Abduh, as a destroyer of the old rather than a creator of the new. Doubtless this evaluation is true, if we are thinking in terms of the building of a new society and the integration of new values with the old. Muḥammad 'Alī was primarily a soldier and an adventurer, who came to Egypt as an officer with an Albanian-Turkish contingent in 1800 and stayed to found an empire and a dynasty for himself by monopolising the resources of the country for his own purposes. Like most early attempts at modernisation, his reforms centred on the military–educational missions to Europe, military and quasi-civilian schools in Egypt, shipyards, arsenals, factories, hospitals, the extension of irrigation and the introduction of new cash crops such as indigo and long-staple cotton, the settlement of the bedouin, and fiscal, legal and administrative reforms. He destroyed what was left of Mamlūk power and created the most powerful fighting force in the Ottoman Empire – with which he conquered Arabia and the Sudan, as well as helping to subdue revolts against the Ottoman Turks in Greece and Crete. Determined to wrest what he considered to be his rights from Maḥmūd II, the Ottoman Sultan, he set about the conquest of Syria in 1831. By 1832 his armies had penetrated deep into Asia Minor as far as Konya, only 150 miles from Istanbul, and it was only French and British might, especially the latter, which saved the Ottoman capital and finally forced him to be content with the hereditary *pashalik* of Egypt.

Muḥammad 'Alī's most lasting contribution to the modernisation of Egypt lay in the educational policies he had adopted. He did not create a national educational system, for his schools were tied to very limited goals: the staffing of his administration and his military machine. Out of his efforts, however, emerged an educated élite that was to become the nucleus of a new intelligentsia able to carry on and broaden his programme. One of the most influential of these 'new men' was Rifā'ah al-Ṭahṭāwī (d. 1873), a graduate of the mosque-university, al-Azhar, who

Muḥammad ʻAlī, Viceroy of Egypt 1805–49 and founder of a dynasty which survived until the 1952 Revolution

had been sent to France to study and who, upon his return to Egypt, published a notable account of his stay there and of political life in France at the time. He was appointed director of Muḥammad ʻAlī's new School of Languages, was a prolific translator and wrote widely on political, social and religious subjects. Under the Khedive Ismāʻīl, Muḥammad ʻAlī's grandson (ruled 1863–79), al-Ṭahṭāwī was again head of the Bureau of Translation and editor of the first educational magazine published in Arabic.

Ismāʻīl, the impatient moderniser, is famous as the builder of the Suez Canal and the improvident spendthrift who aimed at complete autonomy within the Ottoman Empire, but who plunged Egypt so deeply into debt to European financiers that he lost his throne and paved the way for the occupation of his country by the British in 1882. His reign saw vast changes in the outward development of Egypt, as well as the establishment of an embryonic national system of education, including the first government school for girls. He also established the first representative National Assembly in any Muslim country which, though very limited in its powers, began to demand more constitutional controls the deeper the country fell into the clutches of its creditors.

The latter half of the nineteenth century was one of intellectual ferment and new directions of thought throughout the Arab World. The secret of Europe's strength was examined by Khayr al-Dīn of Tunisia (1810–89) in a book, the introduction of which was translated into French under the title: *Réformes nécessaires aux États musulmans.* His conclusion was that prosperity was based upon good government, by which he meant the limitation of the autocratic

Religious minorities in the Middle East

Country	Population (date of census or estimate)	Majority religion (%)	Minority religions (totals)		Total minority excl. Muslim (% of whole)
EGYPT	40,000,000 (1975 est.)	Muslim 92.5% (87.5% Sunnī 5% Shī'ī)	Christians		3,000,000 (7.5%)
			Copts	2,660,000	
			Others	330,000	
			Jews	10,000	
IRAN	32,500,000 (1974 est.)	Muslim 99% (94% Shī'ī 5% Sunnī)	Baha'ī	60,000	325,000 (1%)
			Zoroastrians	25,000	
			Others (*Jews, Christians*)	240,000	
IRAQ	10,400,000 (1973 est.)	Muslim 95% (49% Shī'ī 46% Sunnī)	Christians	400,000	500,000 (5%)
			Others	100,000	
ISRAEL	3,300,000 (1973)	Jewish 88%	Muslim (*maj. Sunnī*)	340,000	410,000 (12%)
			Christians	70,000	
JORDAN	2,580,000 (1973 est.)	Muslim 96% (85% Sunnī 11% Shī'ī)	Christians	100,000	100,000 (4%)
LEBANON	2,600,000 (1973 est.)	—[a]	Christians (maj. Maronite)	1,090,000	—[a]
			Muslim		
			Sunnī	286,000	
			Shī'ī	250,000	
			Druzes	88,000	
			Jews	6,000	
SAUDI ARABIA	8,450,000 (1973 est.)	Muslim 99% (Sunnī)	—		—
SYRIA	6,880,000 (1973 est.)	Muslim 90% (c. 75% Sunnī 15% Shī'ī)	Christians	550,000	600,000 (9%)
			Others	50,000	
TURKEY	38,150,000 (1973 est.)	Muslim 98% (85+% Sunnī)	Christians and Others	75,000	75,000 (2%)

[a]Estimates given for both Christians and Muslims as neither is a majority or a minority in the normal sense.
Middle East and North Africa (Europa Publications, 21st edn., 1974–5).

authority of the ruler by representative institutions. He laboured to show that such reforms were not contrary to the sacred law of Islam and himself helped to frame the constitution of 1860 – the first attempt of its kind in the Islamic World.

The same period saw a revival of the Arabic language and literature. In addition to the translation movement, attention was given to the republication of the Arabic classics, including the *Muqaddimah* of the great Arab historian, Ibn Khaldūn. Another development was the burgeoning of Arabic journalism, whose influence upon the language itself and the evolution of a new lucid, economical and expressive literary style can hardly be overestimated. In addition to the newspapers, a wide variety of literary and scientific/technological magazines came into being. Inspiration for these, as well as a good deal of their material, often derived from the West, though their aim was to contribute to the revival of the East. History and literature provided grist for the editors' mill, but their pages also discussed such current questions as cosmology, evolution, witchcraft, hypnotism and the modernisation of the Arabic language, as well as reporting the latest discoveries of science and technology. Syrian journalists played a significant role in this movement in both Egypt and Lebanon, as is illustrated in the founding of the newspaper, *al-Ahrām*, in 1876, and of the literary magazine, *al-Hilāl*, in 1892 – both still published in Cairo. There were Egyptian publicists too – al-Ṭahṭāwī has been mentioned – and their role became more important as time went on. New standards of excellence were set by Muḥammad 'Abduh (d. 1905) during his short period of editing the Egyptian Official Journal, *al-Waqā'i' al-Miṣrīyah.* 'Abduh is better known as the leading Islamic reformist of his period.

The intellectual influence of the West was introduced to the Arab World through educational missions sent to Europe and European instructors brought in, as we have seen. The role of European and American Christian missionary activity, of longer standing in Syria than in Egypt, should not be forgotten. Scores of schools were opened up, for girls as well as boys, long before governments began to pay attention to the education of the female sex. As a result of their efforts such institutions as the Syrian Protestant College (now the American University of Beirut) and Collège St Joseph sprang up in Lebanon, and later the American University in Cairo and the Ḥikmah University in Baghdad. These schools and colleges, however, did not help to solve the basic problems of a predominantly Muslim society: namely how to explain the decadence of the Islamic East compared to the surging power of the Christian West, how to rejuvenate the East, whether to borrow and what to borrow from the West, and how to reconcile such borrowings with traditional values and norms.

There was little hesitation in borrowing the science and technology of the West, but scant attention was given to the problem of the integration of the new with the old. How to explain the decadence of the Islamic world and how to rejuvenate it were the central questions that engaged the attention of Jamāl al-Dīn al-Afghānī and his illustrious disciple, Muḥammad 'Abduh. Al-Afghānī who, it now seems clear, was in reality of Persian origin, was a revolutionary activist. He strongly believed that the Muslim World could recover its lost glory and power if it would but return to its fundamental teachings and would unite, at the same time availing itself of the science and technology of the West. Because of these views he advocated the overthrow of corrupt Muslim rulers and supported the pan-Islamic pretensions of Sultan 'Abdülḥamīd of Turkey.

Muḥammad 'Abduh, on the other hand, became disillusioned with revolutionary activism and devoted his most productive years to legal and educational reform in Egypt, and to the defence of Islam. For him faith and reason were in complete accord. He advocated the exercise of reason (*ijtihād*), consideration of the public weal (*maṣlaḥah*), and the accommodation of the variant views of the legal schools (*talfīq*), for the re-interpretation of Islam in accordance with the needs of modern society. His followers later split into two main groups: the thorough-going liberal rationalists and the neo-fundamentalists, to the latter of which belongs the Muslim Brotherhood.

Let us turn back in time now to the colonialist period in recent Arab history and the rise of nationalism, for which colonialism was in large measure responsible. The first region to fall into colonial hands was that which we now know as Algeria. The French landed near the city of Algiers on 14 June 1830, and were to stay until 3 July 1963, the day when General Charles de Gaulle recognised Algerian independence. Tunisia was the next part of the Arab World seized by the French, with British connivance at the Berlin Conference of 1878 as a *quid pro quo* for the occupation of the island of Cyprus. The French and British had been cooperating in Egypt to force the will of the creditor nations on the reluctant Ismā'īl, but in the end France backed off and the country fell to the British. In 1875 Britain had bought out Egypt's shares in the Suez Canal, and it was unthinkable that she would allow any other foreign power to dominate this vital link with India and the Persian Gulf. By the turn of the century Britain had added the Sudan to her Empire, forestalling French penetration from the Congo. The two powers worked out an 'Entente Cordiale' in 1904, one consequence of which was the extension of French control over Morocco in the form of a 'protectorate' in 1912. Italy jumped in to grab Libya in 1911, but in the main it was France and Britain who divided up the Arab world between them. They partitioned the remaining Ottoman Arab provinces by the Sykes–Picot Agreement of 1916, the provisions of which, with some change, became the basis for the post-First World War mandates, by which Syria and Lebanon fell to France, and Iraq, Palestine and Transjordan to Britain. The British had long since been dominant in the Persian Gulf and had secured Aden as a coaling station on the Red Sea–India route in 1839. Thus the whole of the Arab world – all except the Yemen and central Arabia – was engulfed by European colonialism.

French colonialism in North Africa differed in certain important regards from British colonial policy in the eastern part of the Arabic-speaking world, or even French policy in the latter area. In North Africa the French embarked upon a massive programme of colonisation – the settlement of French *colons* in the areas 'pacified' by their military forces. This process was carried farther in Algeria than in Tunisia and Morocco, mainly because it had gone on much longer in Algeria than in the other two, although essentially the same policies of expropriation and the invalidation of native tribal rights in order to open up the way for French settlement were followed. Another distinction between Algeria and the other two areas was that the former was declared to be an integral part of France and the Algerians to be French 'subjects', though not French 'citizens'. Tunisia and Morocco, on the other hand, were 'protectorates', with the administration remaining in the hands of emasculated native governments, while the real power lay in the hands of the French resident-general and his officials.

Both France and Britain claimed to be the bearers of light and civilisation – *la mission civilisatrice* – to the dark corners of the earth over which they had extended their sway. Neither power, however, in practice thought of applying the same principles of freedom and equality to their possessions abroad as they did in the homeland. The French claimed to be very tolerant and considerate of their colonial peoples at the social and human levels, and it is true that the colour bar, especially with respect to intermarriage, was not as rigid among them as among the British; but when it came to sharing equal rights and freedom with their subject peoples, the French, if anything, were more adamant than the British.

Neither the French nor the British followed policies of colonisation and assimilation in the eastern Arabic-speaking countries. After the British occupation of Egypt in 1882, ostensibly to save the Khedive Tawfīq from the clutches of 'Urābī Pasha and his fellow 'rebels', real authority lay in the hands of the British pro-consul, Sir Evelyn Baring (later Lord Cromer) and his successors, along with their British advisers. The country remained a nominal part of the Ottoman Empire until the entry of Turkey into the Second World War on the side of the Central Powers, at which time it was declared a British protectorate. Under the pressure of the Egyptian nationalist movement we witness the anomaly of the occupying power unilaterally declaring the 'independence' of Egypt in 1922. Egypt entered into a Treaty of Friendship with Britain in 1936 and joined the League of Nations a year later, although she did not win complete independence until the 1954 agreement for the withdrawal of British armed forces.

The 'mandate' system as set up by the League of Nations was to be 'a sacred trust of civilisation' designed for 'the well-being and development' of the peoples concerned and their preparation for independence. The Mandates agreement of 1920 touched off a bloody revolt in Iraq, which prompted the British to set up Prince Fayṣal, one of the leaders of the 1916 Arab Revolt against the Turks, as the King of a nominally autonomous state. Further concessions were won in the 1930 treaty with Britain, and Iraq was granted a constitution, although she maintained a special relationship with Britain under the terms of the Baghdad Pact until after 'Abd al-Karīm Qāsim's revolt of 1958. In 1936 both Syria and Lebanon were able to reach agreement with France on treaties after the pattern of the Anglo-Iraqi Treaty of 1930, but they were never ratified by the French government. Although the French Mandates in Syria and Lebanon were formally abrogated upon the defeat of the Vichy forces in 1941, De Gaulle's Free French forces seemed as reluctant as the previous régimes to grant them real independence. In 1943 the French Délégué-Général went so far as to arrest the Lebanese president and the majority of his government for their audacity in throwing off the remaining limitations on Lebanese sovereignty. The final evacuation of French forces from the region occurred only after the issuance of a British ultimatum, following the French bombardment of Damascus for three days to quell the rioting that had broken out in protest against France's insistence upon the maintenance of her special interests.

Tunisia. The Ḥabīb Bourguiba Mosque in the President's home town, Monastīr, a striking example of modern Tunisian craftsmanship

Dislodged from the Levant and later from Indo-China, France determined to hold onto her North African territories. A concerted effort had been made toward assimilation and the establishment of French as the language of administration, education and the media. At the political level, however, even the moderate nationalists became disillusioned with French reluctance to grant the indigenous population anything like equality with the *colon* minority. In the post-Second World War period the aim of almost all groups was independence, and when armed resistance finally broke out in 1954 they threw in their lot with the Front de Libération Nationale. Under the pressure of events in Algeria, both Tunisia and Morocco were able to wring their independence from France in 1956, the former under the leadership of Ḥabīb Bourguiba and his Dustūr Party, and the latter when the monarchy under Sultan Muḥammad V (father of the present King Ḥasan II) became the rallying point for the nationalist forces.

By 1963, the year of Algeria's independence, the whole of the Arab world was free of European domination, except for Britain's foothold in Aden, the Aden Protectorate and the Gulf Emirates. Freedom had not been won anywhere, however, without a nationalist struggle. The factors which gave rise to nationalism in the Arab World, as elsewhere, fall into two main categories: the internal and external. The former include the geographic and socio-cultural elements, the most important of which are history, language and religion, while the external factors include the nationalist ideology whose inspiration came from Europe and the political fact of European colonial rule. It would be a mistake to belittle the importance of indigenous values for all Arab nationalist leaders from 'Urābī to Jamāl 'Abd al-Nāṣir (Nasser). Still, it is a noteworthy fact that most of them, such as the early Beirut group described by George Antonius in his *Arab Awakening*, Muṣṭafā Kāmil and Sa'd Zaghlūl in Egypt, and the North African leaders, had either received their education in Europe or in Western-type schools at home, or had drunk deeply at the wells of Western liberal political thought. The fact that the nationalist leaders had turned Western ideology into a weapon against the European powers explains in part why the latter proved to be so helpless in dealing with the nationalist reaction to colonial rule, no matter how weak the opposition. In the period between the two World Wars the entrenched position of the colonial powers looked well-nigh invincible, but within a generation their power to dictate the destinies of these countries had disappeared and their bases been liquidated.

It is a noteworthy fact that the first generation of nationalist leaders who fought for national liberation, especially in the eastern part of the Arab world, were in most cases themselves swept away, along with the liberal-democratic political institutions which they had unquestioningly accepted and operated. The leaders to whom the colonial rulers turned over power were in the main from the rich bourgeois land-owning class, a group of men made in the colonialist's own image and who, by and large, operated the system for their own benefit. It was not so much that democracy failed there, as elsewhere in most of the Third World, as that it had never been given a fair chance to succeed. Nor had the old leaders been seen by the younger, more radical generation to be able to rid their countries completely of foreign bases and foreign influence. Their greatest crime, however, the one that sealed their downfall, was the humiliating defeat they incurred in their united, or rather disunited, military effort to prevent the creation of the State of Israel in 1948, the latter being regarded by the Arabs as the re-embodiment of the Western imperialist presence.

The failure of the first generation of Arab nationalist leaders contributed, along with events in the outside world, to open the door for other ideologies. Their poor performance also served the purposes of the conservative Muslim party which, from the early days of modernisation, had resisted the rising tide of borrowings from an increasingly secular West. This secularising process was clearly visible in the new western-type schools set up by Muḥammad 'Alī and is illustrated by the fact that al-Ṭahṭāwī introduced the study of *fiqh* (Islamic jurisprudence) into the School of Languages, in direct competition with the Azhar University. The Azhar itself could not in the end escape the trend: in 1961–2 it too was transformed, partially at least, into a modern university by the addition of faculties of medicine, agriculture, commerce and engineering. The legal field has likewise undergone far-reaching change through the introduction of mainly French-based legal codes. The progressive displacement of the *sharī'ah* (Islamic law) may be illustrated by such steps as the outlawing of polygamy in Tunisia in 1957 and the incorporation of the *sharī'ah* courts into the national court-system of Egypt in 1956. The traditional status of women has radically altered, especially since the opening to them of educational opportunities up to the highest level, giving them entry into professional, business and even political life.

It was in protest against this tide of Westernisation and secularisation, and the failure of the nationalist leaders to remove the indignity of a foreign imperialist presence and to institute an Islamic way of life, that the Muslim Brotherhood sprang into existence in Egypt in 1928. Under its founder, Ḥasan al-Bannā, it devoted itself in the thirties to religious and social reform: classes for instruction in the true Islam, schools, clinics, small factories and so forth. The troubled political climate during the Second World War, due to enforced cooperation with the British war effort, afforded al-Bannā the opportunity to exercise considerable political pressure. Even King Fārūq (Farouk) began to seek Brotherhood support. In 1952 its leaders demanded the right of veto over the legislation of the new revolutionary régime as the price of cooperation. This was rejected, however, and their organisation was smashed after an attempt upon Jamāl 'Abd al-Nāṣir's life in 1954. That the movement is not dead has been evidenced by plots against the régime discovered since that time. Islamic fundamentalism still has supporters in all Arab countries, and finds its embodiment in such leaders as Libya's radical Colonel Qadhdhāfī and Sa'ūdī Arabia's[2] conservative King Fayṣal.

[2] King Fayṣal was assassinated on 25 March 1975, and was succeeded by his brother, the former Crown Prince Khālid.

Jiddah, Saudi Arabia: modernisation through education: a domestic science (cookery) class and a vocational training school

Communism did not make much progress in the Arab World until after the Second World War. Some Arab thinkers had been influenced by Fabian socialist ideas before the turn of the century, and small Marxist parties sprang up in Egypt, Lebanon, Syria, Iraq and Palestine in the twenties. In the thirties the organisational efficiency of the Fascist states won the admiration of many Arab nationalists, but after the defeat of the Axis Powers and the beginning of the cold war, communist Russia fell heir to some of this popularity and began to be regarded as a possible counterweight to Western hegemony in the area. Stalin, however, had little admiration for Arab nationalism, so it was not until the mid-fifties that Russian policy shifted, when her leaders began to realise the possibility of gaining their political and strategic ends in the area by supplying arms, aid and political support to the Arab countries. The Egyptian arms deal with Czechoslovakia in 1955 was a crucial step, followed by Nāsir's nationalisation of the Suez Canal and the Anglo-French–Israeli invasion of Egypt in 1956, and the agreement with Russia for aid to build the Aswan High Dam in 1958.

In spite of Soviet political gains in the area, helped forward by the colossal blunders of Western political leaders, local communist parties have remained of negligible size and influence except sporadically in Syria, Iraq and the Sudan. They have sometimes been able to play a greater role in the labour movement, as they did in the Sudan until recently. Marxism as a philosophy and interpretation of history has had little attraction for most Arabs, nor do they want to fall wholly within the embrace of the Russian bear any more than they do that of Western 'imperialism'.

Although communism as such has made little headway in the Arab World, a number of Arab governments have turned to some form of state socialism and linked it with Arab nationalism in an attempt to build an independent Arab ideology – 'Arab socialism'. Egypt, Syria, Iraq and Algeria have been the leaders here, with some other Arab states following more or less closely in their train. It is not surprising that the Arabs, like many other areas of the Third World, should reject capitalism with its very close ties with the colonial exploitation of their recent past. Arab socialism may also be seen as a rejection of the monopoly of wealth and privilege enjoyed by the local bourgeoisies, and as a move toward satisfying the rising expectations of the masses. Characteristic steps taken have included land reform, the nationalisation of foreign enterprises and most sizeable local businesses, and the institution of far-reaching state control over the economy. Since political motives have been dominant, the results, as one might have expected, have been mixed. However, in spite of tremendous obstacles such as poverty, ignorance and the scarcity of resources (except in the oil-rich states), coupled with an average population increase of about three per cent per annum (in comparison with a world average of 2 per cent, 1·3 per cent in North America and 0·8 per cent in Europe), most of the Arab states have marked up a creditable increase in their gross national product in recent years.

It has been said that the drive behind Arab nationalism and Arab unity derives to a great extent from the Arab–Israeli dispute. That there is a much broader and more venerable basis for Arab unity in their common language, culture and historical experience, both ancient and modern, should be evident to all. It must be confessed, however, that the creation of Israel by force in the midst of the Arab World, against the opposition of the Palestinians and other Arabs, is one of the dominating factors of their recent history. Israel, whatever ancient rights to the land her people claim, is regarded by the Arabs as an intruder and a bastion of Western 'imperialism'. It is difficult to see how the problem, bedevilled as it is by Great Power rivalries as well, can be solved in the foreseeable future so as to satisfy the two competing nationalisms – Jewish and Arab.

It is a truism to say that the Arab World is passing through a swiftly changing and far-reaching transitional stage. This revolution has gone far beyond the political level to embrace the economic, social, cultural and intellectual aspects of life. All too often, outside observers have emphasised political events, to the neglect of developments in the humanistic field in literature, art, the stage and general cultural self-awareness. These aspects have contributed more to, and are more accurate manifestations of the modern Arab identity than the political cataclysms that shake the area.

The radio, cinema and television have brought the Arabs, as well as others, into the mass age, with both its ugly superficiality and its advantages for the dissemination of knowledge and political consciousness. The amenities and opportunities for both education and employment in the cities, wedded to the drive for industrialisation and development

Morocco. Typical small shops in the old bazaar of Fez

centred in the urban areas, have attracted millions of redundant workers and their families from the countryside to feed the mushrooming urban squalor. A visitor to the metropolitan centres of the Arab World cannot but be impressed with the similarity between them and other cities around the world, in their outward aspects, their urban culture and their human problems.

The clash between modernisation and traditionalism continues, and it is too much to expect political stability when the area is being buffeted by so many conflicting and competing forces, both internally and externally. The Arabs have been awakened to the new age, however, and can be counted on to pursue a course in keeping with their own genius, history and interests, and to use every resource at their command, including their tremendous oil reserves, to accomplish the ends which they consider valuable and necessary.

15

Tribalism and modern society: Iraq, a case study

ALBERTINE JWAIDEH

Arab tribalism suggests the habits and modes of life of desert bedouin who follow a nomadic way of life and for whom blood and kinship ties are constitutive of their every relationship. Except for the relatively small number of bedouin who wander its desert fringes, however, the great majority of the tribesmen of Iraq, both now and in the past, have been settled and semi-settled cultivators of the land. They are heterogeneous in ethnic origin, language, and religion.[1]

Since the beginning of history there have been traces of tribalism among Semitic elements of the population, but it became a general and permanent feature of the life of the agrarian population during the Kassite period, or about 1200 B.C. Whatever forms of tribalism may have existed in earlier periods, once the Arab influence became dominant it assumed more distinctively Arab, or bedouin-like, features. Except for localised and marginal instances, however, the bedouin Arabs have never displaced the indigenous population, but rather were absorbed by it. Indeed, peasants today live in mud houses almost identical with those of the Babylonian farmers and often use similar tools, while fishermen in the marshes dwell in reed huts and punt the high-prowed boats of their Sumerian ancestors. Many features of land tenure and plant husbandry follow practices similar to those codified by Hammurabi, and the conservative outlook of the peasant has been one of the constant features of Mesopotamian history, ancient and modern. All of these characteristics illustrate how many of the components of Mesopotamian life pre-date and are independent of essentially tribal factors. The admixture of Arab blood is an incidental factor; it is the adaptability and utility of tribalism to the pre-conditions of life that accounts for its shape and durability in Iraq.

Intrinsic to nearly all aspects of life and society in the region has been the dominant influence of the twin rivers – the Tigris and the Euphrates. Owing to a sub-tropical climate and low rainfall, agricultural enterprise on the alluvial plain requires irrigation. The dimensions and profile of the plain, as well as the rate of flow of the rivers, preclude cheap and easy 'basin type' irrigation as has been practised in Egypt. Since the combined flood periods of the twin rivers occur between April and June, too late for winter crops and too early for summer crops, a complex system of 'perennial irrigation' is necessary in order to ensure the irrigation and drainage of individual holdings. But the creation and maintenance of an elaborate and efficient network of canals requires an enormous common effort and co-ordinating authorities. A second factor of life for sedentary society on the alluvial plain has been its exposure to the incursions of the hostile tribes of the

[1] The ethnic composition of Iraqi tribes is for the most part mixed and in certain significant instances non-Arab. The non-Arab elements include the Kurds, the largest minority in Iraq (approximately one in seven Iraqis is a Kurd), who are ethnically 'Aryan', descendants of the ancient Medes, speak an Indo-European language, and for the most part are Sunnī Muslims by religion; the Yazīdīs who are Kurdish by ethnic origin and language, but non-Muslim by religion; and the Lurs who are ethnically and by language related to the Persians and by religion Shī'ī Muslims. The Arabic-speaking population is ethnically mixed and includes small minorities of Christians of different varieties; the Muslim majority is made up of the Shī'īs (*ca.* 55 to 60 per cent of the Arab Muslims) who are dominant in the south and the Sunnī Kurds are dominant in the north. When the Sunnī Kurds are added to the Sunnī Arabs, the Muslim population of Iraq is almost equally divided between Sunnī and Shī'ī. There are other minorities in Iraq, which, for one reason or other, are either non-tribal in nature or inconsequentially so – e.g. Türkmans, Jews, Christians, and Mandaeans (Sabaeans).

western desert and the 'barbarian' highlanders to the east and north. Whatever man has achieved in Iraq, he has done it at the price of a constant struggle against nature and against other men, and this struggle forms the very thread of the history of Iraq.

Since the alluvial plain of the lower basin of the twin rivers forms a geographical unity, those periods when the entire region has been under the control of a single, centralised government, able both to shield its domain from external threats and to impose its will internally through an orderly administration of its human and natural resources, have been the times of greatest prosperity. Conversely, governmental disintegration, whatever its nature or cause, has resulted in either devastation at the hands of alien hordes or a deterioration in the canal system, or both, and a diminution in the fortunes of the land generally. It has been precisely during the periods of decline in the power and authority of the central government that Iraqi tribalism has most clearly demonstrated its worth. However strong and benevolent to agriculture imperial governments have been, they have tended to be fragile and have eventually broken apart, while the more primitive tribal structures have been more elastic and have supplied some semblance of order and protection. Indeed, there have been periods when the continuity of Mesopotamian agriculture has been preserved by tribal order alone, and this was especially the case during the nearly four centuries of Ottoman rule.

Before the Ottoman conquest, the centres of imperial power had been either within or reasonably close to Iraq; now, however, Iraq became a remote, frontier province, a rich source of revenue, but peripheral to the major concerns of the authorities in Istanbul. The Ottomans failed to appreciate the role of government in the maintenance and growth of the province's prosperity and the governors of Baghdad were granted limited power so that they could not seek independence. Consequently, the tribes emerged as the dominant force in the country and Ottoman authority extended little beyond the walls of the major cities and towns. Owing to the solidarity of tribal society and its determination to defend its lands against all comers, the history of Turkish rule in Iraq was one of continuous struggle. In order to understand this struggle, therefore, it is necessary to examine the structure of tribal society in Iraq.

The basic unit of tribal society is *al-bayt* (house). Like the English word 'home', *bayt* signifies both the inhabitants and the structure, which might be a tent or a hut made of mud or reeds. The *bayt* consists of all closely related persons living under the same roof and dependent upon one another for their livelihood. A second generation of *bayts* is formed when children marry and they continue to be closely tied to the senior *bayt*. Five generations of *bayts* form a second unit, called a *fakhd*. A *fakhd* takes the name of the original *bayt* or the name of a member who has distinguished himself in the affairs of the tribe. The *fakhd* is headed by a *shaykh* acknowledged for his leadership qualities by all the member *bayts*, including those residing outside the tribal area (*dīrah*). Several *fakhds* descended from a common ancestor form an *'ashīrah*. This larger unit is similarly based on blood ties and holds a common tribal *dīrah*. The *shaykh* of an *'ashīrah* is usually a member of its wealthiest and most powerful *bayt*. Several *'ashīrah*s, having a common origin, form a tribe (*qabīlah*) under the leadership of a paramount *shaykh*.

All the units of this tribal society – the *qabīlah*, the *'ashīrah*, the *fakhd*, the *bayt* – are united by blood ties, but the strength of the bond varies in inverse proportion to their respective size. The *bayt*s of a *fakhd* are bound together by mutual obligations, economic and familial. Claims for redress of any injury or injustice done by a member to a non-member are made against the *fakhd* and become the collective responsibility of all its members. If, for example, a tribesman kills a person from outside his *fakhd*, every member of the victim's family or *fakhd* has the traditional right to avenge the death of the lost relative by killing either the transgressor himself or some other member of his *fakhd*. As the proverb says, 'Blood can be demanded only of those within the five generations.' The *shaykh* of the *'ashīrah* is responsible for settling disputes between *fakhds* and any other matters transcending the authority of the *shaykhs* of *fakhds*. In the same way the paramount *shaykh* of the *qabīlah* has jurisdiction over the *shaykhs* of *'ashīrahs*. Each level of tribal structure retains its autonomy until danger or catastrophe threatens the tribe, in which case the paramount *shaykh* assumes complete control. Regardless of the distance of the relationship, the claims of the tribes having blood ties take precedence over any commitments to outsiders. Hence all conflicts within a tribe cease when it is threatened by an alien group, be it another tribe or the government. An Arab proverb succinctly sums up the nature of tribal relationships: 'Your brother comes before your cousin, but your cousin before the stranger.' In Iraq, furthermore, what are essentially blood ties are reinforced by the fact that land is involved, since individual land holdings are held by virtue of membership in the tribe.

The *shaykhs* play the most prominent role in this society. They are usually drawn from the ruling house within each of the respective units. The *shaykh* is the champion of his tribe and leads it in time of war, with his sons and relatives as his lieutenants. He is responsible for the welfare of his tribe: he is required to maintain a guest house (*muḍīf*) for the benefit of his tribesmen and to provide meals for the indigent; to advance money to those in financial need, especially in the planting season; to determine the size of individual land holdings within the tribal *dīrah* and to supervise the distribution of water resources; to organise labour forces for the digging of canals, the dredging of those in use, the building of dykes for the reclamation of new lands from the marshes, and the strengthening of embankments in times of flood; to post men at all times in order to keep vigil against the danger of overflow; to fix the dates of sowing, harvesting, and threshing; and to arrange transportation to market and the terms of sale. Many of these duties are delegated to deputies, known as *sarkāls*, who act as foremen of groups of labourers.

During Ottoman times appointment to the office of paramount *shaykh* of the *qabīlah* carried special significance, since he was the mediator between the tribe and the government. The choice, however, was a tribal prerogative made in accordance with long established traditions. The government did not normally interfere, but before confirmation the *shaykh* was asked to give certain assurances as to his loyalty, to guarantee full payment of revenues, and to maintain law and order within his tribes. However, even though the government claimed the right to depose him, this provision was of little significance, since the *shaykh* retained his authority only by identifying himself with the interests of his tribe. The general attitude was, 'If the government can enforce its requirements, we will obey. If not, we will ignore it.'

Arab tribal society acknowledges an unwritten customary law. It is obeyed and venerated, since defiance means expulsion from the tribe and the rupture of all family relationships, a fate considered worse than death. Legal disputes are referred to the *shaykh*, who presents matters for the decision of the tribal council consisting of men selected for their wisdom, usually elders, and presided over by the *shaykh* or his deputy. Whenever the council cannot reach a decision, arbitrators, either *'awārif* (village or tribal sages knowledgeable in the settling of disputes), or *furrāḍ* (specialists in tribal law), may be asked to render a decision which is then binding on the parties concerned, with the *shaykh* responsible for implementation. Sometimes the disputants refer their differences to *sayyids* (holy men descended from the Prophet Muhammad), whose verdicts are respected. Whenever the evidence is inadequate for establishing guilt or innocence, the accused is placed under oath. Oaths are taken on the Qur'ān or on the grave of some *sayyid* of local celebrity, or even on the person of the *sayyid* himself. All who hear the oath, as Gertrude Bell has observed, 'know beyond question that if the speaker is forsworn his temerity will bring upon him within the year a judgment greater and more inexorable than that of man'.

Tribal solidarity varied from one locality to another. Where government authority prevailed, usually in close proximity to cities and major towns, the tribal system weakened and ceased to function; in the rich agricultural regions the tribe was closely knit, united under their *shaykh* in resistance to the government. In areas bordering the desert, strength and cohesion were necessary in order to meet the desert nomads on equal terms. When certain crops such as rice required close and effective supervision, cultivators gladly submitted to the absolute authority of their *shaykhs*. Small and weak tribes allied themselves with more powerful neighbours; in this way large tribal confederations under a paramount *shaykh* (*shaykh al-mashāyikh*) were formed, in order to serve collective needs which tribes could not fulfil separately. Such were the Khazā'il of the Middle Euphrates, the Āl Bū Muḥammad and Banī Lām of the Tigris, and the Muntafik in the south. These confederations became so powerful that they could defy the government and defeat its armies. The Muntafik ruled the whole of southern Iraq from the Euphrates to the Tigris and, for a time, the whole region down to and including the city of Baṣra. This powerful principality (*imārah*) consisted of nomadic, semi-nomadic, settled, and marsh-dwelling elements, widely disparate in ethnic origins, firmly rooted in the land and Shī'ī by religion. They owed allegiance to their *amīrs*, the Āl Sa'dūn, a Sunnī family originally from

Mecca and descended from the Prophet, who preserved their bedouin habits and refused to succumb to local influences. The Ottomans, in fact, came to depend upon the Muntafik to defend the frontiers against Persia and the powerful Wahhabis of the desert.[2]

Among the Arab tribes to the north of the alluvial plain, along the Tigris valley, and in the rolling uplands of the rainfall zone, the tribal system resembles that of the south. A different pattern of tribal society, however, is preserved by the Kurds of the north and northeast. For them the basis of tribal unity is common ties with the land rather than the extended family, as is characteristic of the Arabs. The Kurdish population includes both nomadic and settled elements, though the number of the nomads has fallen off rapidly in recent times. Indigenous tribal government among the Kurds may assume one of three forms: a classical tribal group of similar origin under an 'Āghā'; a tribe under a chief of different descent; and a tribe whose religious chiefs combine secular with religious authority.

How the process of change within traditional societies in modern times is to be viewed is a matter open to divergent interpretations. It is usually explained in terms of either modernisation or westernisation. 'Modernisation' carries the connotation of the adaptation of older, more primitive societies to newer modes of life, whereas 'westernisation' denotes the adoption by non-western societies of the ways of life and habits of mind characteristic of western technological societies. The one view sees the primary factors inducing societal transformation as indigenous to the society itself, whereas the other view places primary stress on exogenous factors. But since the adequacy of such concepts depends upon the evidence of history, an examination of the change which the traditional tribal society of rural Iraq has undergone over the last one hundred and fifty years is in order.

Long before the nineteenth century western traders, diplomatic representatives and missionaries had resided in the port city of Baṣra and to a lesser extent in Baghdad, and an occasional western traveller found his way through the countryside. But the penetration of the interior from the 1830s onwards as a result of the concession of steamboat navigation rights to Messrs Lynch Bros, and the opening of the Suez Canal in 1869, led to an eightfold increase in the total volume of Iraqi trade between 1870 and 1914. The fact that the rapid growth in export trade was primarily in agricultural products meant that the rural population was indirectly affected. Furthermore, Iraq had long been astride the mail route between Great Britain and India, and this led in the 1860s to the laying of telegraph lines connecting Iraq with Turkey, Iran, and India. The tribal areas lost some of their former isolation and were made more vulnerable to outside interference in their affairs. However, these essentially external influences had little direct effect on the fabric of Iraqi tribal life.

The impact of the West during this period was greater on the urban population than on rural areas, and was more economic than social in nature. If that portion of the urban community associated with trade prospered and grew, the hand-craft industries declined as a result of competition from foreign manufactures and hence urban growth slowed. But the impact was greatest on the urban upper and middle classes, although these were not and had never been tribal. It would therefore seem that it is among the factors indigenous to Ottoman and Arab relationships that the primary causes of social transformation in this period must be sought.

A perennial concern of the Ottoman government throughout the nineteenth century was the modernisation of its governmental institutions in order to facilitate the re-imposition of direct rule over the many diverse peoples of the empire, that is to say, to reverse the trend of the previous two centuries toward increasing autonomy under indigenous or semi-independent local rulers, and to establish a sound fiscal basis for its bureaucratic order. The government approached this task with caution and its performance was at best fitful and inconsistent. Its efforts were not directed toward the initiation of social change as such, but toward the consolidation and maintenance of Ottoman hegemony. Just as the various local rulers had established themselves on the basis of the control of the land within their domains, so the land provided the key to success or failure in the realisation of Ottoman objectives; only by wresting control of the land could the Ottomans establish their authority and meet the fiscal requirements of an expanding bureaucracy and a modern army. So far as Iraq was concerned, Ottoman policies were not successful, yet the actions taken were to have a decisive influence on the shape of social change.

[2] See the previous chapter on 'The Modern Arab World'.

Since 1747 the Ottoman governors of Iraq had been virtually independent Mamlūks or Georgian freedmen. By 1831 Persia had dropped its designs on Baṣra and the Wahhābī menace had declined, and hence the central government no longer needed Arab assistance and felt strong enough to challenge the power of the Mamlūks. Baghdad was occupied, the last of the Mamlūk governors, Dā'ūd Pasha, removed, and shortly thereafter the Kurdish principalities in the north of Iraq were eliminated and the semi-autonomous governors of Mosul (the Jalīlī family) deposed. Thereafter the government assumed control of the administration in Baghdad and the governors were appointed directly from Istanbul with instructions to break the power of the tribal confederacies and increase revenues. But the Turks had no consistent policy other than to divide and rule, setting various tribes within a confederation against one another and creating dissension among the *shaykhs*, who were induced to compete for the lucrative tax collection rights arbitrarily auctioned off by the governor of Baghdad. These actions met with only limited success, and created a wall of hostile and defiant tribesmen.

So far as the transformation of tribal society is concerned, the governorship of Midḥat Pasha (1869–72) was of crucial importance. First, he initiated the administrative system of municipal and provincial government. Accordingly, Muntafik became a District with Nāṣir Pasha Āl Sa'dūn, the Amīr of the confederacy, as Lieutenant-Governor, which brought to an end the long-standing independence of the Sa'dūn principality. Second, Midḥat introduced the Ottoman Land Code, by means of which he hoped to tie the cultivators (*fallāḥīn*) to the land, weaken the hold of the *shaykhs* over them, and bring them into direct contact with the government. He also believed that it would result in greater prosperity for both government and *fallāḥīn*. Until then the possession of tribal land was not based on grants or written documents but on the claims of tribes, from time immemorial, to land acquired either by conquest or by the settlement and cultivation of previously unoccupied lands. Ownership was a corporate affair, resting on the ability of the tribe as a whole to hold and defend its lands. The individual *fallāḥ* held such land as he cultivated by virtue of his membership in the tribe; and hence the methods and conditions of tenure were defined by tribal tradition. This was the situation *de facto*, but not *de jure* in the view of the Ottoman government and its courts. In their view, most tribal lands were state-owned (*mīrī*), and hence the government claimed a share of the produce as tax and an additional land-owner's share. The Ottoman Land Code of 1858 was the only legal basis on which Midḥat could rest in trying to reform the system of land-tenure. Under its provisions, he sought to allocate land to the *fallāḥīn* themselves, who were issued title deeds (*tapu sanads*) granting legal right of possession of the land only (the usufruct), while the final ownership or servitude (*raqabah*) remained vested in the government.

These innovations produced far-reaching social and economic changes which began to crystallise during the last thirty years of Ottoman rule. Tribesmen saw no value in mere 'scraps of paper' conferring rights which, in their view, they had always possessed and exercised freely, and they declined registration, while those better acquainted with the law, such as the Sa'dūns or the inhabitants of the cities, applied for and received title deeds to a great part of the tribal lands. Thus an additional class of absentee landlord, laying claim to a share of the yield, was created. Relationships within the tribe began to alter: the status of the *shaykhs* who had accepted title deeds to tribal lands shifted perceptibly from that of champions of their tribesmen to that of landlords, while tribesmen could take less pride in the shared possession of land by virtue of tribal membership and became increasingly mere tenants. The Land Code did not prevail, however, for in all other respects tribal custom continued to govern the rights connected with the land and also all social relationships. Indeed, neither the *tapu* holders nor the government could enforce their claims through the machinery of the Ottoman administration and the judiciary, and if they wished to do so they had to rely on tribal authorities such as the lesser *shaykhs* and *sarkāls*. While the great tribal confederations had been shattered and the power of the paramount *shaykhs* broken, and in some instances individual tribes fragmented, the tribal structure remained the only effectual basis for ordering the life of the rural population, and the only defence of the tribesmen against the insidious rapaciousness of *tapu* holder and government alike.

With the British occupation of Mesopotamia in 1914, the exogenous and indigenous factors contributing to social change became intermingled. While Western influence was predominant among the urban élites and the pace of this development rapidly accelerated until it became overwhelming, indigenous factors associated with the land continued to determine the pattern of social change in tribal areas, and hence the gap between urban and tribal societies widened.

British policy was directed initially toward the consolidation of British authority in the area and subsequently, once independence became imminent, to the transmission of power to friendly elements which could be relied upon to support British interests. The administrative system introduced by Midḥat became in British hands an efficient means of imposing the will of the government, while the use of aircraft and armoured vehicles facilitated the more effective surveillance and control of tribal areas.[3] The systematic exaction of revenues, which the Ottomans had claimed but had never been able to realise, produced returns three and a half times greater in 1920 than those of 1911. The collection of revenue per capita in Muntafik increased more than fifteen-fold from 1916 to 1919: never before and never since has the proportion of taxation been so high in the tribal areas. However, government services did not keep pace with this dramatic increase, since the inflated salaries of British personnel and the provision of the amenities they required took a substantial part of the budget. The oppressiveness of this state of affairs was a prime factor in precipitating the bloody and costly tribal insurrection of 1920, which led subsequently to the granting of national rule.

In regard to the land, British policy was essentially conservative; it made a genuine attempt to ascertain established practice, and tried to standardise and stabilise it by giving it the force of law. But in consequence of this, customs of only recent and rather dubious origin became entrenched in law; and even customs of older and firmer origin changed their nature. *Shaykhs* holding leases became virtual landlords of tribal lands by law, as they had previously been by tribal custom; but whereas they had been responsible to the tribesmen so long as their position was based on tribal custom, now their position was guaranteed by the government and they could appeal to it in any dispute with the *fallāḥīn*. The balance of power was therefore tilted still further against the *fallāḥīn*, and the landlords (many of whom now moved into the towns and cities and became absentees) amassed great wealth.

The social and political consequences were even more important than the economic consequences. The British to some extent reversed the policy of the Turks by strengthening the hand of the tribal *shaykhs* whom they used to exercise control over the area. Meanwhile, the relation of the *shaykhs* to their tribesmen had radically changed. In fact, during the insurrection of 1920, the enmity of the insurgent *shaykhs* and tribesmen was directed, not only against the British, but also against those *shaykhs* and *sarkāls* who had exploited the new situation for their personal aggrandisement. This feeling was exacerbated by the habit of settling unfavourably the claims of *shaykhs* who had sided with the Turks in the Great War or who had participated in the insurrection, thereby weakening their position, while those who had been cooperative were rewarded with generous settlements and their position strengthened. A similar policy was followed down to 1958. Whereas formerly the relationship between *shaykh* and tribesmen had been tribal in the fullest sense, with both status and income accruing to the office of the *shaykh*, and not to his person, now it became mainly economic, a relationship of landlord and tenant. This new relationship was codified by the Land Settlement Law of 1932, by which settlement of title to tribal lands was made to the *shaykh*. Because the more powerful *shaykhs* were also members of Parliament – indeed it was a Parliament of *shaykhs* rather than a parliamentary democracy – the government supported the claims of landlords. This enabled the consolidation and extension of their landholdings until the vast size of estates, particularly in the irrigation zone, became the most striking characteristic of landownership in Iraq. This made for conservatism in social policy, and alienated the mass of the people from their rulers.

Iraq had become virtually two nations governed by two sets of laws; one for landlords and urban dwellers and another for the tribesmen who were tied in law to the land. A law of 1933 provided that no *fallāḥ* in debt to his landlord could leave the land; he had become in effect a serf and not properly speaking a tenant, since he had no security or freedom of action. This contrasted sharply with his

[3] Glubb Pasha (Glubb, Lieutenant-General Sir John Bagot. *War in the Desert: An R.A.F. Frontier Campaign*. London: Hodder and Stoughton, 1960, p. 69), points to Iraq in 1921, as the first instance in which air-forces were employed in the place of ground troops for internal security duties following the insurrection.

Iraqi tribesmen near Ctesiphon (al-Madā'in)

former status, as a tribesman with rights to a share in the land communally held. The only escape was to leave the tribal *dīrah* entirely. This gave impetus to a rural exodus: some were attracted to Kuwait when its oilfields were opened; but the majority flocked to the cities, particularly to Baghdad, once oil revenues in the 1950s began to generate development projects and demand increased for labourers in the construction industry. Emigration from 'Amārah, which had been in progress since the 1920s, greatly accelerated in the 1950s, reaching the rate of ten lorry-loads a day leaving for Baghdad. This led to a decline in agricultural yields in the south, diminished population growth relative to other areas of the country, and contributed to the phenomenal increase in the population of Baghdad with its festering slums. Those who left the tribal areas cut their former ties and ceased to be tribal: they now became a part of a new order, where social change followed different patterns.

Under the circumstances, riots and insurrection became endemic to the area. When an attempt was made to introduce reform legislation in 1937, however, the *shaykhs* threatened open rebellion and brought the government down. The government under the old order was powerless, since not only did any measure it might propose for dealing with this situation face almost certain defeat in Parliament, but the *shaykhs* could also still arouse the tribes to rebel against change, using as a pretext the age-old issue of the much hated taxation. In these circumstances, the overthrow of the government by violence became almost inevitable.

On 14 July 1958, the military under General 'Abd al-Karīm Qāsim led a social and political revolution. Within six weeks an Agrarian Reform Law was decreed. Its objectives were twofold: (1) to destroy the power of the large, landholding *shaykhs* and to raise the standard of living and the social status of the *fallāḥīn*; and (2) to increase the proportion of agricultural production as a component of the national income. In order to facilitate these objectives, all landholdings in excess of certain acreages, varying in accordance with the means of watering, were to be expropriated and redistributed in small, family-sized plots to the individual *fallāh*. To date, however, the terms of the law have only partially been fulfilled and it is generally deemed to have been a failure. Modelled after the Egyptian Agrarian Reform Law of 1952, it was not suitable for agricultural conditions in Iraq. It left the individual *fallāḥ* without capital, supervision, or the basis for co-operative work; the government negated the basis of tribal order without substituting a viable alternative. The results were a decline in crop yields necessitating the importation of food staples, the rapid depletion of the soil owing to salinity and hence the abandonment of many plots by *fallāḥīn* and continued emigration to the cities. The irony in the present situation is that, generally speaking, crop yields are greater and the *fallāḥīn* more contented on middle-sized estates where the *shaykh* continues to supervise the labour, provides services ranging from the extension of credit to the marketing of produce, and arbitrates disputes. In fact, traditional practices have been reintroduced in some areas in order to stimulate agricultural production and to bring the land back into cultivation, though admittedly as a temporary expedient.

Except for the transformation in the role of many of the *shaykhs*, the structure of tribal society and its traditions remain firmly established. Tribal conservatism entails resistance to change. Yet change is urgently necessary if Iraq is to provide for its future generations. Once the oil resources are depleted, the only resource remaining will be the land, and it will perhaps need to provide the economic base for the support of a population double the present one. The prerequisites for the successful realisation of that objective are governmental stability, the construction of an extensive flood-control and canal system which will maximise usage of water resources, drainage schemes for the desalination of the land, and a social structure adaptable to change yet suited to the requirements of collective effort. The task of providing irrigation and drainage schemes is formidable and costly, but is within the capacity of modern hydrological engineering and of the government to fund them while there are adequate oil revenues. The task of overcoming the social obstacles to newer and more efficient techniques of cultivation is more difficult and calls for greater delicacy. The challenge of the future is not the adoption of western social structures and attitudes, but a social transformation which will make for a freer and more prosperous life, will preserve the positive attributes of the older society, and function within the limitations indigenous to the region. A modern society which secures a firm foundation for the resuscitation and future prosperity of this once famous land must conform to the requirements of irrigation imposed by the twin rivers. It could then once again realise the meaning of the affectionate invocation of an ancient Sumerian seer:

> O thou river who didst bring forth all things,
> When the great gods dug thee out,
> They set prosperity on thy banks.

The Shah of Iran visiting development areas in southern Iran

16

Iran

W. G. MILLWARD

The basic patterns of traditional society and culture that have dominated, until recently, those areas of the Middle East inhabited by peoples of Iranian stock are of diverse origins and relative antiquity. It can be argued plausibly, for example, that certain traits of character, mental attitudes, moral values and social customs exhibited or practised by many Iranians today reflect the inheritance of the Zoroastrian past and the legacy of the imperial memories of Achaemenian and Sasanian times. Nevertheless, though scholars may differ over the degree of its relevance and application, there is general agreement that the cultural matrix of traditional Iranian society was, as it still is today (though to a rapidly diminishing extent), the ethical and spiritual complex of Islam. The framework of this complex was erected in the two centuries that followed in the wake of the Arab conquests of Iraq, the Iranian plateau and Central Asia in the mid-seventh century of our era. After this period of relative quiescence, while the Persians were gradually adjusting to the radical changes wrought in their social and cultural system from the impact of this Arab, tribal and basically nomadic invasion, their Iranian spirit reasserted itself in the form of a series of politically independent states and dynasties and, on the cultural plane, in a linguistic and literary recrudescence symbolised by the *Shāhnāmah* of the poet Firdawsī (d. 1020). This Iranian spirit, further tried and tempered by devastating incursions from without by Turks, Mongols and Afghans and by innumerable internecine conflicts, has carried over into the twentieth century and in the process enabled the Iranians to manifest an innate sense of their own centuries-old identity and their distinctness *vis-à-vis* their neighbours. Among the most salient national characteristics of the Iranians, therefore, are their capacity for survival and their sense of being different.

But a threat to the survival-power and self-confidence of Iranians in modern times has arisen from the impact of Western social and political ideas and as the consequence of an all-out espousal, on the part of their government, of policies of modernisation and technical development. The chief result of this impact has been to introduce, as the most striking and significant facet of social and cultural experience in contemporary Iran, the factor of change, an ongoing process which threatens ultimately the very foundations of the traditional social order. Yet, while changes in this sphere of Iranian life are important and central, we should not be blinded to the corresponding relevance and importance of tradition and continuity. Large areas of the national life in Iran are still heavily influenced, even dominated, by the moral values of Islam and by traditional folkways. The reason why change has tended to monopolise the attention of students of the contemporary scene in Iran is the fact that the process runs so deep and has effects so far-reaching; thus, for a second time, after the passage of roughly thirteen centuries, Iranians are facing a type of change which seems certain to transform the basic pattern of their traditional social order. How long the process will take to effect this transformation is difficult to predict. There is conclusive evidence that the social and class structure of Iranian society has already sustained radical change in the last several decades, chiefly in the rapid growth and expansion of the professional middle class. In any conflict between continuity and change, between tradition and modernity, the end-result can only be viewed and properly evaluated from the vantage point of history. In certain spheres the process has gone far enough already to ensure that the nature of Iranian society in the near future will be generically different from its traditional version in the recent past.

In order to appreciate the significance of Western-inspired change on the social and cultural life of the modern Iranian, on his intellectual and psychological orientations and his spiritual inclinations, one must first cast a brief look backwards in time and consult the historical record. The interpretation of this record depends of course on one's viewpoint, but if we take our cue from leading spokesmen generally accepted by Iranians themselves, we may more easily understand the insider's perception of this process, when it began and how far it may have proceeded. One prominent Iranian writer believed that his people, in common with many other easterners, have always had a basic predisposition in a westerly direction.

> History reveals that we have always had our gaze fixed firmly on the west. . . This multi-dimensional 'we', during these ages, has constantly had the west in view – the shores of the Mediterranean, Greece, the Nile valley, Lybia, and the far-west, i.e. Europe and the amber seas of the north. We, the inhabitants of the Iranian plateau, have been but a small portion of this great entity, and as such have always set our sights on the west. . . Perhaps our westward orientation arises from the fact that we have always been waiting expectantly, in this dry expanse of ours, for Mediterranean clouds. Although the east is the source of enlightenment, still, for us, inhabitants of the Iranian plateau, the rain-bearing clouds have come always from the west.'[1]

Among other reasons he adduces for the directional bias of Iranians in favour of the west are a recoil and escape from the cloying embrace of mother India and the constant pressure of destructive incursions from eastern nomads. In this same writer's view it was roughly three centuries ago that the spirit of rivalry and equality of competition with westerners which animated this basic predisposition westward, was transformed into an attitude of inferiority and submissiveness. As a result of crushing military defeats at the hands of the Ottomans and the Russians (who are considered a part of the Western world for the purposes of this essay); the sectarian and obscurantist tendencies of the clerical élite who exercised excessive influence in the declining years of the Ṣafavid dynasty (1629–1722); the decline of the transit trade routes from the east after the circumnavigation of Africa (1498); and the rising aggressiveness of Western colonialism – for all these and other reasons, the Iranian body politic was debilitated by chronic anaemia and susceptible to the germ of a sickness with which it is still afflicted, 'Westomania', i.e. the condition or state of being 'struck' by the West. The major symptom of this illness (of which we will hear more later) is an abject servility to the dictates of technology and the machine and to their Western origins.

Many Iranians consider this interpretation of the historical record exaggerated and extreme. Most of the same factors, however, are accepted by more conservative scholars to explain the eastern, especially the Iranian, predisposition toward the West in modern times and their preoccupation with the acquisition of modern techniques. Another respected scholar cites all but one of these same historical antecedents to explain the 'backwardness' of Iran and her 'ignorance' of the new knowledge and techniques being developed in the West during the seventeenth and eighteenth centuries. In his view it was the crippling and senseless losses inflicted on Iran in defeats at the hands of the already technologically superior Russians which attracted the attention of many Iranian leaders to the need to acquire the rudiments of modern science and the facilities of the new mode of civilisation.[2] The solution to the problem devised by the authorities of a later period was to send a select group of students to England, and still later to France and Germany, to acquire knowledge of new sciences useful 'to themselves, their political leaders and their country in general'. This policy, begun in 1811, has continued up to the present as the major vehicle for the acquisition of modern science and technology and for the insemination of Western standards and values at virtually all levels of national life.

It was in the nineteenth century too that actual contacts between Iran and Western countries, particularly European, were gradually extended through the vehicles of trade and diplomacy. Westerners first came to Iran as travellers and missionaries, then as diplomats and commercial concessionaires, later as occupation troops and finally, in ever-increasing numbers, as technical experts, advisers and teachers.

[1] Jalāl Āl-i Aḥmad, *Gharbzadagī*, (Tehran, 1341/1962), pp. 12, 18.

[2] Farīdūn Ādamīyat, *Fikr-i āzādī va muqaddimah-yi nahẓat-i mashrūṭīyat*, (Tehran: Sukhan, 1340/1961), pp. 21–3.

At present there are some fifteen-thousand-odd foreigners of Western provenance living and working in Iran, ostensibly assisting in the process of development and modernisation. At the same time there are more than twenty thousand Iranians studying abroad (mostly in Western countries), hoping to add to their country's modernising potential. The two World Wars brought Iran firmly within the orbit of the Western powers and subjected her to the exigencies of international *Realpolitik*. The legacy of these war-time experiences still influences the conduct of most Iranians in their contacts with foreigners. Though they are anxious to avail themselves of the many advantages of modern education, scientific advances and industrial development as these are known in the West, many individual Iranians still harbour resentment (often less than thinly disguised) at having to acquire them from people whom they regard primarily as the imperialists who occupied their country in the Second World War and forced the abdication of their ruler, and who have in any case exploited them economically for centuries. Above all, they accept the desirability of Western technical know-how but reject the values on which most Western societies are based.

The net result of this expanding contact over the years with representatives of the so-called 'developed' or 'progressive' countries, including Russia, has been the transformation of many basic structures and attitudes of the traditional Islamic society of Iran. Under the influence of the activities and writings of men like Mīrzā Muḥammad Ṣāliḥ, Amīr Kabīr, Mīrzā Ḥusayn Khān Sipahsālār, Mīrzā Malkum Khān and Jamāl al-Dīn Asadābādī, certain elements of the population were motivated to seek actively the reform of the political system in Iran, particularly with a view to limiting the arbitrary power of the autocratic Qājār Shāhs. Whereas the movement for reform and modernisation, along Western lines, of the military, bureaucratic and financial systems of the traditional order came primarily from the ruling authority of the day, the demand for limitation on the power of the sovereign and the establishment of a constitutional government based in law was strongest among the ranks of the middle and lower classes who had suffered most from the ruler's oppression. Drawing partly on the egalitarian aspects of Islamic tradition and partly on the inspiration of the theories of Western political philosophy (and some of their practical models), the Persian Constitutional Revolutionary Movement gathered momentum during the early years of the twentieth century; and it succeeded finally in 1906 (under the leadership of Western-oriented secularists like Ḥasan Taqīzādah and liberal Islamic clergymen such as the two Sayyids Ṭabāṭabā'ī and Bihbihānī) in forcing on the sovereign acceptance of a Fundamental Law which would provide for constitutional government representative of popular wishes, and a check on the monarch's arbitrary and unilateral exercise of power. In the years that followed up to 1925, many Iranians learned from painful experience the lesson that reform and change in political affairs cannot be accomplished merely by the promulgation of a document, nor by the setting up of a formal body or council for specific political activities. What is required is a broad base of popular support amongst all classes of the society for the principles and values behind the changes. Since this was lacking in Iran in the early years of this century it proved impossible to make real the changes envisaged in the Constitution of 1906. As a consequence, from 1925 to the present, the country has been governed by a new dynasty, the Pahlavīs; Riẓā Shāh (Reza Shāh) and his son Muḥammad Riẓā (Reza) Shāh, have both exercised power according to the traditional methods of authoritarian government developed and refined over the centuries by Persian kings, and patterned more specifically on the model of the 'web-system' of the Ṣafavid dynasty in the Islamic period.

Since 1925 the ruling authority of Iran has vigorously espoused the policies of modernisation and development. By fiat from above, changes have been decreed in virtually all sectors of Iranian life designed to bring Iran into line with the example of the developed and industrialised nations of eastern and western Europe and North America, i.e. the West (Japan has only recently been accepted as a tutelary exemplar). The basic reforms were accomplished by royal decree under Riẓā Shāh, and included remodelling, wholly or in part, the judiciary, the bureaucracy, education, communications and industry. The philosophy of 'social engineering' implicit in these measures for the physical reconstitution of Iranian society has been continued under the leadership of the present Shah and his advisors, including many young technocrats who have been co-opted into the political élite. Muḥammad Riẓā Shāh, building on the new foundations laid down by his father, and blessed with the incalculable good fortune of unlimited revenues from Iran's abundant oil reserves, has attempted to create a new infrastructure for Iranian society. The philosophy behind his actions and the specific policies for the attainment of his objectives have been spelled out in two books, *Mission for My Country* (London, Hutchinson and Company, 1960) and *The White Revolution* (Tehran, Imperial Pahlavi Library, 1967). As the French title of the latter book (*La révolution sociale de l'Iran*) suggests, the basic objective, in addition to increasing the agricultural productivity and industrial capacity of Iran, and securing the state financially and militarily, is to bring about a thoroughgoing social revolution. There is an undeniable aura of welfarism, of concern for the interests and aspirations of all sectors and classes of society, and even a note of high moral purpose reflected in the pages of this book. It is undeniable that many of the measures proposed for the improvement of the lot of the masses – particularly the basic programme of land reform – have already begun to bear fruit. What is missing in both these books is a clear statement of the principles of moral value which inspired the social changes they propose; in short, a new system of social values which will undergird and support the new social edifice created by the reconstructive efforts of the two Pahlavī monarchs and their governments. There is still an urgent need for official sanction and support for a social value system which will be congruent with and supportive of the new structure called 'modern Iranian society'. More important still, and more vital in the short term, is the need also for a practical programme for the inculcation of these values in the minds of the younger generation.

It is clear that the changes effected in the pattern and structure of Iranian society by Pahlavī blueprints have concerned what we might call the external or the institutional-organisational frame of reference. Plans have been laid and more or less fulfilled, by such government agencies as the Plan Organisation, for the reform and extension of social services, the expansion of steel production, the exploitation of various natural resources, and many other laudable objectives. These are concrete signs of material and physical progress. What is equally obvious is that little or no account has been taken of how to cope with the problems of the persistence of traditional attitudes and moral values in the minds of the mass of the population, who are expected to function within the fabric of the physical and organisational framework of the new society. The problem of value-lag is not an unknown phenomenon even in Western societies. It is, however, the most important feature of contemporary Iranian society, since it is more acute in degree and affects all levels of the total structure.

The problem of value-lag and moral disequilibrium as a result of the over-rapid changes required by westernisation and industrial development are best illustrated, in the context of contemporary Iran, in those areas of society represented by the family and child-rearing, education and mental health. Despite the existence of newly established structures deriving from early efforts in modernisation, many traditional attitudes and their value-sanctions still persist even in more public spheres such as business, bureaucratic administration, and the law as it relates to personal status. Since with Iranians however, as with most other peoples, politics is fundamentally and inextricably bound up with these areas of concern, it may serve as an instructive example of the present situation. In theory and in practice there have been many changes in the structure and administration of government in Iran since the Constitution was granted in 1906. But closer observation reveals that these changes have been for the most part nominal and superficial. The traditional system and power-relationships it embodies remain virtually intact. Despite the wide expansion of government services and in the ranks of the bureaucracy, the creation of quasi-ministerial agencies to handle specific tasks such as planning for development, and the changes of nomenclature for various divisions and posts of the government, effective decision-making power remains in the hands of the Shah – at the centre of the political process – in all areas of public policy. The co-option of 'new men' into the government, members of the new class of the professional–bureaucratic intelligentsia, many of whom have had some foreign (usually Western) experience and education has brought about a noticeable increase in administrative efficiency in such areas as the National Iranian Oil Company, the Plan Organisation, and other government agencies. The effect in the more traditional branches of the administration is less marked so far.[3]

[3] For the problem of the clash between the new and the old in government in Iran, see, James A. Bill, *The politics of Iran: groups, classes and modernization*, (Columbus, Ohio: Merrill, 1972), chapters 2–4.

The 'T' jetty at Kharg Island, Iran's deep-water terminal in the Persian Gulf, which is capable of handling oil tankers larger than any so far built

Persepolis, ruins of the Achaemenid palace. In the background are tents erected for the 2,500th Anniversary celebrations of the founding of the Persian state

Of all the political philosophies and ideologies of the Western world none has had a more potent influence on the mind of Iranians, rulers and ruled alike, than that of nationalism. The lure and blandishments of this nineteenth- and early twentieth-century political preoccupation of the West, were strong for Iranians, with their long tradition of recurrent national and imperial sovereignty stretching back over nearly twenty-five centuries. Riẓā Shāh made nationalism and the celebration of the glories of Achaemenid and Sasanid Persian imperial tradition a cornerstone of his nation-building programmes. The same concern for the cultivation of a sense of national self-awareness and identity has been exhibited by the present king from the beginning of his reign, and was made the subject for an international celebration in October of 1971, when he gave an elaborate and expensive open-house in Tehran and Shiraz (Persepolis) to commemorate 2500 years of Iranian monarchical tradition. But, beyond a certain point, the glories of pre-Islamic Iran can only be extolled at the expense of those of the traditional Islamic society. The inflexible and hierarchical social structure of Sasanid Iran and the Zoroastrian values on which it was based were vehemently rejected by the peasantry and other oppressed elements of Iranian society in the seventh century, when Islam arrived promising in theory greater equality, mobility and freedom. Though Iranians for the most part chose to assert their individuality and separateness under the banner of Islam by opting for the Shī'ite rite thereof during the hegemony of the Ṣafavid dynasty, they nonetheless have always been at pains to stress also their full membership in the Islamic community and to emphasise their unique contributions to the highest achievements of Islamic culture and civilisation. By playing too much on the theme of nationalism and the glories of ancient Persia, Iran in recent times has suffered a significant estrangement from her Arab neighbours and other co-religionists. Many of her differences with the Arab countries are based primarily on conflicting political persuasions, but the excessive emphasis on national identity based on ethnic and linguistic particularity and pre-Islamic social and cultural traditions has served to loosen the bonds of brotherhood in Islam and produced a wide and enduring fissure in the bedrock of Islamic cultural unity.

The impact of nationalism and modernisation in the realm of religion is difficult to measure effectively. Certainly recent Iranian governments have had religious policies calculated to reduce and eliminate the role of religion, and of its custodians, in political affairs, presumably out of zeal to imitate most Western models of the modern nation-state. Traditionally the clergy, through its highest-ranking members, have played an influential role at the centre of power in the Islamic society of Iran. Riẓā Shāh sought deliberately to alter this clerical role by excluding them from his counsels and striking at their economic viability by withdrawing from them control of the administration of justice and education, and by seizing *waqf*-properties (mortmain) and their revenues and placing them in the hands of a government department. The present king has continued the policy of disestablishing the Muslim clergy from their niche in the traditional social structure. Other methods employed to achieve this objective have been the personal appointment of *imām-i jum'ahs* (chief religious functionaries) in the cities and principal towns of the country, the supervision and control of many seminaries and clerical training grounds (especially those attached to universities), and the banishment or exile of key leaders who represent potential foci of opposition to government reform programmes. The government has obviously not overtly attempted to influence official doctrine. By its policies of modernisation and social change, however, it has in effect transformed the role traditionally played by religion as the sanction for all social relations and interaction. Religion has been excluded from the realm of temporal affairs, and its custodians economically emasculated and cut off from many of their traditional sources of support. Since Islamic law has been virtually superseded (except for a residue in the civil code) by new codes of law based on European models, the Shī'ite clergy in Iran are now relegated to the single role of providing spiritual guidance for the believing masses. Iranian adherence to the sectarian Shī'ite rite of Islam, which incorporates as a matter of official doctrine the principle of legitimate dynastic succession in the temporal and spiritual headship of the community of believers (a principle which is duplicated in the Iranian political tradition), clearly serves the interests of national identity; but the government has recently limited clerical attempts to propagandise and missionise by closing down such mission centres as the Ḥusaynīyah Irshād, for fear, it is alleged, of offending the sensibilities of the Sunnī Muslim majority in neighbouring Arab states, Turkey and Afghanistan.

Another characteristic feature of religious life in Iran since the acceleration of modernisation following the Second World War has been a concomitant increase in the incidence of secularism. In traditional terms the concept of secularism is redundant in a truly Islamic society. Since, ideally, Islam relates to and rules upon all aspects of the believer's and the society's existence, there is no room for the secularist in traditional society. He is a contradiction in terms. The fact remains, however, that there has always been a subtle strand of freethinking and nonconformism in the warp and woof of Iranian history. The rebellions associated with the names of Mānī and Mazdak in Sasanian times were in effect social protests against the stifling conformity exacted by the Zoroastrian establishment. In Islamic times there were numerous examples of the healthy scepticism of independent spirits, whose position most people would associate with the poetry of 'Umar Khayyām. It is significant that Khayyām was more famous in his homeland as a scientist. In the mental and spiritual climate created by the exclusion of religion from the public domain, and by the heavy emphasis attached to scientific study and enquiry on the road to modernisation, it is natural that this historical penchant for freethinking and indifference to formal religion should find greater scope. Young people who no longer receive the traditional diet of religious instruction in their modernised education programmes set down by the Ministry of Education, are not so much anti-religious as areligious in their outlook. They regard formal religion and the values and duties it prescribes as irrelevant to the style of life they wish to live. The same attitude is prevalent among the technically trained and scientifically oriented new generation, some of whom are members of the present political élite responsible for guiding development and modernisation programmes.

Ironically, attempts to modernise and reformulate traditional Islamic doctrines, to make them more relevant and comprehensible to the new generation, have only recently begun in Shī'ite Iran. In lands of Sunnī tradition such as India and Egypt, the challenge of science and secularism was felt and met around the turn of the century (and even earlier) through the efforts of men like Muḥammad Iqbāl and Muḥammad 'Abduh. This suggests that Iran may be approximately half a century behind many of her Muslim neighbours in the confrontation with secularism; and since science and technology have advanced dramatically and unpredictably in the last fifty years, it may prove necessary for her religious leaders to increase their efforts to combat those forces which tend to erode the relevance of religion in the national life. They may take some encouragement from the fact that secularism in Turkey and Egypt seems to have declined in recent years.

In the domain of literature there have been two major trends apparent in Iran since the beginning of the nineteenth century and the opening of contact with the West. The influence of Western standards came first in the realm of content and ideas. Returning students, travellers and diplomats filled their literary testaments (usually in the form of travelogues and diaries) with descriptions of Western society and institutions and the ideas on which they were allegedly based. By the turn of the century many political concepts such as democracy, liberalism, socialism, republicanism, constitutional government and the rule of law, even if imperfectly understood in some cases, had been appropriated and made an integral part of the vocabulary and intellectual equipment of many Iranian writers. They even found expression in highly traditional forms, as witness the work of poets like Bahār, 'Ārif and 'Ishqī.[4] Since literature has traditionally been a conservative art form where conventions are slow to change, it was not until the early years of this century that Iranian writers tried their hand at adopting Western literary forms and genres. A sharp break with the canons of traditional Persian poetry came in the person of Nīmā Yūshīj (d. 1959), who first experimented with new verse forms and eliminated rhyme. Every style of poetic expression known in the Western world has been attempted by someone or other among the last several generations of Persian poets. But the battle between the partisans of traditional Persian verse and the so-called 'New Wave', the devotees of the new poetry, continues apace. In the realm of prose, the short-story has been successfully adapted by a number of writers of the first rank, such as Jamālzādah and Chūbak. It is generally agreed, however, that the novel and the drama have yet to be thoroughly assimilated and made an integral part of the Persian literary canon, notwithstanding the appearance of several outstanding examples of both genres by excellent writers.

[4] See Yaḥyā Āryanpūr, *Az Ṣabā tā Nīmā*, 2 vols. (Tehran: Kitābhā-yi jaybī, 1350/1971), 2:332–81.

A developed and highly articulated literary corpus requires an educated populace with consistent reading habits. Iranians are a people with a long, respected and in some areas unparalleled literary tradition. Poetry has always held pride of place among the Iranians as a vehicle for literary creativity and will probably continue to do so for some time to come. With the spread of literacy, the extension of facilities for education, and the development of a broadly-based political consciousness and social awareness, the popularity of and demand for varied prose forms should increase significantly. At the moment there is a sizable demand only for the products of the daily press and the weekly and monthly illustrated magazines. These latter frequently contain articles dealing with purely literary matters, and sometimes a mixture of literary, social and human-interest themes in the form of interviews with prominent literary figures. It has to be emphasised that no Iranian writer of literary merit has yet been able to earn his living solely by writing. Most prominent figures of the present generation are either of independent means or earn their primary livelihood in a related profession such as teaching or journalism.

The use of literature as a vehicle for social criticism has yet to strike deep roots in Iran. There are isolated examples of attempts to use the novel to point up certain social abuses and inequities (Āl-i Aḥmad's *Nūn va'l-Qalam* ['N' and Pen] and *Nafrīn-i Zamīn* [The Curse of the Earth]). But on the whole comment on and criticism of public policy and of the persistence of social problems and inequalities is rigidly controlled by state censorship. The destructive and inhibiting effect of censorship on the creative processes of the artist discourages most writers from seriously turning their attention to social themes. Those who persist find that they must cloak their references and allusions to such matters in symbolic and metaphorical language to by-pass the censor – a device which frequently precludes being fully understood by the reading public. To escape these limitations, some socially conscious and critical writers have chosen or felt obliged to live abroad. There is a school of thought in Iran, as there is elsewhere, that believes literature has nothing to do with political issues and social problems and should be restricted to the non-controversial realm of nature and aesthetics. Their ideal is a poet like Suhrāb Sipihrī. But this school of thought is in the minority even in Iran, and its support is declining. The new spirit of enquiry and curiosity fostered by the scientific approach, and the new educational curricula of Iranian schools, will produce an increasing number of citizens who wish to see no limits placed on the creative impulses of the writer or poet. When the tastes and values of such people prevail modern Persian literature will no doubt develop and mature and take its place in the caravan of world literature.

What of the present situation and the prospects for the future? Is contemporary Iran still a 'West-struck' society doomed to follow the directions required by technology and industrial development? Can Iranians manage to preserve, in the face of the continuing pressures exerted by modernisation and change, their essential core of identity as shaped over the centuries? Most Iranians who admit to the existence of this problem agree with the basic diagnosis made by Jalāl Āl-i Aḥmad a decade ago. But unless they also share his pessimism, they would not agree with his predictions for the future. The majority of Iranians, modern and traditional alike, believe that change is inevitable. Those who are products of the last three generations of the modern educational system would add that it is also desirable. Development in all spheres is the declared objective of the present authorities. In a recent interview with a Western newsman, the Shah predicted that by the decade of the 1980s there would be two developed and sophisticated industrial nations in Asia: Japan and Iran. Even discounting the not unnatural partisanship of these claims, Iran may have a better chance than most Third World countries of success with its development plans. The record of the last decade in several fields is impressive by international standards. There can be little doubt of the continuing survival-power of the Iranian today. The question of the moment for most intellectuals is what the new costs of survival will be in the rush of enthusiasm for change. The basic problem remains: what role should be given to science, technology and industrial development in the overall scheme of modern Iranian society? How can Iran develop its human and natural resources without falling prey to the same disabilities that have too often been unintended by-products of development in the West? Clearly slavish imitation of Western examples is not the way. But with so many Westerners living in the country and directly involved in the development process, can this be avoided? A number of Iranian thinkers sincerely believe that the present course will lead to disaster.

According to one, if the mechanisms and techniques used for development in the West are applied uncritically in Iran, the very least that can be expected is more psychic disorientation and a greater incidence of mental illness.[5] The need for change, even the transformation of the traditional structure of Iranian society and the value systems on which it was based, is recognised and accepted by a majority of Iranians educated in the state school system since 1950. It is even widely regarded as an accomplished fact. Where they do not agree is on the following questions: what shape should the new structure have? What weight should be given to technology and industrialisation in contrast to the humanities in education and social planning? Which traditional values should be retained and which rejected? How can new systems, techniques and values, adopted in the process of modernisation, be made congruent and harmonious with the Iranian spirit, as it has been refined and tested by the vicissitudes of the ages? Despite many prophecies of doom, it seems likely that the technocrats will have their way in the foreseeable future, leaving the matter of value-adjustment to take care of itself. This arouses the anxieties of those who believe that technical and industrial development have their own inexorable logic and momentum, and that the consequences are frequently disastrous in the realm of human values. Whether the new society presently emerging in Iran has sufficiently stable institutions to withstand a prolonged period of value-conflict between traditional and modern standards is an open question.

[5] Riz̤ā Ārāstah (Reza Arasteh), *Naqsh-i ʻilm va Ṣanʻat dar tajdīd-i ḥayāt-i millathā*, (Tehran: Shirkat-i Sahāmi-i Intishār, 1347/1968), p. 100.

Sultan Sulaymān the Magnificent and his army before Sigetvár in Hungary on his last campaign, 1566. From a sixteenth-century Turkish manuscript

17

Turkey: from cosmopolitan empire to nation state

ELEAZAR BIRNBAUM

The peak period of Ottoman Turkish power in Europe is usually considered to be the reign of Sultan Sulaymān (*Süleymān*)[1] the Magnificent (1526–66). His empire encompassed the Turkish heartland of Asia Minor and all the other Muslim lands around the Mediterranean from Syria to Algeria, as well as Arabia and parts of Iraq and Iran, while the Black Sea was almost surrounded by Ottoman lands. Much of south-eastern Europe, including the whole of the Balkans, was his. The Ottoman armies struggled with Christendom's forces in Hungary and besieged Vienna in 1529. Western statesmen and writers have often expressed satisfaction that Europe was 'saved from the Turkish hordes'. The Turks gradually relinquished most of these lands in the following centuries. Recently, however, they have made a new but peaceful 'invasion' of central and western Europe. In the late 1960s and the early 1970s, hundreds of thousands of Turks poured in, not as conquerors, but as workers, providing much needed manpower in factories. In 1972 there were half a million of them in Federal Germany alone, and smaller numbers in other countries. Another million are waiting impatiently to go to Europe. One might be tempted to say that now Europe is being economically saved *by* the 'Turkish hordes'.

The country we call Turkey is geographically 97 per cent in Asia and only 3 per cent in Europe. Between these continents it has acted as a bridge across which there has been a two-way traffic of peoples, ideas and armies throughout recorded history. This land has variously been the centre or the possession of several major empires – Hittite, Persian, Greek, Roman, and then Byzantine, that bulwark of Christendom against an expanding Islam. Not long after the death of Muḥammad in Arabia in 632, Muslim *ghāzīs* (*ġāzī* = fighter in Islam's Holy War) were pushing against Byzantium's land frontiers in south-eastern Anatolia; three times they besieged Constantinople. Among these warriors, Arabs and other converts to Islam, there were not yet any Turks. It was only somewhat later that the Turkish peoples made contact with Islam, when they gradually migrated westward from their east central Asian homelands, and reached the Iranian-speaking areas of Transoxania in Central Asia. Many of the Turks soon became eager Muslims. They proved to be excellent soldiers, and from the ninth century onwards they were recruited by the local rulers, first as royal bodyguards, later into fighting units. Before long Turks constituted the main military forces of the Islamic world.

In the eleventh century Turkish *ghāzīs*, having crossed Iran, were pressing on Byzantium's eastern frontiers, and when these were breached in 1071 they continued westward across Asia Minor, often assisted by the local Christians who were very discontented with Byzantine rule. The *ghāzīs* had several motives. In expanding the Abode of Islam, they were fulfilling a major religious duty. If they should die in battle they were assured of paradise, and if they survived they would obtain booty. The conquerors established small states, piecemeal, in many parts of the peninsula, and it became steadily Islamised and Turkicised, by immigration, settlement, and increasingly by conversion of the Christian population. The distinctive features of Islamic civilisation took root: the social organisation and administration, the educational system, and the architecture. As these were consolidated in the hinterland, the borders were being

[1] The italicised forms in parentheses throughout the chapter represent the Turkish spelling of Islamic names and terms.

constantly pushed further west by enthusiastic *ghāzīs*.

One of the *ghāzī* states was destined to play a major role in world history for six centuries. It was founded in north west Asia Minor, reputedly about 1299, by a certain 'Os̱mān (also 'Uth̲mān, Otman – whence the European form Ottoman) and expanded rapidly; in 1354 its armies crossed the Dardanelles. In hardly more than a century the Ottomans were holding most of the Balkans. The great capital of Eastern Christendom, Constantinople (Istanbul), long isolated, its population dwindled, its grandeur dimmed, was captured in 1453. This conquest had real symbolic significance: it proclaimed to the world the triumph of Islam and dramatically confirmed that the Ottoman Empire had become the greatest Muslim power and a major force in Europe.

Acquisition of territory was not the Ottomans' only talent. To the conquered lands they brought a sophisticated civilisation, and often created stability and prosperity where there had been little before. As each area was conquered there was an influx, from the hinterlands, of Ottoman administrators, teachers, judges and all the other personnel of an Islamic state. The land was divided up amongst Muslim fiefholders, though non-Muslim peasants might continue to farm it as sharecroppers. The fiefholders had to go and fight as cavalrymen for the Sultan when required, and to bring along their own fighting men, the number depending on the size of the fief. Quite early, the need for a permanent infantry was felt and the *devshirme* (*devşirme*, levy) system was introduced. Every few years a certain number of teenage peasant boys were forcibly conscripted from the Sultan's Christian subjects. The most intelligent were selected for training in the Palace schools, while the remainder were sent to work for Turkish farmers for several years, so that they might learn Turkish and assimilate to Islamic ways. They were then recalled to join the Janissaries, the famous crack regiments of the Turkish regular army.

The forced levy of boys may seem cruel, but for the boys themselves it opened the door to the possibility of fame and fortune. Those trained in the Palace schools received an outstanding education, both general and special, lasting up to 15 years. For several centuries after the conquest of Istanbul in 1453 most of the highest offices of state were filled almost exclusively by the *devshirme* élite: the Grand Vezir (who was deputy to the Sultan himself) as well as the military commanders, provincial governors and leading administrators were, nearly all of them, former Christian peasant boys. Their privileged position was so much envied that some Muslim fathers smuggled their sons into the *devshirme*. Routine civil service functions were, however, mainly carried on by born Muslims.

In medieval Europe, non-Christians generally had few rights or none. Any security that they enjoyed was essentially at the discretion of the local ruler or bishop and could be withdrawn at any time. In the Ottoman Empire the situation was quite different. Islamic law stipulates religious tolerance for Christians and Jews, and security for their lives and property under certain conditions, the chief of these being that they pay certain special taxes and behave with due respect to the Muslims. The non-Muslim communities were considered religious-national groups (called *millet* in Turkish). They were governed by their own traditional laws, which were administered by their own religious leaders. These leaders had two functions: they represented their people before the government and at the same time acted for the government in passing on its decrees to their communities. The main *millet*s were Greek Orthodox, Armenian and Jewish. Their members did not have legal equality with Muslims, yet the system did provide some real legal protection. The various communities lived as largely self-contained entities, side by side, in reasonable harmony.

To sum up: in its heyday the Ottoman Empire, stretching over a vast area of Europe, Asia and Africa, had a fairly efficient administration, which gathered the taxes needed to maintain the troops, who were still extending the frontiers. The public aspects of a vibrant civilisation were expressed externally in magnificent stone buildings. Justice was dispensed, religious colleges flourished, scholars composed learned treatises, histories and biographies in Turkish, Arabic and Persian, while poets created verse with increasing skill. Artists embellished the books, and fine craftsmen the buildings. The Sultan's educated subjects were much impressed by the way the state and its legal system were reorganised during the reign of Sulaymān and bestowed on him the appellation Ḳānūnī, 'the Lawgiver'. European observers, for their part, marvelled at the efficiency with which his empire was run, at the disciplined valour of the army, the sobriety of the Turks, and, above all, at the splendour of the cities and the court.

Aya Sofya, Istanbul. The great sixth-century Byzantine church of Hagia Sofia, transformed into a mosque in 1453. The Ottomans added the four minarets and the royal tombs (foreground)

They called him 'the Magnificent'.

Yet the period of its glory already contained the seeds of its decay. The complex organisational machine which enabled the huge empire to function began to lose its flexibility. Officials and hierarchies became entrenched and self-perpetuating impediments to necessary change. In post-Renaissance Europe, rapid technological progress had started, but in the Ottoman Empire people in authority were already saying that what ensured success for their ancestors should still be good enough for them. Another major factor in the Empire's decline was a fall in the quality of the Sultans. For its first 250 years the Empire had only ten Sultans, a sequence of outstandingly able men who achieved much during long reigns. Princes would be sent off to govern provinces, and the one who had proved ablest and most dynamic would most likely become the next Sultan, while the rest would be judicially executed to prevent the rebellion of potential rivals. At the beginning of the seventeenth century, however, the law of succession was changed. Henceforth the oldest surviving member of the imperial family succeeded to the Sultanate, often after years of waiting in comfortable imprisonment, without the opportunity to learn in practical ways about government, politics and warfare, or to get to know his future subjects. When such men suddenly found themselves in supreme command they were often unfit for the responsibility. Palace intrigues now came to determine policy, and official posts were obtained by bribery, or were sold to the highest bidder. The once-loyal Janissaries grew increasingly undisciplined and inefficient. Many took part-time jobs, got married, enrolled their children in the corps and prevented others entering. Instead of fighting at the frontiers, they preferred to stay at home, frequently demonstrating for higher pay and against any change or reform, and interfering in politics.

Soldiering, government, farming and handicrafts were traditional Turkish occupations, while commerce was left largely to local Christians and Jews, and to Europeans. From the sixteenth century onwards, European merchants began to receive charters ('capitulations') granting them trading rights, freedom of religion, self-government under their own consuls, and exemption from Ottoman taxes and laws. As the Empire grew weaker, the European governments whose subjects had received the capitulations used them increasingly to interfere in Ottoman affairs. Administration deteriorated and the Treasury was constantly empty, so the government permitted tax farmers to buy the right to collect taxes. These men then reimbursed themselves by extorting money from the peasants so ruthlessly for short term gains, that there were peasant revolts on the one hand and abandonment of farmland on the other. At the same time the products of Europe's flourishing new industries flooded the Empire and undercut the local craft industries, with grave effects on the economy. Internal decline was accompanied by defeats at the frontiers. From the eighteenth century onwards the Ottomans were generally in retreat. This decline had become manifest with the loss of Hungary and southern Poland in 1699. The Balkans were lost piecemeal throughout the nineteenth century and after; all the Arab and North African provinces were detached, bit by bit, from 1830 to the end of the First World War.

Ottomans worried about the causes of their decline; some blamed the machinations of European powers. Others saw the defeats as divine punishment for religious laxity and neglect of traditional ways, and urged a return to piety. The adoption of European military technology was promoted in some quarters; elsewhere there were calls for the restoration of the institutions of the empire to the glory of their state in the days of Sulaymān. The deep conservatism at all levels of the Establishment, as well as of the vast majority of the people, made any modernisation appear like 'surrender to infidels'. Turkey had become the Sick Man of Europe and many European powers did not mind if he became still more sick, as this enabled them to extend their own influence. Some of them actively encouraged the centrifugal forces within, to hasten its fragmentation. In the forefront of these forces were the ideas released by the French Revolution in 1789, and closely related were the nationalist currents in Europe which gradually infected all the minority *millets* except the Jews. In response to the nationalisms of the minorities, there was an attempt in the latter part of the nineteenth century to develop a sense of Ottoman (not Turkish!) patriotism, uniting the Sultan's subjects of all religious denominations. Both the new patriotism and pressures from Europe were among the causes for the proclamation of equality for all citizens, which was written into the Constitution of 1876.

The forces of change grew stronger. As the nineteenth century wore on, young officers, who were sent for advanced military training to France, brought back more than the technical and linguistic knowledge they had been sent to acquire. They returned to Istanbul full of dangerous thoughts about liberty, reform, and parliamentary democracy. A major reform, called the *Tanẓīmāt* ('Reorganisation'), began in 1839 and some westernisation beyond the purely military field became official policy. In former times, the Ottoman Empire's self-image had been that of an essentially *ghāzī* institution, the embodiment of a militant Islam, whose functions had been to raise the money needed for the army, to dispense justice and to subsidise the theological educational system. Now for the first time the state began to feel responsible, like contemporary European states, for encouraging economic development, public works, and general and special education. Another major change was recognition of each man's rights and duties as an individual, not merely as a member of his group. Western and secular ideas were disseminated by the new media – newspapers and magazines – and by books, including translations from French and English.

Towards the end of the nineteenth century and the beginning of the twentieth, two movements which attracted the intelligentsia were Ottomanism and Pan-Islamism. The former failed because the non-Muslims preferred their own minority nationalisms, the latter because it not only obviously excluded non-Muslims, but because even the Muslim Arabs preferred Arab nationalism. Partly as a reaction against these minority currents, and the gradual detachment of the non-Turkish provinces from the Empire, and partly as a result of interest aroused by the studies of the ancient (pre-Muslim) Turkish past by a number of European Turcologists during the later nineteenth and early twentieth centuries, a purely Turkish nationalism developed. Ideological foundations were supplied by Żiyā Gökalp, whose ideas were adopted in the years before the First World War by the young army officers known to Europeans as the 'Young Turks'. The term Turk, which in Ottoman times had come to mean an illiterate peasant, was now being used with pride.

Gazi Mustafa Kemal, first President of Turkey (left), with his comrade-in-arms and successor, Ismet Pasha, Ankara 1925. They later assumed the surnames Atatürk and Inönü

Reforms delayed the Empire's collapse but could not prevent it. Its alliance with the losing side in the First World War brought final disaster. Even the Turkish heartland was invaded in 1919 and about to be dismembered. The crisis produced the man of the hour: Mustafa Kemal (later surnamed Atatürk, 'the Father Turk', 1881–1938) who inspired the dispirited population, and reorganised the broken army. The invaders were driven out and Turkish sovereignty over Asia Minor and Eastern Thrace in Europe gained international recognition. Istanbul was felt to be too closely bound up with the old régime and too cosmopolitan, with its many non-Turkish inhabitants liable to influences from abroad, and also too physically vulnerable, to serve any longer as capital. It was therefore replaced by Ankara, the centre of resistance, deep in Turkish Anatolia.

Under Atatürk's influence the Sultanate was abolished (1922), and soon afterwards the religious institution of the Caliphate (1923); the great leader became the first President of the new Turkish Republic. Thus ended the longest lived and largest of all Islamic empires.

By comparison with its predecessor, which had encompassed many lands, peoples, languages and religions, the Republic is small and almost homogeneous. Its territory is a compact block, the whole of Asia Minor with a small adjacent area of Europe. At present over 90 per cent of its population are Muslim Turks (mostly Sunnite, some Shi'ite). The main minorities are also Muslims: about 7 per cent Kurds, and 1.5 per cent Arabs living in the east and south-east frontier areas. The remaining Christians (Greeks, Armenians) and Jews live mostly in the large urban centres, especially Istanbul and Izmir.

In the Ottoman Empire the Turks had been the standard bearers of Islamic-Oriental culture. Atatürk built his new Turkey on different foundations. He wanted it to jettison most of its imperial history, and to become a 'progressive and civilised nation . . . a part of civilisation', by which he meant Europe, whose culture he conceived as essentially secular and international. In 15 years he and his friends pushed through an incredible series of sweeping measures to show practically and dramatically that Turkey was now irrevocably of the West. Introduced with such force and speed that opposition forces were unable to organise effective resistance, new laws abolished the Islamic religious establishment, the religious colleges and the powerful dervish orders and the endowments of all these groups were appropriated for secular state purposes. The *sharīʿah* (Islamic law) and its courts were replaced by legal codes imported from Europe and administered by new secular courts. Traditional oriental clothing was proscribed, the western calendar was adopted, and Sunday became the weekly day of rest. Writing is a powerful instrument of civilisation and transmitter of tradition. The Arabic script had been used by the Turks since they became Muslims a millennium earlier. In 1928 the Latin alphabet was abruptly introduced and the Arabic script forbidden for the writing of Turkish. The new letters quickly found acceptance since they were better adapted to the vowel structure of the Turkish language and made it easier to learn reading and writing. But this reform has cut off the new generations of Turks from their Ottoman and Islamic past, since very few are now able to read books in the old script. The consequences of all these great cultural breaks are incalculable.

Traditionally Turks had shown little interest in commerce, which had been mainly in the hands of the minority *millets*, but when most of these departed or were removed from Turkey by the early 1920s there was an economic vacuum. The Turks lacked (and still seem to lack) the business instincts necessary to run the state's economy properly. This is evident even more in public than in private enterprise. The state factories for major industries are not very successful because of poor planning, market research and distribution, and the unimaginative timidity of an overdeveloped bureaucracy. Business generally is much inhibited by an excessive number of government regulations and officials. Most salaries are now so incredibly low that it is only the least dynamic section of the literate population that takes civil service posts. The consequences are obvious. The economy is very unbalanced. Some 70 per cent of the population is engaged in agriculture, which produces only 35 per cent of the gross national product and a mere 1 per cent of taxation. Only 25 per cent of the farmers are beyond subsistence farming, agricultural methods being outdated and the yields poor. The small percentage of rich farmers who have disproportionately large holdings are so influential politically that they almost escape taxation. Atatürk once described the Turkish peasants as 'the real masters of the country', but that is still far from being the case. Every year another 200,000 of them drift to the cities in search of jobs, where they

Turkish peasants near Hatun Saray, in south-central Anatolia

Istanbul street scene at Eminönü. The great Sulaymanīye Mosque and its colleges built by Sultan Sulaymān crown the hilltop, and at its bottom stand the mosque and college built by his minister Rüstem Pasha

establish vast shanty-towns on the outskirts. (They constitute 45 per cent of the population of Istanbul and 65 per cent in Ankara). Many are unemployed or underemployed, barely surviving as bootblacks, vendors of chewing gum or knick-knacks. Some of Turkey's economic problems are clearly related to the rapid population increase – nearly 3 per cent a year – while the job-creation rate lags far behind. And yet the country is rich in mineral and other natural resources, whose efficient exploitation has hardly begun. The labour shortage in western Europe has had the effect of partly reducing the unemployment problem; in the past few years many Turks have gone to work in European factories, returning to Turkey later with their savings.

Turkish respect for soldiers is probably a relic of the *cbāzṭ* tradition. Five of Turkey's six presidents have been military men. While they became civilians on assuming office, they owed their prestige to their previous careers. Atatürk was certainly the most remarkable of their number. He was, in principle, a democrat, but in practice authoritarian. He established a one-party system as the only possible way of forcing his reforms through an acquiescent parliament. To allow free expression and due representation to spokesmen for the powerful and popular forces of Islamic traditionalism and conservatism would, he feared, prevent the passage into law of his proposals for westernisation. Real multi-party democracy did not begin until 1945. The elections in 1950 brought to power a party which got mass support from the traditionalist majority of the electorate on a programme that made many concessions which were incompatible with that of Atatürk, although it paid homage to his memory and acknowledged, in principle, the secular nature of the State. Since that time there has been ceaseless political in-fighting. The party struggle involves complex factors, but the cleavage between secularists and traditionalists is very real. However, the biggest parties contain some of each, and, as elsewhere, personalities often play a greater part than principles. The rise in people's incomes is neither keeping pace with inflation, nor with the expectations raised by politicians, as well as the increasingly influential mass media: newspapers, advertising, and radio. The 'transistor revolution' of the late 1960s, the recently built network of good roads and cheap bus transport, have all been major factors in bringing once remote areas of Turkey into daily contact with the outside world.

While the parliamentary system has proved to be fairly democratic, it has not been able to produce governments which could bring order to the economy or deal effectively with the acute social problems. Hence the growth of extremism in the 1960s and early 1970s at both ends of the political spectrum. Left-wing radical students have met in bloody clashes with various combinations of nationalist, racist and religious elements. When the governments of the day have proved incapable of handling the situation, the army has several times intervened and temporarily taken charge. It continues to consider itself as the guardian of the Turkish revolution and the trustee of Atatürk's reforms.

The position of religion in the Turkish republic is one of its most intractable problems. That a Turk should be a Muslim seems not only natural but inevitable to Turks of all classes. To this day a 'non-Muslim Turk' would seem a contradiction in terms, even to the most secularised Turkish intellectuals, who accept only the cultural heritage of Islam, without believing in its doctrines or observing its precepts.

The Ottoman Empire was the Turkish expression of militant Islam, and in that lay the secret of its growth and civilisation. Some Ottoman writers of the past blamed the Empire's decline on failure to observe Islam adequately; they prescribed more enthusiastic observance as a sure cure. Atatürk's diagnosis was precisely the opposite: he claimed that it was Islam that had kept the Turks backward and 'uncivilised' *vis-à-vis* Europe, and that nothing less than total secularisation of both the state and the people's attitudes could bring the country to health.

The secularist intelligentsia, though influential far beyond its numerical proportion, is still a fairly small group. The vast majority of Turks, in towns and villages, remain enthusiastically attached to Islam, even though their theological knowledge is weak, and that of their local teachers is now rarely much stronger. The closure of the religious colleges (*medreses*) in 1924 deprived the population of a regular supply of knowledgeable teachers of Islam. Their place has often been taken by comparatively ignorant men, some of them fanatical and/or heterodox. The Faculty of Theology set up at Istanbul University, in 1933, and later transferred to Ankara University, has also not produced either the kind or the quantity of teachers needed by the masses. Nevertheless religious feeling remains very strong:

crowds of worshippers of all classes fill the mosques in both town and country. Atatürk's name is invoked not only by secularists but by many naive religious people too. A copy of a rare photograph of that arch-secularist with his hands raised in prayer, at some public function, hangs on the walls of many little coffee houses and private homes.

The villagers and urban lower classes feel very Muslim, and so do the majority of industrial skilled workers, technologists and technocrats. Only a small percentage of Turks – and these are mainly in the intelligentsia, higher bureaucracy, and the rich business community – as yet fully hold the western value system and mentality, whose adoption has continued to be the official policy for half a century, and on which depends the development of Turkey into a Western nation. The nature of the humanities, their place in the educational system and national life, and their relative importance *vis-à-vis* technology, have not yet been decided. Amongst university students and elsewhere an identity crisis has grown. Often they are not anti-religious but areligious. Lacking as they do the deeply rooted sense of security of the traditional Muslim, they realise that they are not yet the Europeanised Turks envisaged by Atatürk. They now feel unsure what their Turkishness really means and wonder whether it provides enough meaning for their lives. A moral vacuum needs to be filled. In this situation the current ideologies fashionable among students in Europe and North America have reached them too, although they look strangely rootless in the context of Turkish history and society. With little support from the minority of Turks working in industry, students and intellectuals run a variety of radical left-wing movements advocating various brands of communism and socialism, some involving guerilla action. Although the amount of support they have won is small and its base narrow, it has been sufficient to bring about a strong rightist and traditionalist backlash, and, as we have already mentioned, the resultant clashes have brought intervention by the army.

The Ottoman Empire had three parallel flourishing literatures. The highly polished court type, in the mainstream of classical Islamic literatures, was cultivated and understood only by the intellectual, political and administrative élite, while the folk and religious literatures were popular among wider sectors of society. Since the middle of the nineteenth century, Western influences on Turkish literature, both in form and content, have been constantly growing, while the court and religious streams have dried up. Modern Turkish poetry has passed through all the currents of European fashion, sometimes in combination with elements of the old traditions of Turkish folk literature. In the past half century novels, and above all, short-stories have gained literary success and popularity, and many of them have, by their subject matter, created social awareness, in pinpointing problems in Turkish society.

In spite of their differences, most Turks feel pride in Turkishness, which in their eyes is synonymous with physical courage, hardiness, generosity, hospitality, sobriety and honesty, and indeed these qualities are widespread. There is some truth in the observation that there are several co-existing Turkeys. Most of the political, administrative and economic power is held by the comparatively small middle class – officials, intellectuals, army officers and an increasing number of businessmen – living in the three or four largest cities. Quite a different country is the Turkey of the small towns. The third and largest Turkey is that of the 35,000 small villages, and these contain over 70 per cent of the population, who live a hard farming life, mostly near subsistence level. Amongst the peasants in eastern Turkey, polygamy is not uncommon, even at the present time. Most village marriages are solemnised only by the local *imām*, in spite of the fact that nothing but monogamous marriage is legally recognised by the authorities.

All the Turkeys are, in practice, still essentially male societies in their public life, although women have complete legal equality, and have been playing an increasing role. For decades there have been some women professors, doctors, lawyers and teachers. The proportion is rising as more women are receiving higher education. (At present 20 per cent of the university students are women.) In towns many who would formerly have stayed at home now act as typists, shop assistants, bank clerks, telephone operators and factory workers.

In her foreign policy Turkey has consistently followed the course set by Atatürk, and, as a result has enjoyed more than half a century of peace. In spite of her religious, cultural and linguistic heritage, she has carefully avoided pan-Islamic and pan-Turkish involvements. For instance she recognizes Israel's existence, *de facto*, and there is a flourishing trade between the countries, yet she maintains good relations with the Arab states. The population at large is in sympathy with the Arabs, yet the intellectuals generally admire Israel, holding it up as an example to their own country, in proof of their contention that it is possible to be a Western island in a Levantine sea. Turkey maintains 'correct' relations with the Soviet Union, refusing to become involved in the plight of the Turkic peoples of Soviet Central Asia. Turkey's membership of several European economic and military organisations, as well as her alliances with some Western powers, are psychologically important to her, making her feel that she is recognised by the West as a Western community.

Turkey's great imperial past has given her a tradition of good administrators, soldiers and scholars. The present situation demands a revival of that tradition, yet first class men cannot be found to staff the civil service unless the government will provide them with a living wage. An understanding of economics, and the courage to frame and carry out long term policies will have to be developed. It is equally vital for Turkey to discover a way in which the deep devotion of most of her people to their religious heritage can find its due place, without retarding unduly the social and economic changes on which the country's prosperity depends. If the Turks can utilise fully those qualities of common sense, discipline and fortitude which have long characterised them, their country can overcome its difficulties, and contribute substantially to the wellbeing of the Middle East and of Europe.

18

Khātimah

G. M. WICKENS

The title of this final chapter is appropriate in a very obvious sense, for it is the Arabic word for 'end', 'conclusion', 'finis'. But more than that, it has a very pregnant sound in the cultural world of the Middle East of which we have been speaking in this book. It is a variant form of a word meaning 'signet' or 'seal'; and the latter word is commonly used to designate Muḥammad as the last, the ultimate of the Prophets, the messenger who put the 'final stamp' on God's word to man. By an extension also to be found in other cultures, the society founded and maintained in accordance with that final message has tended to look on itself as being also 'the last word'. It would not always claim to be perfect (indeed, Islam makes ample allowance for human imperfection), but it has traditionally seen itself as alone in the world in being on the right, the only right, lines.

In considering the Middle East – that great, cosmopolitan world, largely Islamic in culture – this finality, this 'certainty' (to use another Islamic key-word), has to be sensed as the most significant general attitude over most of the last fourteen centuries. Indeed, this is true, even now, wherever and insofar as that culture is religiously informed. One might go even further: even where religion, to the outside or superficial observer, might not appear to be overwhelmingly important (e.g. in modern Egypt or Turkey), it is often inherently and instinctively so for a great many people; and in a culture where politics and religion have for so long been 'twins' (as yet another Islamic expression has it), religion is very easily subsumed into the newer philosophies of nationalism and revolution. This is, of course, particularly so with a religion which, whatever outsiders may argue as to its origins and development, comes – in the eyes of the true believer – direct from the Author of all Being, and is especially maintained and cherished by Him. That is to say, in political terms: it owes absolutely nothing to Western societies or to reactionary elements within the Middle East itself, but can rather be seen as a standing, authoritative criticism of them.

In themselves, these are not specifically Islamic phenomena. In the West residual Christian and Jewish awarenesses still come to the surface in various ways whenever a community feels threatened by war, or internal upheaval, or racial persecution. What is peculiar to Islamdom is the steady intensity of this feeling of finality and certainty at virtually every period of history. The Iranian ever-open door to innovations and heresies of all kinds; the reconquest of Spain by the Christians; the Mongol invasions; the Turkish military and political ascendancy: all these, and many other 'calamities', have been bewailed at one time or another. But to the millions who felt conscious of the inner, essential, God-guaranteed virtue of the Islamic way of life, none of these worldly vicissitudes has seemed to have much real significance in the ultimate scheme of things.

Even the terrible and mounting humiliations which that way of life has suffered from the West, over the last three centuries or so, seem in themselves not to have shaken this trust in finality and certainty. If they had produced a greater shock, there might have been a quicker and more thoroughgoing collapse of the old order and the adoption of a new one – a sort of Middle East parallel to the Japanese two-stage revolution, that of the late nineteenth century and that of the post-1945 period. At long last, however, it would seem that the trance-like confidence *has* been broken, though the realisation of what has happened is still not fully or generally conscious.

One factor has been the very slowness and unevenness of modernisation itself, the Middle East's patently accelerating inability to catch up with the West, even in those areas that Islam has accepted as beneficial, or at least neutral, to itself. But paradoxically there is also another factor in this malaise, namely the West's own massive loss of nerve as to its courses and purposes, whether political, social, economic, cultural or spiritual. If the Middle East lacks both a clear goal and the ability to realise it, the West suffers from the ability to realise virtually any goal if it could only decide which one it wanted. The Middle East is by now too far Westernised to draw back, but not sufficiently so to attempt to control its own fate and devise its own solutions – as, once again, the Japanese might seem to be doing.

History offers few, if any, parallels to what we now see happening to the Middle East. First, we have a once great and vigorous and original culture that has gradually run down, but without ultimate decay and with frequent splendid revivals. Eventually it comes, not always obviously and consciously, to be dominated by a culture that may or may not be its equal, but which is technically more efficient and set on a course of geometrical acceleration towards ever greater efficiency. No successful synthesis occurs, merely a congeries of odd misfits and loose juxtapositions. At the same time, the dominated culture is neither replaced nor insulated: by and large, it retains its own functions and its confidence until a very late date, before succumbing to a thousand complex cross-currents of discord and violence from both within and outside. One might wish to compare this process with the long-drawn-out agony of the Roman Empire, but such a comparison would be in many ways inappropriate. The Middle East culture has been richer and more original than the Roman, and without any of the latter's inner decadence and degradation, particularly as it views the human condition. Secondly, the Middle East, if it is now collapsing, is not doing so essentially from internal contradictions and unresolved tensions: indeed, we have said that, within its own terms, it has often worked too well for its own good, and that a little internal friction (like the secular vs. the religious in the West) might have given greater forward momentum. Finally, the enemy at the gates has not been, as with Rome, a barbarian force at a lower cultural level, but a higher and virtually irresistible power in every effective sense.

Now, if we are not to run the risk of losing perspective, we should elaborate somewhat on this socio-psychological question of self-sufficiency and indifference to non-conforming reality. Let us take three very different examples – one allegedly dating from the seventh century, one from the sixteenth–seventeenth, and one from the twentieth. The second Caliph, 'Umar (634–44), is the classic figure, especially for conservative and fundamentalist Islam, of the Islamic ideal of simple piety and righteousness. It was during his Caliphate that many Islamic institutions assumed their traditional form; at the same time he directed the first, and perhaps the most impressive, expansion of Islam in terms of territorial coverage. One of the conquests achieved at this time was that of Egypt, and in this connection there is an account, probably apocryphal and doubtless exaggerated, of wanton destruction wrought on the great Graeco-Egyptian libraries at Alexandria. Later ages – justly or unjustly, but certainly with general approval – attributed to 'Umar an unashamed defence of such vandalism: 'What do these books matter? If they support the Qur'ān they are superfluous; if they disagree with it, they lie.' Such an attitude sees truth as simply black and white, divided by a line; quite apart from the question of whether there can be absolute right and wrong, existential reality is given no depth; there is no recognition at all of the vast neutral area of life on which, conceivably, the Qur'ān cannot be employed as any sort of meaningful measure. This is the extreme attitude of Islamic self-sufficiency – one that, in the nature of things, could not be maintained everywhere or indefinitely, but one that in greater or less measure is characteristic and constantly recurring.

Between the notional date of that reference and our next occurs the great blossoming of a vigorous and original Islamic civilisation, say between 800 and 1100, when all sorts of 'outside' ideas and influences were assimilated and used as springboards for new achievements. Not every facet of life was scrutinised afresh in a brighter, clearer light; but at virtually all times during these three centuries there was someone, or some group, with a lively and open curiosity about large and important aspects of reality, whether Islamic or pagan or infidel. Even then, of course, sooner or later things had to be fitted – if they were to remain permanently acceptable – into an Islamic pattern of some kind, whether natural or somewhat synthetic. There was not, and there would never be, comfortable room for thoroughgoing incongruity or mutually tolerant plurality. At the same time, with a few exceptions, Islam rarely knew the *violent* pressures to conformity and consistency that distinguished much of Western culture, with its xenophobia, religious persecution and witch-hunts.

Our next reference is a quotation from the British Orientalist Bernard Lewis,[1] discussing the outwardly much more enterprising and open Turkish attitude, in or about the seventeenth century, towards Western innovation. 'Turning', he says, 'from gunnery and typography to knowledge and ideas, we find far fewer traces of Western influence, for it is here that the Muslim rejection of Christianity and all that came from it was most effective. Though clever with their hands in making useful devices like guns, clocks and printing presses, the Europeans were still benighted and barbarous infidels, whose history, philosophy, science and literature, if indeed they existed at all, could hold nothing of value for the people of the universal Islamic Empire. During the reign of Mehmed II there was indeed the beginning of a scientific renaissance, but under his successors, in the words of a modern Turkish writer, "the scientific current broke against the dikes of literature and jurisprudence".'

'In these dikes there were, however, a few small leaks, through which some knowledge of the West percolated into the circles of Muslim scholarship.'

Now, in this estimate of the Islamic Middle East's reaction to the essentially non-Islamic, we are dealing with a rather different situation from the supposed one of the Caliph 'Umar and the libraries of Alexandria. Something like 1000 years had passed, and the Middle Eastern world had reached yet another – and probably its ultimate – peak of internal culture and sophistication. That culture was by now the equal of any in wealth, political organisation, military ability, intellectual, literary and artistic development – in short, in practically any sphere of traditional human activity. With the wisdom of hindsight, *we* know that it was wrong in assuming itself to be the only culture worth mentioning; for if it was easily the equal of two or three others among its contemporaries, they on their side were obviously fit to stand the comparison too. But like the established American culture of the present day, it felt itself under no compulsion to bother with these or other comparisons; for, like that culture, it saw itself as the measure of all things, and felt an inner assurance that whoever did not ultimately go *its* way was damned. (Two words of qualification here: one must remember, once again, that all societies have something of this attitude – it is the degree that matters; and secondly, there is a difference between seventeenth-century Islam and the modern U.S.A. in that the latter has to some extent generated its own forces of self-criticism and dissent.) One may say, then, that by comparison with the early centuries this is a more sophisticated and outwardly justified feeling of self-sufficiency; but it is still essentially the same feeling, reinforced indeed by a millennium of basically unchallenged triumph.

What we also know now, again with the wisdom of hindsight, is that whether or not the Middle East could afford to ignore the West's achievements in areas coinciding with its own (religion, government, art, literature, thought, and so on), it certainly made a critical mistake in not realising what was utterly new in that peculiar culture's manifold workings. What the Middle East saw as amusing, and sometimes useful, gadgets were in fact the by-products of a whole new and dynamic way of life: of new ways in living (economically, socially and politically), and of new ways of looking at the physical world, at society, and at man himself. The initial key-breakthroughs were not always conscious or deliberate; but, once made, they were self-sustaining, mutually reinforcing, and necessarily tending to constant acceleration. Not only would nothing in the West ever be the same again; even the changes themselves would not last for any length of time before giving way, ever more rapidly, to new changes. Moreover, in the not-so-very-long run, everything would become subject to this process of change and relativity – not just technology and socio-political organisation, but art, literature, thought and behaviour.

It is this all-or-nothing inclusiveness of modern Western civilisation, this necessary tendency to affect everybody and everything, that makes it so difficult for radically different cultures to adopt, even where they keenly wish to do so. Bernard Lewis refers above to 'a few small leaks' in the dikes of traditional Middle Eastern culture, 'through which some knowledge of the West percolated'. From 1600 or so to our own day these leaks have remained,

[1] See *The Contemporary Middle East*, ed. B. Rivlin and J. S. Szyliowicz (New York, Random House, 1965), p. 118. The original source is Lewis's *Emergence of Modern Turkey*, but the more general reference provides a better setting for present purposes.

growing in both size and number; but until very recently the dikes have remained too. There have been, especially in the last 150 years, innumerable individuals in and from the Middle East who have thoroughly grasped one or more facets of Western culture; there have even been some who have become as wholly at home in that culture as the most gifted and integrated of Western minds. There have also been societies, or segments of societies, that have adopted varying measures of Western culture and tried to make them their own, either in a radically new start or in a blending with the traditional culture. But to date no Middle Eastern society has thoroughly transformed itself, becoming like Japan a peer and a challenge to the West: there is plenty of tinkering with the works, but the essential mainspring of transformation has never been properly fitted into the social machine or wound to a point of dynamic and irreversible tension.

You do not Westernise or modernise (even if you want to, and large segments of the Middle East are by no means sure that they do want to) simply by creating a nation-state, or trying to spread literacy, or introducing the French or the Swiss legal codes, or by instituting universal suffrage, or by building airports or railways or foundries or factories, or by educating your best young people in Europe or America (or in the European or American traditions). Nor can the transformation be brought about by imitating communist movements elsewhere, or copying Hollywood movies and television shows, or even by an eager adoption of way-out art and literature. Moreover, whatever apparent good or evil may result from such measures, taken separately or together, trouble must inevitably come from attempts to introduce them alongside the old ways – the old social hierarchies of town and village, segregation of the sexes, intricately structured human relationships created out of different needs and conditions, faithful observance of traditional religious duties, particularly the day-long fasts in the month of Ramaḍān, and so on. Modern Western culture is every bit as jealous and exclusive towards its servants as was the God of the Ancient Hebrews: if you hope for the rewards, you must give the wholehearted devotion expected, no matter where it may lead; and changes of heart and mind come hardest of all to fundamentally agricultural societies.

Our third example of the self-sufficient attitude, prevailing despite everything right up until recent times, comes from a modern Egyptian short-story writer, Maḥmūd Taymūr. Here was a man of educated family, thoroughly well versed in the traditional culture and subsequently educated in Europe, particularly France (where he came under the influence of the supreme short-story craftsman, Guy de Maupassant). His stories are a sort of magic mirror, not only of Egyptian life in itself, but – less consciously – of the interaction between that life and the lives of the many foreigners resident in Egypt in the period following the outbreak of the First World War. The term 'magic' should be stressed, for Maḥmūd Taymūr is no direct realist, but removes his raw material to a distance and endows it with a simple, dreamlike beauty of observation and expression. We take the lesser-known, but splendidly worked story entitled 'The Tavern-Singer'. It tells of a tempestuous youthful romance with a street-waif who subsequently became a beautiful night-club *chanteuse*. The background to the story is the Cairo of 1915, full of Allied troops on their way to take part in the Middle East campaigns against the Turks. The fulcrum of the action is the fact that the girl-singer is, and enjoys being, a favourite with the British officers passing through. But the story develops along lines that this brief summary would not lead one to expect. Unlike the young Middle Eastern writers of to-day, Taymūr reveals no rabid nationalistic feelings, no violent resentment of foreign troops on his native soil. (Nor, be it said, does he hopefully applaud their presence as his likely champions against Ottoman-Turkish domination.) They are simply there, like the Nile or the weather. The narrator does not even show rancour at coming off the loser after a quarrel over the girl with one of her British admirers. What is really extraordinary about his attitude is this (unless one sees it in the framework of self-sufficiency of which we have been speaking): despite a clearly implied knowledge of English, of the inner workings of the lives of these soldiers, and of the global factors that have brought them to Cairo – despite all this, he refers again and again merely to their external characteristics: their red, 'wooden' faces, their harsh voices, yellow teeth, foul-smelling pipes, their pushing onto streetcars, and so on. There is no hatred: once, indeed, there is a quiet note of compassion for them 'as lambs going to death with a song on their lips'. But they are a phenomenon having no ultimate significance either in his own life or in the life of which it is part. And this, be it remembered, is a story by one of the most delicate and sensitive writers of twentieth-century Egypt.

Former President Nixon has characterised the Middle East situation generally as potentially very much more dangerous than that in South-East Asia. He doubtless had his own reasons for saying this, and he might have been hard pressed if asked to give some solid grounds for the statement. Nevertheless, it is very difficult to disagree with the statement in itself. None of the non-Western areas of the world – Africa and Asia particularly – enjoys anything like even the relative stability and security of the West in general. But in no other area besides the Middle East does one find such an explosive combination of what might be called socio-psychological elements. Here we have a civilisation that was once, and for long, great in every sense, expansive and dominating. (One could, for example, regard the whole of European history, from 650 to 1650, as in one sense a long battle not to go under to the Middle Eastern Joneses – there was for a thousand years little question of keeping up with them!) Then, when this civilisation ceased to be truly great, expansive and dominating, it still continued to be valid, and to function reasonably well, for those who lived within its bounds – so well, indeed, that most of its adherents scarcely realised, if at all, that its great days were over. Even the few rulers or intellectuals who were curious about, and felt an admiration for, certain things they could see outside, all too often saw the problem of change and updating as a matter of detail and of externals – something that could be accomplished piecemeal and by legislation and technical improvements.

Things have not worked out. The magnitude of the real problem has come to light not in the frustrations of the struggle with imperialism, or economic penetration, or the Arab–Israeli conflicts, but in much simpler, more fundamental things. This culture once produced of its own originality some of the world's greatest buildings, works of art and ingenious craftsmanship, superb manuscripts: these were its traditional skills. Now, in the 1970s, they are largely dead, without being replaced by or developed into their counterparts in modern Western terms. (Much the same is true for literature, thought, and the life of the spirit.) While enigmatic and once heavily exploited China engages in atomic and rocket research, and gives aid and advice to underdeveloped nations; while Japan, even after a disastrous defeat in war, and with few natural resources, floods the West with cheap, but superbly engineered cars, cameras and ships; the once great Middle East can, *of its own unaided self*, no longer produce a really decent building or machine. Even a well-produced book is still a rarity, outside one or two centres like Beirut and Cairo.

This has nothing to do, basically, with energy or interest or natural aptitude. The story of the Middle East past that we have told leaves no doubt that these qualities are as freely available in the Middle East as elsewhere, quite apart from the fact that countless individual Middle Easterners at the present day, of all races and traditions, exhibit such qualities abundantly in their daily lives. There are competent, even brilliant, Middle Eastern thinkers, architects, doctors and artists, but their skills run all too often to waste in their own society. Many Middle Easterners are fully conscious, while the majority may well feel an unconscious certainty, that they could do great things – as they have done them before – if only circumstances were otherwise. Neither they nor we, nor any other group, clearly understands what is amiss or how to put it right. It is this that makes the Middle East at once dangerous and important.

People who can look back on great accomplishments and forward to great potential do, as a simple psychological fact, become dangerous in their frustration if that potential is thwarted – no matter from whom or what the thwarting arises. Such frustration, of course, only exacerbates the original problem, and a vicious circle develops.

As we have said above, no one person or group of persons can fully grasp the problem or offer practical solutions. History neither poses simple questions nor offers simple answers – if, indeed, it offers answers at all. The Middle East's real difficulties will not be solved by American presidents or visiting senators, or even by aid-missions. Equally, they will not be solved by Soviet party-secretaries or visiting commissars or advisers – nor, for that matter, by the comments of professors, whether Middle Eastern or from the Western or Eastern blocs. They are human problems that will work themselves out, one way or another, over a long time, and with pain and difficulty and uncertainty. But any working out that comes must be by the Middle East itself, within the Middle East, and in Middle Eastern terms of reference.

If the West itself ultimately fails before such a

working out comes about, no sort of solution is likely ever to be reached, for the West's failure would assuredly drag the rest of the dependent world down with it. This possibility, it must be obvious, is in many ways greater than that of a disaster coming from the Middle East, or of the Middle East continuing to fumble along in its present squalor and confusion. The West now faces on a massive scale its own socio-psychological frustrations: the breakdown of social peace and order, and of traditional political and social structures; the collapse of moral, intellectual and artistic standards as traditionally received for centuries; the waste and pollution of resources; overpopulation; and so on. Unlike the problems of the Middle East, this has not been a case of slow ageing from within, compounded by a failure to grasp new, outside solutions. The West's is a threatened sudden collapse, a stroke at the very height of power and growth. The great hope is, of course, that the West's own dynamic will act quickly enough to correct the malfunction before it becomes disastrous.

If this hope is realised in any practical degree, the West will both save itself and give others hope for their own salvation. In these matters, one does not save others: one tries to save oneself while letting others get to Heaven in their own way. One may, indeed must, try to understand and sympathise with the difficulties and the efforts of others; one may even try to help them, especially if requested. But much the most important contribution is to refrain from hindrance and criticism. The key to such self-restraint, even more than to sympathy and helpfulness, is knowledge and understanding.

Nor are these judgments invalidated, or even seriously qualified, by the events of October 1973 and the related (though not wholly consequential) oil-crisis. In the long run, the more or less stalemate outcome of the October war, with its nearer equalisation of Israeli and Arab morale, and its decisive demonstration of the all-round limits of realistic possibilities, can only be to the good. Again, though painful in the short run, it is also ultimately healthy for the West to be brought finally to face the realities of the resources picture, particularly where non-renewable resources are involved. However feeble and shortsighted its reaction, the West (and the world at large) can never again ignore the problems of consumption-rates, price-scales, ownership and control, and their effects on its accepted life-style. It is reasonable to hope too that, in their dramatically new-found financial, economic and political strength the governments of the Middle East will maintain their present diplomatic firmness, skill, self-control and concern for a good world-image. Their effective place in world-affairs now seems assured for the foreseeable future.

It is hoped that these chapters, by their breadth and variety and historical depth, have given at least some basis for such knowledge and understanding to those who feel concern for their not so remote neighbours.

Suggested background reading

N.B. Many of the books cited have excellent critical bibliographies. P. = *paperback edition.*

Abbouchi, W. F. *Political Systems of the Middle East in the 20th Century*. New York, Dodd Mead; Toronto, Burns and MacEachern, 1970.

Covers more ground than its title suggests, and builds up from a good background.

Antonius, George. *The Arab Awakening*. New York, Putnam, 1961; New York, Capricorn, 1965 P.

A classic statement of the development of Arab nationalism.

Arberry, Arthur J. *Classical Persian Literature*. London, Allen and Unwin; New York, Macmillan, 1958.

Contains much translated material.

Arnold, Thomas W. and Guillaume, Alfred, (edd.). *The Legacy of Islam*. London, Toronto, New York, Oxford University Press, 1931, repr. 1965.

Berger, Morroe. *The Arab World Today*. New York, Doubleday; London, Weidenfeld, 1962; 1964P.

Good on everyday social aspects.

Bombaci, Alessio. *The Literature of the Turks, I*. Translated by K. R. F. Burrill. The Hague (Netherlands), Mouton, 1976. (Near and Middle East Monographs series, 3).

Good survey, from pre-Islamic Turkic literature down to modern early Republican writing. Some extracts in translation.

The Cambridge History of Islam (edited by P. M. Holt, Ann K. S. Lambton, Bernard Lewis), 2 vols., Cambridge, New York, Cambridge University Press, 1970.

Chapters by various specialists on the whole spectrum of Islamic history up to the twentieth century.

Coulson, Noel J. *A History of Islamic Law*. Edinburgh, Edinburgh University Press; Chicago, Aldine, 1964 (Islamic Surveys series).

A masterly survey which incorporates the most recent research on the subject.

Davison, Roderic H. *Turkey*. Englewood Cliffs, New Jersey, Prentice-Hall, 1968. (The Modern Nations in Historical Perspective series).

Short but clear historical survey, with useful essay on further reading.

Fakhry, Majid. *A History of Islamic Philosophy*. New York, Columbia University Press, 1970.

A comprehensive general account.

– *Islamic Occasionalism and its Critique by Averroes and Aquinas*. London, George Allen & Unwin, 1958.

An excellent study of the controversy over the nature of causation in medieval Islam. It presupposes some background in philosophy.

Geertz, Clifford. *Islam Observed; Religious Development in Morocco and Indonesia*. New Haven, Yale University Press, 1968.

Gibb, Elias John Wilkinson. *A History of Ottoman Poetry*. 6 vols. London, Luzac, 1900–9 repr. 1958–67.

A detailed survey of classical poetry. Many translations in late nineteenth-century style. Vol. 1 is excellent study of the conventions of classical Islamic poetry.

Gibb, Hamilton Alexander Rosskeen. *Arabic Literature: An Introduction*. 2nd ed. Oxford, Clarendon Press; Toronto, New York, Oxford University Press, 1969.

Gives a concise and excellent statement of the cultural and intellectual milieu in which medieval Arabic literature developed.

– *Mohammedanism: An Historical Survey*. London, Oxford University Press, 1961 (and repr.); New York, Oxford University Press, 1962.

Grube, Ernest J. *The World of Islam*, London, Hamlyn; New York, Toronto, McGraw-Hill, 1966 (and repr.) (Landmarks of the World's Art series).

A good overview of Islamic art which enables the reader to compare the art of the different cultural areas.

Halman, Talât Sait (ed.), see *Review of National Literatures* and *The Literary Review*.

Hodgson, Marshall G. S. *The Venture of Islam*. 3 Vols. Chicago, 1974.

A comprehensive and sometimes provacative survey of Islamic civilisation.

Holt, Peter M. *Egypt and the Fertile Crescent, 1516–1822: A Political History*. London, Longmans; Ithaca, Cornell University Press, 1966.

The best survey of Arab lands under Ottoman rule.

Hotham, David. *The Turks*. London, Murray, 1972.

A perceptive journalist's description of the modern Turks in the light of their past.

Hottinger, Arnold. *The Arabs: their History, Culture and Place in the Modern World*. London, Thames and Hudson;

Berkeley, University of California Press, 1963.
The modern history of the Arab world explained in terms of the earlier cultural heritage.

Hourani, Albert. *Arabic Thought in the Liberal Age, 1798–1939.* London, Toronto, New York, Oxford University Press (for the Royal Institute of International Affairs), 1962; 1970P.
Perceptive and well-written; selected bibliography.

Husayn, Taha. *An Egyptian Childhood.* (Tr.) E. H. Paxton, London, 1948; *The Stream of Days* (Tr.) H. Wayment, London, 1948.
The autobiographical account by a leading twentieth century Arab writer and intellectual of his childhood and religious education in al-Azhar. This is a translation of the work originally entitled *Al-Ayyām*, vols. I and II.

Ibn Khaldun. *An Arab Philosophy of History: Selections from the Prolegomena of Ibn Khaldun of Tunis.* (Tr.) Charles Issawi. London, Murray; New York, Paragon, 1950 (and repr.) (Wisdom of the East series).
The translation includes selections relating to Islamic theology and philosophy.

Ireland, Philip Willard. *Iraq: a Study in Political Development.* London, Jonathan Cape, 1937.
An authoritative study of the modern history of Iraq.

Issawi, Charles, (ed.). *The Economic History of the Middle East, 1800–1914: A Book of Readings.* Chicago, University of Chicago Press, 1966; P.
An excellent symposium; includes many selections on Iraq, though the one on Land Tenure is dated; excludes North Africa.

Itzkowitz, Norman. *Ottoman Empire and Islamic Tradition.* New York, Knopf, 1972.
How the Ottomans themselves saw their society and its institutions.

Kamshad, Hassan. *Modern Persian Prose Literature.* Cambridge, New York, Cambridge University Press, 1966.
Covers the last sixty years, with a special study on Ṣādiq Hidāyat (Sadegh Hedayat).

Kinross, Lord (Balfour, Patrick, Baron Kinross). *Atatürk: the Rebirth of a Nation.* London, Weidenfeld; New York, Morrow, 1966.
Essential for understanding both the creator of modern Turkey and his creation.

Lerner, Daniel. *The Passing of Traditional Society: Modernizing the Middle East.* New York, Free Press of Glencoe; Toronto, Collier-Macmillan, 1958; 1964P.

Lerner, Ralph and Mahdi, Muhsin (edd.). *Medieval Political Philosophy: A Sourcebook.* New York, Free Press of Glencoe; Toronto, Collier-Macmillan, 1963; Cornell University Press P.
The first part includes reliable translations from the Arabic of the Islamic philosophers, Alfarabi, Avicenna, Ibn Bajja, Ibn Tufayl and Averroes.

Levy, Reuben. *An Introduction to Persian Literature.* New York and London, Columbia University Press, 1969.
Essays arranged by theme, rather than a comprehensive treatment.

Lewis, Bernard. *The Emergence of Modern Turkey,* 2nd ed. London, New York, Oxford University Press, 1968.
A brief historical survey of the Ottoman Empire precedes a first class account of Turkey from the beginning of westernisation (late eighteenth century) to 1950.

– *The Arabs in History,* 4th ed. London, Toronto, Hutchinson, 1966; New York, Harper, 1966 P (Harper Torchbooks).
Concise and readable sketch.

– *The Middle East and the West.* London, Weidenfeld; Bloomington, Indiana University Press, 1964; 1968 P. (Indiana University International Studies series).
A good introduction to the Middle East.

Longrigg, Stephen Hemsley. *Iraq, 1900 to 1950: A Political, Social, and Economic History.* London, New York, Toronto, Oxford University Press, 1953.
The standard history by one with a first-hand knowledge of the country and its people.

– *The Middle East: A Social Geography,* 2nd ed., incorporating new material by James Jankowski, London, Duckworth, 1970.
A good basic book for all purposes.

Macdonald, Duncan Black. *The Religious Attitude and Life in Islam.* Chicago, University of Chicago Press, 1909; repr. Beirut, Khayat, 1965.

Mahfuz, Najib. *Midaq Alley, Cairo* (Tr.) Trevor Le Gassick. Beirut, Khayat, 1966.
A novel by a leading modern Egyptian novelist about the people living in a small Cairo street.

al-Marayati, Abid (and others). *The Middle East: its Governments and Politics.* Belmont, California, Duxbury Press, 1972.
A useful quick reference book, with some good chapters, but uneven in coverage and treatment.

Mez, Adam. *The Renaissance of Islam.* (Tr.) Salahuddin Khuda Bukhsh and D. S. Margoliouth. Patna, 1937 and repr.
Fascinating survey of Islamic civilisation at one of its highpoints.

Nicholson, Reynold Alleyne. *A Literary History of the Arabs.* (2nd ed.) Cambridge, Cambridge University Press, 1930, repr. 1966; 1969 P.
Although somewhat outdated, this is still the most comprehensive general introduction to medieval Arabic literature, noted for the abundance of its readable translations.

Nolte, Richard H. (ed.). *The Modern Middle East.* New York, Atherton Press; London, Prentice-Hall 1963.
Amongst useful essays on social, political and economic problems, this book contains H. B. Sharabi's *The Crisis of the Intelligentsia in the Middle East.*

Patai, Raphael. *The Arab Mind.* New York, Scribner, 1973.
Emphasises human factors in politics and economics.

Peters, F. E. *Allah's Commonwealth.* New York, Simon and Schuster, 1973.

Qur'ān. *The Koran Interpreted.* (Tr.) A. J. Arberry. London, Toronto, New York, Oxford University Press, 1964 (The

World's Classics series).

Review of National Literatures, Vol. IV, no. 1, Spring 1973: *'Turkey from Empire to Nation'*. Editor Talât Sait Halman. Jamaica (New York), St. John's University, 1973.
This special issue contains outlines of Ottoman and modern Turkish literature, folk poetry and drama.

Rice, David Talbot. *Islamic Art.* London, Thames and Hudson, New York, Praeger, 1965; P (World of Art series).
A good pictorial introduction to the art of most of the Islamic countries.

Rivlin, B. and Szyliowicz, J. S. (edd.). *The Contemporary Middle East: Tradition and Innovation.* New York, Toronto, Random House, 1965 P.
Over 50 essays on various topics, very well arranged and classified, and often 'easy to read'. Much original material translated.

Rypka, Jan (and others). *History of Iranian Literature.* Reidel, Dordrecht, 1967; New York, Humanities Press, 1968.
Comprehensive and authoritative, but Marxist-biased in places, and not always well translated.

Saunders, John J. *A History of Medieval Islam.* London, Routledge and Kegan Paul; New York, Barnes and Noble, 1965.
A readable and generally accurate account.

Schacht, Joseph and Bosworth, C. E. (edd.). *The Legacy of Islam.* 2nd ed. London, Toronto, New York, Oxford University Press, 1974.

Smith, Wilfred Cantwell. *Islam in Modern History.* Princeton, Princeton University Press, 1957; New York, New American Library, 1959 P (and repr.) (Mentor Books).

The Literary Review, Vol. 15, no. 4, Summer 1972. Rutherford, N. J., Farleigh Dickinson University 1972.
This special issue (guest editor T. S. Halman) is devoted to translations of the works of modern Turkish authors (8 short-story writers, 24 poets), with an informative introduction by the editor.

Thesiger, Wilfred. *The Marsh Arabs.* New York, Dutton; London, Longmans, 1964.
A fascinating and well-written account of seven years with the primitive tribesmen who live in the marshes of southern Iraq.

Von Grunebaum, Gustave E. *Classical Islam, a History, 600–1258.* London 1970.
Stimulating and percipient; much attention to cultural factors. Translation from German awkward and inaccurate in one or two places.

Warriner, Doreen. *Land Reform and Development in the Middle East: A Study of Egypt, Syria, and Iraq.* London/New York, Oxford University Press (Royal Institute of International Affairs), 1957.
The standard work on the subject, but somewhat dated.

Watt, William Montgomery. *Islamic Philosophy and Theology.* Edinburgh, Edinburgh University Press; Chicago, Aldine, 1962 (and repr.) (Islamic Surveys series).
Largely an account of the development of Islamic theology in its social context.

– *The Influence of Islam on Medieval Europe,* Edinburgh, Edinburgh University Press, 1972.
Several minor inaccuracies.

Index and glossary

Note: All names beginning with *al-* or *Āl-* are indexed under the capital letters immediately following